CARL PHILIPP EMANUEL BACH EDITION

Series I · Volume 18
Keyboard Sonatas, 1744–1747

CARL PHILIPP EMANUEL BACH AUSGABE

Editionsleiter
RACHEL W. WADE

Herausgeber
E. EUGENE HELM

Music Department
OXFORD UNIVERSITY PRESS
Oxford and New York

CARL PHILIPP EMANUEL BACH EDITION

General Editor
RACHEL W. WADE

Co-ordinating Editor
E. EUGENE HELM

Music Department
OXFORD UNIVERSITY PRESS
Oxford and New York

Werkgruppe I

WERKE FÜR SOLO-TASTENINSTRUMENT

Band 18

CARL PHILIPP EMANUEL BACH
(1714–1788)

Sonaten für Tasteninstrument

H. 40 (W. 62/6)
H. 43 (W. 65/15)
H. 46 (W. 65/16)
H. 47 (W. 65/17)
H. 48 (W. 65/18)
H. 49 (W. 65/19)
H. 51 (W. 65/20)

Herausgegeben von
DAVID SCHULENBERG

Series I

SOLO KEYBOARD MUSIC

Volume 18

CARL PHILIPP EMANUEL BACH
(1714–1788)

Keyboard Sonatas

H. 40 (W. 62/6)
H. 43 (W. 65/15)
H. 46 (W. 65/16)
H. 47 (W. 65/17)
H. 48 (W. 65/18)
H. 49 (W. 65/19)
H. 51 (W. 65/20)

Edited by
DAVID SCHULENBERG

Oxford University Press, Walton Street, Oxford OX2 6DP, England
Oxford University Press Inc., 200 Madison Avenue, New York, NY 10016, USA

Oxford is a trade mark of Oxford University Press

Library of Congress Cataloging-in-Publication Data
Data available

ISBN 0–19–324018–1

The preparation of this volume was made possible in part by a grant from the National Endowment for the Humanities,
an independent federal agency of the United States of America.

The silhouette of Carl Philipp Emanuel Bach on the front cover is by an anonymous contemporary (Pölchau Collection,
Deutsche Staatsbibliothek, Berlin/DDR).

Printed in Great Britain on acid-free paper
by St Edmundsbury Press Ltd., Bury St Edmunds, Suffolk.

CONTENTS · INHALT ·

PREFACE

TO THE CARL PHILIPP EMANUEL BACH EDITION

THE aim of the Carl Philipp Emanuel Bach Edition is to publish the complete works of the composer in a form that most closely represents his intentions. Editorial additions to the primary source of each work have been made only when demanded by the necessity for musical authenticity or clarity. The edition is divided into ten series:

    I Solo Keyboard Music
   II Concertos and Sonatinas
  III Chamber Music with a Leading Keyboard
       Part
   IV Solo Sonatas for Wind or String
       Instruments
    V Trio Sonatas
   VI Other Chamber Music
  VII Symphonies
 VIII Works for Solo Voice(s)
   IX Major Choral Works
    X Choral Works for Special Occasions

Only works known to be authentic are included; with a few exceptions these works exist in autographs, are cited in Bach's writings, or are included in the catalogue of his estate, which was based on his own records. Works are identified by Helm number, but subsidiary reference may be made to the Wotquenne number (see 'H.' and 'W.' in the list of abbreviations). The numbers given in the titles of works are those found in the catalogue of the composer's estate.

If an authentic variant or revision of a work exists, it is included in the same volume; any arrangement or alternative version for a different scoring is given in the series appropriate to its medium of performance. Cadenzas are included in the body of the music only if found in the primary source; however, if one of the authentic cadenzas compiled in ms. 5871 of the Bibliothèque du Conservatoire Royal de Musique, Brussels (H. 264) is specifically indicated for the work in question, that cadenza appears at the foot of the page containing the fermata.

Fundamental to the approach of this edition is minimal editorial intervention. However, two centuries of change in musical notation demand certain modernizations in the representation of Bach's music. Such changes are tacit and include the fol-lowing: the regularization of clefs; the deletion of redundant accidentals within a bar; the repetition of an accidental across a barline where it would have been considered implicit in the eighteenth century; the normalization of beaming where notes sharing one beam are stemmed in two different directions; the regularization of dynamic indications (e.g., changing *forte* and *for:* to *f*); the full notation of passages indicated by abbreviations in the primary source; the deletion of rests supplied occasionally in the upper stave of keyboard parts during tutti sections of concertos; and the modernization of spelling and punctuation in vocal texts. The layout of the instruments in the score usually follows that of the primary source.

Alterations that are the result of editorial decisions rather than notational modernization are made explicit. Any change not found in the sources is given in square brackets; if it is found in at least one alternative source, it is given in parentheses and its source identified in the List of Variant Readings. Any editorial changes that cannot easily be indicated in the score itself, such as the rewording of titles, are listed in the Critical Commentary. In general, the C. P. E. Bach Edition refrains from attempting to regularize discrepancies between the various parts in slurring, articulation, or dynamics, because of the abundant evidence that what Bach wrote or omitted was usually intentional. Not only are there many autograph sources where such 'discrepancies' recur extensively, but there are also manuscripts in which the copyist's efforts to regularize have been rejected by the composer's corrections, deletions, or erasures.

The Critical Commentary comprises descriptions of sources and a List of Variant Readings. Sources are discussed in the order of their importance to the edition, with a detailed account of each one: its layout and format (if not upright), title page, history, unusual features, and relation to other sources of the work. Only those sources of the most reliable provenance are included in the List of Variant Readings, which deals primarily with specific details of pitch, rhythm, ornamentation, marginalia, deleted notes, and erasures. Variants in performance indications such as slurs, strokes, dynamics, and bass figures are usually summarized more generally in the description of the sources rather than itemized, and only if their importance warrants it.

For citation of particular bars, the movement number is given in roman numerals, followed by the bar number in arabic (e.g., II. 47). In the List of Variant Readings, the precise location of each variant is indicated by bar number, instrument, and a 'note-and-rest number', as explained in the list of abbreviations. Pitches are referred to by Helmholtz's system, as shown here.

US note values and English equivalents

whole-note	semibreve
half-note	minim
quarter-note	crotchet
eighth-note	quaver
sixteenth-note	semiquaver
thirty-second-note	demisemiquaver

PREFACE

TO SERIES I · VOLUME 18

DURING the years 1744–7, C. P. E. Bach continued to expand the technical and expressive vocabulary of the keyboard sonata, the genre that he had already established as his own special domain with the prints of the 'Prussian' and 'Württemberg' sonatas of 1742 and 1744 respectively. Although Bach would publish no further collections of sonatas until 1760, one of the seven sonatas edited in this volume was issued in 1762 as part of an anthology of keyboard music, two others appeared in unauthorized prints after 1760, and most were also widely distributed in manuscript copies.

Four of the present works—H. 40 (W. 62/6), H. 46 (W. 65/16), H. 47 (W. 65/17), and H. 51 (W. 65/20)—are extraordinary virtuoso pieces from a group that has been described as 'serious' and 'experimental'.[1] The three others, H. 43 (W. 65/15), H. 48 (W. 65/18), and H. 49 (W. 65/19), are simpler in their technical demands and expressive aspirations. Although all four 'serious' works have been published, H. 40 (in F minor) was the only one to appear in an authorized print during the composer's lifetime. The seven sonatas appear in the present volume in the order in which they are listed in the catalogue of Bach's estate.[2]

Nothing is known about the occasions for which any of these sonatas may have been written. But the dichotomy between 'light' and 'serious' sonatas might be traced to the customary distinction between music for the *Kenner* (experts), including Bach himself, and that meant for wider distribution among the *Liebhaber* (amateurs). Bach's keyboard

publications of the 1760s tended towards the lighter type of work; nevertheless, the 'serious' sonata H. 40 appeared in the serialized anthology *Musikalisches Allerley*, which contained generally lighter pieces. This might have reflected a modest resurgence of interest in contrapuntal music among the literate public, as evinced by the contemporary writings of Friedrich Wilhelm Marpurg; H. 40 opens with one of the few first movements in any of Bach's keyboard sonatas to contain a significant polyphonic element.

Two of the other 'serious' sonatas, H. 46 in C and H. 47 in G minor, contain innovations that look forward to some of Bach's later keyboard works. In both sonatas, the first two movements are played without a break (as in many contemporary *sinfonie*), and each incorporates an improvisatory type of music into the sonata cycle—quasi-recitative in H. 46, fantasia in H. 47.[3] The three lighter sonatas also point forward, in a sense, since they suggest that Bach was already finding it advisable to blunt his style in order to create easier or more accessible music. But these pieces are by no means entirely insignificant. The witty final movement of H. 43 is far from simple, and the first movement of H. 48, with its alternations between running motion and short syncopated figures—the latter regarded by some contemporary writers as a form of *tempo rubato*[4]—employs an easier version of a device Bach had used in the first movement of H. 37 (W. 52/4), the F sharp minor sonata of 1744. H. 49 might be one of the first of his keyboard sonatas whose earliest known form contains varied reprises; embellished repetitions of the sort found in the last movement would become a major concern of Bach in the works of the 1750s. But the varied reprises in this sonata may date from

[1] D. M. Berg, 'The Keyboard Sonatas of C. P. E. Bach: An Expression of the Mannerist Principle' (Ph. D. diss., State University of New York at Buffalo, 1975), pp. 96–7. Works will be referred to by their numbers in the Helm thematic catalogue (H. in the List of Abbreviations), and (upon first mention) by the number in the Wotquenne thematic catalogue (W. in the List of Abbreviations).

[2] *Verzeichniss des musikalischen Nachlasses des verstorbenen Capellmeisters Carl Philipp Emanuel Bach* (Hamburg, 1790); facs. edn. annotated R. W. Wade as *The Catalog of Carl Philipp Emanuel Bach's Estate. A Facsimile of the Edition by Schniebes, Hamburg 1790* (New York, 1981) [hereinafter cited as the *Nachlassverzeichnis*]. Dates of composition are taken from the *Nachlassverzeichnis*.

[3] For a more detailed analysis, see D. Schulenberg, 'C. P. E. Bach through the 1740s: the Growth of a Style', in *C. P. E. Bach Studies*, ed. S. L. Clark (Oxford, 1988), pp. 217–31.

[4] Marpurg, *Anleitung zum Clavierspielen*, 2nd ed. (Berlin, 1765; facs. ed., Hildesheim, 1970), p. 40; G. S. Löhlein, *Clavier-Schule, oder kurze und gründliche Anweisung zur Melodie und Harmonie* (Leipzig und Züllichau, 1781), ii, 129, 131.

considerably later than that; indeed, it is unlikely that this sonata dates from the 1740s at all, at least in its surviving form.

Autograph manuscripts survive only for H. 46 and H. 49 and have served as the principal sources for those works; the manuscripts are in Berlin (Staatsbibliothek Preußischer Kulturbesitz, Mus. ms. Bach P 1131) and Kraków (Biblioteka Jagiellońska, Mus. ms. Bach P 771) respectively. For H. 40, the edition follows the print in *Musikalisches Allerley*, while manuscript copies by Bach's copyists have served for the remaining works. These copies all appear in the Berlin manuscript Staatsbibliothek Preussischer Kulturbesitz, Mus. ms. Bach P 775; each copy was revised or at least overseen by the composer.[5]

Except in the case of H. 49, the sources of these sonatas transmit variant readings that reflect revisions made at various times by the composer. It is clear from these variants that Bach added ornaments, appoggiaturas, cautionary accidentals, and other performance indications on one or more occasions, and occasionally made changes in the pitches themselves. The sonata in G, H. 43, and to a lesser extent the sonata in F minor, H. 40, underwent particularly substantial revisions that involved the rewriting, though not the replacement, of several passages. While it is impossible to set a date for any of the revisions, those in H. 40 were made prior to the publication of the revised version in 1762; some of the revisions in the other works, especially H. 49, may not have been carried out until the last few years of Bach's life.[6]

The revisions in the first movement of H. 43 were sufficiently extensive that the early version must be given separately. Otherwise, readings from earlier versions are to be found in the lists of variant readings. Very often these readings involve the *absence* of ornaments or other performance signs present in the main text. The particular sources that preserve early versions are noted in the critical commentary for each sonata; variant readings common to these sources can be presumed with some confidence to belong to an authentic early version, with exceptions as noted in the

commentaries. Variant readings that could not be accommodated within the lists of variant readings have been given as musical examples at the end of each list, referred to by example number. Sources containing more than one work are described fully only once.

Unfortunately, the loss of all but one of the early autographs makes it impossible to be certain of the readings of the early versions. Even in the autograph of H. 46, in which Bach's original entries date from the 1740s, it is not always possible to distinguish original entries from revisions except by consulting early copies. The autograph of H. 49 is a fair copy and probably dates from late in Bach's Hamburg period (1768–88), and therefore provides no assistance in determining any earlier form of the work.

The latest readings in all seven sonatas include the ornament signs that Bach discussed in depth in the first part of his *Versuch über die wahre Art das Clavier zu spielen* (Berlin, 1753).[7] But the vaguer indications *tr*, *t*, and *+*, which are present at various points in the earlier versions, were not always replaced. Particularly notable is the frequent use of the sign *+* in H. 43 and 46. Although this sign was used to indicate the mordent in many eighteenth-century prints (including the unauthorized print of H. 48), Bach appears to have employed it as the equivalent of a hastily written *t*. While the edition of H. 46 follows the autograph, giving 'plus' signs, later copies of the work, including two by Bach's copyist Michel, generally substitute the abbreviations *t* or *tr*; hence all three signs seem to be synonymous. In the principal source of H. 43 Bach himself appears to have approved the substitution of *tr* for *+* in at least one passage.[8]

---

[5] The sources designated 'US Wc' (used for H. 43, H. 46, and H. 48) were examined in person; otherwise the editor worked from microfilms.

[6] Regarding Bach's process for revising works, see P. Fox, 'C. P. E. Bach's Compositional Proofreading', *The Musical Times*, 129 (1988), 651–5.

[7] Facs. edn., ed. L. Hoffmann-Erbrecht, 4. Auflage (Leipzig, 1978); English trans. as *Essay on the True Art of Playing Keyboard Instruments* by W. Mitchell (New York, 1949).

[8] Bars 8 and 75 of the first movement show *+* and *tr*, respectively; Bach entered revisions into the lower stave in both bars without altering the ornament signs in the upper stave. The problem is discussed further in the critical commentaries for H. 43 and H. 46. C. P. E. Bach noted the equivalence of '*tr*' with the cross sign in the autograph of the concerto H. 421 (W. 18) of 1745 (see R. W. Wade, *The Keyboard Concertos of Carl Philipp Emanuel Bach* (Ann Arbor, 1981), p. 67), and W. F. Bach used the same sign, e.g., in the autograph of his concerto for two harpsichords F. 10, dated 'around 1740' by P. Wollny, 'Studies in the Music of Wilhelm Friedemann Bach: Sources and Style' (diss., Harvard University, 1993), pp. 123–5.

The works edited here present few special problems of interpretation for players familiar with Bach's keyboard music. Many questions will be answered by consulting Bach's *Versuch*, of which the first volume appeared in 1753, after the composition but probably well before the final revisions of these sonatas. Models for the realization of the cadenzas called for at the fermatas in the slow movements of H. 40 and 43 can be found in Quantz's *Versuch einer Anweisung die Flöte traversiere zu spielen* (Berlin, 1752),[9] and in several works of Bach's, including the *Sechs Sonaten mit veränderten Reprisen* (Berlin, 1750).[10] Players may also note that each half of the first movement of H. 46 ends in a bar containing just two beats, despite the time signature 'C'.

The most significant question of interpretation concerns the instrument on which the music is to be played. Although the presence of three dynamic levels (*f*, *p*, and *pp*) in two of the works (H. 40 and H. 47) implies the use of fortepiano or clavichord, the only instrumental designation in the contemporary sources is *cembalo*. But Bach appears to have used the latter as a generic term for any stringed keyboard instrument.

During the preparation of the present volume, C. P. E. Bach scholarship has seen significant advances, especially in the evaluation and identification of sources. Every effort has been made to incorporate matter that has come to light while the volume has been in preparation, but it has proved impossible to incorporate full reports on a number of secondary sources.

The editing of this volume was facilitated by a grant to the editor by the National Endowment for the Humanities, a federal agency of the United States Government that supports study in the humanities, history, and other fields. The editorial centre of the C. P. E. Bach Edition has also been supported by a grant from this agency.

The editor is grateful to Ulrich Leisinger for carefully reading the galley proofs and generously supplying valuable information from his own ongoing research about many sources seen by the editor only in photographic reproduction. The editor also thanks Rachel Wade and E. Eugene Helm for advice and assistance, and the editorial staff of Oxford University Press for their help during the publication process. Thanks are due also to Elias N. Kulukundis, who provided a microfilm of a source in his possession, and to the following libraries for making their collections available and supplying copies: Vienna, Gesellschaft der Musikfreunde; Brussels, Bibliothèque du Conservatoire Royal de Musique; Brussels, Bibliothèque Royale Albert I; Staatsbibliothek zu Berlin—Preußischer Kulturbesitz, Musikabteilung mit Mendelssohn Archiv (formerly Berlin, Deutsche Staatsbibliothek und Staatsbibliothek Preußischer Kulturbesitz) Preußischer Kulturbesitz; Bonn, Beethoven-Archiv; Gotha, Forschungs- und Landesbibliothek; Munich, Bayerische Staatsbibliothek; Kiel, Schleswig-Holsteinische Landesbibliothek; Leipzig, Musikbibliothek der Stadt; London, the British Library; the Hague, Gemeente Museum; Kraków, Biblioteka Jagiellońska; Ann Arbor, University of Michigan; New Haven, Yale University Library; Washington, DC, the Library of Congress.

---

[9] Facsimile of the Berlin, 1789, edition (Kassel, 1953); English trans. as *An Essay on Playing the Flute* by Edward J. Reilly (London, 1966).

[10] H. 136–40, 126; W. 50. Ed. E. Darbellay (Winterthur, 1976).

ABBREVIATIONS
USED IN THIS VOLUME

a. corr. (*ante correcturam*)	before correction
A Wgm	Vienna, Gesellschaft der Musikfreunde, VII 3872/1 (H. 47); VII 3872/14 (H. 48); VII 43745 (H. 46)
acc.	accidental
AmB 54	Berlin, Staatsbibliothek Preussischer Kulturbesitz, Musikabteilung, Amalienbibliothek 54 (H. 51)
Anon. 301, 302 (etc.)	anonymous copyists as referred to by the system used in Paul Kast, *Die Bach-Handschriften der Berliner Staatsbibliothek*, Tübinger Bach-Studien, Heft 2/3 (Trossingen, 1958)
app., apps.	appoggiatura, appoggiaturas
arp.	arpeggio, arpeggio sign
B Bc	Brussels, Bibliothèque du Conservatoire Royal de Musique, 5883 MSM (H. 43, 46, 47, 48, 49, 51)
B Br	Brussels, Bibliothèque Royale Albert Iᵉʳ, ms. II 4094 (H. 40)
BNba	Bonn, Beethoven-Archiv
BWV	Bach-Werke-Verzeichnis; index number assigned to works in Wolfgang Schmieder, *Thematisch-systematisches Verzeichnis der musikalischen Werke Johann Sebastian Bachs*, 2nd ed. (Wiesbaden, 1990)
CPEB	Carl Philipp Emanuel Bach
CPEBE	Carl Philipp Emanuel Bach Edition
corr.	corrected, correction (see also a. corr., p. corr.)
D KIl	Kiel, Schleswig-Holsteinische Landesbibliothek, Mb 48/2 (H. 40), 52/4 (H. 46), 53/2 (H. 47), 53/4 (H. 48)
D LEm	Leipzig, Musikbibliothek der Stadt, Sammlung Gorke, Nr. 346 (H. 40)
D Mbs	Munich, Bayerische Staatsbibliothek, Mus. ms. 1794 (H. 46, 51), 1795 (H. 40)
dyn., dyns.	dynamic marking(s)
E.	Ruth Engelhardt, *Untersuchungen über Einflüsse Johann Sebastian Bachs auf das theoretische und praktische Wirken seines Schülers Johann Philipp Kirnberger* (Erlangen-Nürnberg, 1974)
ENK	manuscript in private possession (Elias N. Kulukundis, Greenwich, Connecticut, USA) (H. 47)
F.	Martin Falck, *Wilhelm Friedemann Bach* (Leipzig, 1913; R Lindau, 1956)
GO1	Gotha, Forschungs- und Landesbibliothek
H.	E. Eugene Helm, *Thematic Catalogue of the Works of Carl Philipp Emanuel Bach* (New Haven, 1989)
HB	print of H. 48 by Huberti: *Six sonates pour le clavecin* (Paris, [c.1761])
JAMS	*Journal of the American Musicological Society*
JSB	Johann Sebastian Bach
KN	print of H. 51 by Kühnel: *Grande Sonate pour le Clavecin, ou Fortepiano* (Leipzig, [c.1802])

M20, M23	Washington, DC, Library of Congress, Music Division, M20.A2M684 (H. 46); M23.B13.W65(16) (H. 46)
MA	*Musikalisches Allerley von verschiedenen Tonkünstlern* (Berlin, 1760–3) (H. 40)
Mb 48/2, 53/4, etc.	see D KII in this list
note-and-rest no.	A system of location used in the lists of variant readings to indicate a particular note or rest in the C. P. E. Bach Edition. This number is calculated by counting each note and rest from the barline, including tied notes and notated ornamental notes but not those implied by an ornament symbol.
om.	omitted
orig.	originally
orn.	ornament, ornament sign
p., pp.	page(s)
P 212 (H. 47), P 359 (H. 43, 47, 51), P 367 (H. 40, 46), P 368 (H. 40, 46, 51), P 414 (H. 40), P 673 (H. 48), P 775 (H. 43, 46, 47, 48, 51), P 790 (H. 40), P 1134 (H. 48)	Call numbers (all preceded by 'Mus. ms. Bach') in Berlin, Staatsbibliothek Preußischer Kulturbesitz, Musikabteilung (see also 'H.' in this list of abbreviations)
P 365 (H. 40), P 369 (H. 43, 49), P 1131 (H. 46)	Call numbers (all preceded by 'Mus. ms.Bach') in Berlin, Deutsche Staatsbibliothek (see also 'H.' in this list of abbreviations)
P 771	Kraków, Biblioteka Jagiellońska, Mus. ms. Bach P 771 (H. 49)
p. corr. (*post correcturam*)	after correction
RL	print of H. 51 by Rellstab: *Trois sonates pour le clavecin ou pianoforte* (Berlin, [c. 1792])
US NHu	New Haven, Yale University Library, Lowell Mason Collection, ms. 5009 (H. 40)
US Wc	Washington, DC, Library of Congress, Music Division, M23.B13.W65(15) case (H. 43), M23.B13.W65(18) (H. 48)
vol.	volume
W.	Alfred Wotquenne, *Thematisches Verzeichnis der Werke von Carl Philipp Emanuel Bach (1714–1788)* (Leipzig, 1905/R 1972)
Wq. n. v.	index number assigned to works by C. P. E. Bach that lack 'W.' numbers in Paul Kast, *Die Bach-Handschriften der Berliner Staatsbibliothek*, Tübinger Bach-Studien, Heft 2/3 (Trossingen, 1958)
52/5, 52/6, 52/7	Kiel, Schleswig-Holsteinische Landesbibliothek, ms. Mb 52/5 (H. 51), 52/6 (H. 51), 52/7 (H. 51)
3872/2, 43753	Vienna, Gesellschaft der Musikfreunde, VII 3872/2 (H. 43), VII 43753 (H. 43)

VORWORT

ZUR CARL PHILIPP EMANUEL BACH-AUSGABE

DIE Carl Philipp Emanuel Bach-Ausgabe hat es sich zum Ziel gesetzt, sämtliche Werke des Komponisten in einer Form zu veröffentlichen, die seinen eigenen Angaben so nahe wie möglich kommt. Die Primärquellen für jedes Werk sind darum nur in solchen Fällen editorisch ergänzt worden, wo dies im Sinne musikalischer Authentizität oder Klarheit geboten war. Die Ausgabe gliedert sich in zehn Werkgruppen:

    I Werke für Solo-Tasteninstrument
   II Konzerte und Sonatinen
  III Kammermusik mit führender
       Klavierstimme
   IV Solosonaten für Bläser oder
       Streichinstrumente
    V Triosonaten
   VI Sonstige Kammermusik
  VII Symphonien
 VIII Werke für Solo-Singstimme(n)
   IX Hauptwerke für Chor
    X Gelegenheitswerke für Chor

Nur solche Werke sind aufgenommen worden, deren Authentizität gesichert ist; von wenigen Ausnahmen abgesehen, sind diese Werke in Autographen überliefert, in Bachs Schriften zitiert oder im Verzeichnis des musikalischen Nachlasses aufgeführt, das auf seinen eigenen Aufzeichnungen beruht. Im allgemeinen sind die Werke durch Helm-Nummern gekennzeichnet; gelegentlich wird zusätzlich auf Wotquenne-Nummern verwiesen (siehe 'H.' und 'W.' im Abkürzungsverzeichnis). Die in den Werktiteln aufgeführten Nummern entstammen dem Nachlaßverzeichnis des Komponisten.

Soweit authentische Varianten oder Abänderungen eines Werks vorliegen, sind diese in denselben Band aufgenommen worden. Unterschiedliche Einrichtungen oder alternative Fassungen eines Werks für eine andere Besetzung erscheinen in der Werkfolge für die entsprechende Besetzung. Kadenzen werden nur dann als Werkbestandteil aufgenommen, wenn sie einer Primärquelle entstammen; wenn jedoch eine der in ms. 5871 der Bibliothèque du Conservatoire Royal de Musique, Brüssel, (H. 264) gesammelten authentischen Kadenzen ausdrücklich einem bestimmten Werk zugeordnet ist, so erscheint diese unterhalb

des Notentextes auf der Seite, die die Fermate enthält.

Es ist das leitende methodische Prinzip dieser Ausgabe, editorische Eingriffe auf ein Minimum zu beschränken. Ein zweihundertjähriger Wandel in musikalischer Notation macht allerdings einige behutsame Modernisierungen in der Druckwiedergabe von Bachs Musik erforderlich. Änderungen dieser Art, die stillschweigend vorgenommen worden sind, sind unter anderem folgende: die Vereinheitlichung von Notenschlüsseln; die Streichung überflüssiger Vorzeichen innerhalb eines Taktes; die Wiederholung eines Vorzeichens über einen Taktstrich hinweg, wo es im 18. Jahrhundert implizit vorausgesetzt worden wäre; die Normalisierung der Balkensetzung, wo auf einen Balken verteilte Noten in zwei verschiedene Richtungen gehalst sind; die Vereinheitlichung dynamischer Angaben (z. B. die Umwandlung von *forte* und *for:* in *f*); die vollständige Notation von Passagen, die in der Primärquelle in abgekürzter Form enthalten sind; die Streichung von Pausen, die gelegentlich im oberen Liniensystem der Klavierstimme in tutti-Abschnitten von Konzerten auftreten; und die Modernisierung von Schreibweise und Interpunktion in Vokal-Texten. Die Anordnung der Instrumente in der Partitur folgt im allgemeinen derjenigen der Primärquelle.

Änderungen, die sich aus editorischen Entscheidungen und nicht aus der Modernisierung der Notation ergeben, werden als solche kenntlich gemacht. Jede Änderung, die nicht auf Quellen beruht, ist in eckige Klammern gesetzt; wenn eine Änderung aus mindestens einer gesicherten Quelle hervorgeht, ist sie in runden Klammern wiedergegeben; die Quelle wird in der Liste der Lesarten nachgewiesen. Jede editorische Änderung, die nicht problemlos in der Partitur selbst hervorgehoben werden kann, wie z. B. die Umformulierung von Titeln, wird im Kritischen Kommentar aufgeführt. Überhaupt wird in der C. P. E. Bach-Ausgabe Abstand genommen von dem Versuch, Unstimmigkeiten zwischen verschiedenen Stimmen im Hinblick auf Bindung, Artikulation oder Dynamik auszugleichen, da eine Fülle von Belegen für die Tatsache spricht, daß im allgemeinen hinter dem, was Bach niederschrieb oder ausließ, eine Absicht stand. Dies ist nicht nur zahlreichen Autographen zu entnehmen, wo derartige 'Unstimmigkeiten' in beträchtlicher Zahl immer wieder auftreten, sondern diese Absicht wird zusätzlich durch Manuskripte bestätigt, in denen der Komponist selbst die Bemühungen des Kopisten um Vereinheitlichung durch Korrekturen, Streichungen oder Ausradierungen zurückgewiesen hat.

Der Kritische Kommentar enthält eine Beschreibung der Quellen und eine Liste abweichender Lesarten. Die Quellen sind in der Reihenfolge ihrer Wichtigkeit für die Ausgabe abgehandelt. Über jede einzelne wird dabei detailliert Auskunft gegeben; Anlage und Format (wenn nicht Hochformat), Titelseite, Überlieferung, ungewöhnliche Eigenschaften und ihre Beziehung zu anderen Quellen werden beschrieben. Die originale Orthographie ist ohne Veränderung beibehalten. Nur solche Quellen sind in die Lesartenliste aufgenommen, die im höchsten Maße als gesichert gelten dürfen. Die Lesartenliste enthält im wesentlichen Einzelheiten über Tonhöhe, Rhythmus, Verzierungen, Marginalien, getilgte Noten und Ausradierungen. Varianten in den Aufführungshinweisen wie Bindungen, Striche, dynamische Angaben und Baßbezifferungen sind meist eher summarisch in der allgemeinen Quellenbeschreibung und nicht im einzelnen aufgeführt, und dies nur, wenn es durch ihr Gewicht gerechtfertigt erscheint.

Beim Zitieren bestimmter Takte wird die Satznummer in römischen Ziffern, die Taktnummer anschließend in arabischen angegeben (z. B. II. 47). Die Lesartenliste ermöglicht die Bestimmung der genauen Position einer Variante durch Angabe von Taktzahl, Instrument und einer 'Noten-und-Pausen-Nummer', wie in der Abkürzungsliste erläutert. Tonhöhen werden nach dem Helmholtz-System angeben, wie auf S. x dargestellt.

VORWORT

ZU WERKGRUPPE I · BAND 18

Carl Philipp Emanuel Bach hatte sich mit der Veröffentlichung der Preußischen und der Württembergischen Sonaten in den Jahren 1742 und 1744 als ein Spezialist der Klaviersonate erwiesen und fuhr in den Jahren von 1744 bis 1747 fort, Technik und Ausdruck der Gattung zu entwickeln. Bach ließ zwar bis 1760 keine weitere Sonatensammlung drucken, eine der sieben hier vorgelegten Sonaten erschien aber 1762 in einer Klavieranthologie, zwei weitere wurden nach 1760 in einer nicht autorisierten Ausgabe veröffentlicht, und die meisten dieser Werke waren auch in Abschriften weit verbreitet.

Vier Kompositionen dieses Bandes — H. 40 (W. 62/6), H. 46 (W. 65/16), H. 47 (W. 65/17) und H. 51 (W. 65/20) — sind äußerst virtuos und stammen aus einer Werkgruppe, die in der Literatur als 'ernst' und 'experimentell' charakterisiert wird.[1] Die drei anderen — H. 43 (W. 65/15), H. 48 (W. 65/18) und H. 49 (W. 65/19) — sind in Hinblick auf Technik und musikalischen Ausdruck schlichter. Obwohl alle vier 'ernsten' Werke im Neudruck vorliegen, gab es zu Bachs Lebzeiten nur von der f-Moll-Sonate (H. 40) eine autorisierte Ausgabe. Die sieben Sonaten werden hier in der Reihenfolge wiedergegeben, in der sie im Nachlassverzeichnis erscheinen.[2]

Es ist nicht bekannt, aus welchem Anlaß die Sonaten komponiert wurden. Die Einteilung in 'leichte' und 'ernste' Sonaten kann jedoch auf die zeitübliche Unterscheidung von Musik "für Kenner" auf der einen Seite, zu denen selbstverständlich auch Bach zählte, und Kompositionen für ein breiteres Publikum von Liebhabern auf der anderen Seite zurückgeführt werden. Die Klavierwerke, die Bach im Laufe der 1760er Jahre veröffentlichte, sind eher der 'leichteren' Kategorie zuzuordnen. Trotzdem ist die 'ernste' Sonate H. 40 in der Sammlung *Musikalisches Allerley* erschienen, die ansonsten vor allem anspruchslose Werke enthielt. Dies könnte auf ein beschränkt wiederauflebendes Interesse des gebildeten Publikums an kontrapunktischer Musik zurückzuführen sein, wie es sich auch in den zeitgenössischen Schriften Friedrich Wilhelm Marpurgs zeigt. Der erste Satz dieses Werks ist einer von wenigen Eingangssätzen in Bachs Sonaten mit stark polyphonen Elementen.

Zwei weitere 'ernste' Sonaten, H. 46 in c-Moll und H. 47 in g-Moll, weisen Neuerungen auf, die den späteren Stil von Bachs Klavierwerken bereits erahnen lassen. Bei beiden folgt der zweite Satz unmittelbar auf den ersten — ein Verfahren, das in der Sinfonik der Zeit oft zu finden ist — und sie bereichern den Sonatenzyklus um improvisatorische Momente in Gestalt eines Rezitativs (H. 46) bzw. einer Fantasie (H. 47).[3] Auch die drei leichteren Sonaten weisen in die Zukunft, erwecken sie doch den Eindruck, als habe Bach bewußt schon hier seinen Stil vereinfacht, um leichte und eingängigere Musik zu schreiben. Unbedeutend sind diese Stücke jedoch keineswegs: Das geistreiche Finale von H. 43 ist alles andere als anspruchslos; der erste Satz von H. 48 mit dem Wechsel von Läufen und kurzen synkopierten Phrasen (was von den Theoretikern der Zeit als ausnotiertes *Tempo rubato* interpretiert wird[4]) ist die einfachere Variante einer Kompositionstechnik, deren sich Bach im ersten Satz der fis-Moll-Sonate (H. 37 bzw. W. 52/4) bedient hatte. H. 49 könnte die erste Sonate sein, die schon in der ältesten überlieferten Fassung "veränderte Reprisen"

---

[1] Darrell M. Berg, 'The Keyboard Sonatas of C. P. E. Bach: An Expression of the Mannerist Principle' (Diss. State University of New York at Buffalo 1975), S. 96–97. Die Werknummern beziehen sich auf den Helm-Katalog (abgekürzt 'H.'), bei der ersten Nennung auch auf das Wotquenne-Verzeichnis (abgekürzt 'W.'). Siehe das Verzeichnis der Abkürzungen.

[2] *Verzeichniß des musikalischen Nachlasses des verstorbenen Capellmeisters Carl Philipp Emanuel Bach* (Hamburg 1790), im Folgenden zitiert als *Nachlassverzeichnis*; Reprint hrsg. von R. W, Wade: *The Catalog of Carl Philipp Emanuel Bach's Estate: A Facsimile of the Edition by Schniebes. Hamburg 1790* (New York 1981). Kompositionsdaten sind diesem Verzeichnis entnommen.

[3] Eine ausführliche Analyse findet sich bei D. Schulenberg, "C. P. E. Bach through the 1740s: the Growth of a Style", in: *C. P. E. Bach Studies*, hrsg. von Stephen L. Clark, Oxford 1988, S. 217–231.

[4] F. W. Marpurg, *Anleitung zum Clavierspielen*, 2. Auflage (Berlin 1765; Reprint Hildesheim 1970), S. 40; G. S. Löhlein, *Clavier-Schule, oder kurze und gründliche Anweisung zur Melodie und Harmonie* (Leipzig und Züllichau 1781), Bd. 2, S. 129 und 131.

enthält. In den 1750er Jahren gehören ausgezierte Wiederholungen, wie sie im Schlußsatz dieser Sonate zu finden sind, zu Bachs kompositorischen Hauptanliegen. Die veränderten Reprisen könnten in diesem Fall allerdings auch wesentlich später entstanden sein. Es erscheint sogar eher unwahrscheinlich, daß diese Sonate — zumindest in der erhaltenen Gestalt — aus den 1740er Jahren stammt.

Nur die Autographe von H. 46 und H. 49 sind überliefert und dienten als Hauptquelle für die Edition dieser beiden Werke. Die Handschriften werden in der Staatsbibliothek zu Berlin (Mus. ms. Bach P 1131) bzw. in der Biblioteka Jagiellońska in Krakau (Mus. ms. Bach P 771) aufbewahrt. Unsere Ausgabe von H. 40 hält sich an den Abdruck im *Musikalischen Allerley*. Die restlichen Stücke folgen Abschriften von Bachs Kopisten aus dem Konvolut Mus. ms. Bach P 775 der Staatsbibliothek zu Berlin; Bach hat jede dieser Kopien selbst revidiert oder zumindest durchgesehen.[5]

Außer im Fall von H. 49 sind durch die Quellen für all diese Sonaten unterschiedliche Fassungen überliefert, die offenbar auf verschiedene, zeitlich auseinanderliegende Revisionen durch den Komponisten zurückzuführen sind. Aus den Unterschieden der Lesarten geht hervor, daß Bach im Laufe der Zeit Verzierungen, Appoggiaturen, Warnungsakzidentien und andere aufführungspraktische Hinweise ergänzte, gelegentlich auch die Noten veränderte. Die Sonate in G-Dur (H. 43), teilweise gilt dies auch für die f-Moll-Sonate H. 40, wurde besonders stark revidiert, wobei ganze Passagen umkomponiert, wenn auch nicht völlig durch andere ersetzt worden sind. Es ist nicht möglich, diese Revisionen genau zu datieren. Die Änderungen in H. 40 wurden aber spätestens zur Drucklegung 1762 vorgenommen. Die Überarbeitung einiger anderer Werke, dies gilt insbesondere für H. 49, stammt möglicherweise erst aus Bachs letzten Lebensjahren.[6]

Die weitreichenden Revisionen im ersten Satz von H. 43 machten es notwendig, die ältere Fassung separat wiederzugeben, während sonst die Lesarten der Frühfassungen im Kritischen Bericht angemerkt werden. Oft unterscheiden sich die Frühfassungen nur durch das "Fehlen" von Verzierungen und anderer Artikulationszeichen vom Haupttext. Auf die Quellen der frühen Fassungen weist der jeweilige Kritische Bericht hin. Mit ziemlicher Sicherheit kann man abweichende Lesarten, die von einer ganzen Gruppe von Quellen geteilt werden, auf authentische Frühfassungen zurückführen; Ausnahmen sind im Kritischen Bericht angeführt. Abweichungen, die im Lesartenverzeichnis nicht dargestellt werden konnten, werden als Musikbeispiele wiedergegeben. Diese werden durchnumeriert und am Ende jedes Lesartenverzeichnisses zusammengefaßt. Quellen, die mehr als ein Werk enthalten, werden nur einmal vollständig beschrieben.

Leider ist es nicht möglich, die Lesarten der Frühfassungen zweifelsfrei wiederherzustellen, da die Urschriften mit einer einzigen Ausnahme verlorengegangen sind. Aber selbst im Falle des Autographs von H. 46, das im wesentlichen in den 1740er Jahren entstanden ist, kann man nicht immer zwischen originalen Einträgen und Revisionen unterscheiden, ohne die frühen Abschriften zum Vergleich heranzuziehen. Beim Autograph von H. 49 handelt es sich hingegen um eine Reinschrift, die in den letzten Jahren von Bachs Hamburger Aufenthalt (1768–88) entstanden ist und folglich zur Rekonstruktion einer etwaigen Frühfassung nicht herangezogen werden kann.

Die spätesten Fassungen aller sieben Sonaten verwenden die Verzierungszeichen, die Bach im ersten Teil seines *Versuchs über die wahre Art das Clavier zu spielen*[7] (Berlin 1753) eingehend beschrieben hat. Die mehrdeutigen Zeichen tr, t und +, die sich in den Frühfassungen verschiedentlich finden, wurden dabei allerdings nicht konsequent ersetzt. Besonders auffällig ist der häufige Gebrauch des Symbols + in den Sonaten H. 43 und H. 46. Obwohl dieses Zeichen in vielen Drucken des 18. Jahrhunderts, z.B. in der unautorisierten Ausgabe von H. 48, einen Mordent bezeichnet, scheint es bei Bach eher für ein flüchtig geschriebenes t zu stehen. Während sich die hier vorgelegte Ausgabe von H. 46 an das Autograph hält und die 'plus'-Zeichen getreu wiedergibt,

[5] Die Quellen zu H. 43, H. 46 und H. 48 der Library of Congress wurden vom Herausgeber im Original eingesehen; für die übrigen Quellen standen Mikrofilmaufnahmen zur Verfügung.

[6] Zu Bachs Revisionsmethode siehe P. Fox, "C. P. E. Bach's Compositional Proofreading", *The Musical Times*, 129 (1988), S. 651–655.

[7] Reprint, hrsg. von L. Hoffmann-Erbrecht, 4. Auflage, Leipzig 1978. Englische Übersetzung von W. Mitchell unter dem Titel *Essay on the True Art of Playing Keyboard Instruments* (New York 1949).

ersetzen späte Abschriften, darunter auch zwei von Bachs Kopist Michel angefertigte, das Symbol durchweg durch die Zeichen *t* oder *tr*, so daß es sich wohl um synonyme Bedeutungen handelt. In der Hauptquelle von H. 43 scheint Bach mindestens bei einer Passage den Austausch von + durch *tr* autorisiert zu haben.[8]

Interpreten, die mit Bachs Klaviermusik vertraut sind, werden bei den vorliegenden Werken kaum auf besondere Probleme stoßen. Viele Fragen lassen sich beantworten, wenn man Bachs *Versuch* konsultiert, dessen erster Band im Jahre 1753, d.h. nach der Entstehung, aber mit einiger Sicherheit vor der letzten Revision der Sonaten erschienen ist. Muster für Kadenzen über den Fermaten der langsamen Sätze von H. 40 und H. 43 sind in Quantz' *Versuch einer Anweisung die Flöte traversiere zu spielen*[9] (Berlin 1752) und einigen Werken Bachs, insbesondere den *Sechs Sonaten mit veränderten Reprisen*[10] (Berlin 1760), zu finden. Auffallend ist, daß trotz des vorgezeichneten Viervierteltakts beide Hälften des ersten Satzes von H. 46 mit einem Zweivierteltakt schließen.

Für die Aufführungspraxis ist die Frage nach dem intendierten Instrument wohl am wichtigsten. Obwohl man bei zwei Werken (H. 40 und H. 47) aufgrund der abgestuften Dynamik (*f*, *p* und *pp*) an das Fortepiano oder Clavichord denken wird, lautet die Instrumentenbezeichnung in allen Quellen "Cembalo", die aber bei Bach offenbar als Oberbegriff für alle besaiteten Tasteninstrumente steht.

---

[8] In den Takten 8 und 75 des ersten Satzes steht + bzw. *tr*; in beiden Takte hat Bach Revisionen im unteren System eingetragen, ohne die Verzierungszeichen im oberen System zu ändern. Das Problem wird im Kritischen Bericht zu H. 43 und H. 46 ausführlich erörtert. Im Autograph des Konzerts H. 421 (W. 18) aus dem Jahre 1745 wies C. P. E. Bach auf die Synonymität von *tr* und + explizit hin (vgl R. W. Wade, *The Keyboard Concertos of Carl Philipp Emanuel Bach*, Ann Arbor 1981, S. 67). W. F. Bach benutzte das 'Plus'-Zeichen ebenfalls, zum Beispiel im Autograph seines Konzerts für 2 Cembali (Fk. 10), das P. Wollny auf die Zeit um 1740 datiert ("Studies in the Music of Wilhelm Friedemann Bach: Sources and Style", Diss. Harvard University 1993, S. 123–125).

[9] Reprint der Ausgabe Berlin 1789 (Kassel 1953). Englische Übersetzung von Edward J. Reilly mit dem Titel: *An Essay on Playing the Flute* (London 1966).

[10] H. 136 — 140, 126; W. 50. Hrsg. von E. Darbellay (Winterthur 1976).

Während der Erstellung des vorliegenden Bandes hat die Carl Philipp Emanuel Bach-Forschung erhebliche Fortschritte, vor allem bei der Quellenbewertung, gemacht. Erkenntnisse, die erst im Verlauf der Bandherstellung bekannt wurden, sind soweit wie möglich berücksichtigt. Es erwies sich aber im nachhinein als unmöglich, vollständige Quellenbeschreibungen für viele Sekundärquellen aufzunehmen.

Die Edition dieses Bandes wurde erleichtert durch die Unterstützung des *National Endowment for the Humanities*, einer staatlichen Einrichtung der amerikanischen Regierung, die u.a. geistes-wissenschaftliche und historische Forschungen fördert. Das *Editorial Centre* der Carl Philipp Emanuel Bach-Ausgabe wurde von dieser Behörde gleichfalls bezuschußt.

Der Herausgeber dankt Ulrich Leisinger für eine gründliche Durchsicht der Druckfahnen und für die großzügige Überlassung von Informationen über Quellen, die für die Edition nur als Reproduktionen vorlagen. Der Herausgeber dankt auch Rachel Wade und E. Eugene Helm für Rat und Unterstützung sowie den Mitarbeitern von Oxford University Press für ihre Hilfe während der Bandherstellung. Dank gebührt weiterhin Elias N. Kulukundis, der dem Herausgeber einen Mikrofilm einer in seinem Besitz befindlichen Quelle überließ, sowie den folgenden Bibliotheken, die Zugang zu ihren Sammlungen gewährten und Kopien zur Verfügung gestellt haben: Gesellschaft der Musikfreunde Wien; Bibliothèque du Con-servatoire Royal de Musique Brüssel; Bibliothèque Royale Albert I. Brüssel; Staatsbibliothek zu Berlin — Preußischer Kulturbesitz, Musikabteilung mit Mendelssohn Archiv (ehemals Deutsche Staatsbibliothek Berlin und Staatsbibliothek Preußischer Kulturbesitz Berlin); Beethoven-Archiv Bonn; Forschungs- und Landesbibliothek Gotha; Bayerische Staatsbibliothek München; Schleswig-Holsteinische Landesbibliothek Kiel; Musikbibliothek der Stadt Leipzig; British Library London; Gemeente Museum Den Haag; Biblioteka Jagiellońska Krakau; University of Michigan, Ann Arbor; Yale University Library, New Haven, Connecticut; Library of Congress Washington, DC.

Übersetzt von Eike Wernhard und Ulrich Leisinger

Sonata in F minor
H. 40 (W. 6216)

Carl Philipp Emanuel Bach

Printed in Great Britain

OXFORD UNIVERSITY PRESS, MUSIC DEPARTMENT, WALTON STREET, OXFORD OX2 6DP

2

6

8

Sonata in G major
H. 43 (W. 65/15)

Carl Philipp Emanuel Bach

Prestissimo

16

* *e'* in five sources (see List of Variant Readings).

Sonata in G major
H. 43 (W. 65/15)

Early Version (First Movement)

Sonata in C major

H. 46 (W. 65/16)

Carl Philipp Emanuel Bach

Allegretto

Sonata in G minor
H. 47 (W. 65/17)

Carl Philipp Emanuel Bach

Sonata in F major
H. 48 (W. 65/18)

Carl Philipp Emanuel Bach

Allegro di molto

40

Sonata in F major
H. 49 (W. 65/19)

Carl Philipp Emanuel Bach

Alla Polacca

Sonata in B flat major
H. 51 (W. 65/20)

Carl Philipp Emanuel Bach

Adagio

52

CRITICAL COMMENTARY

Sonata in F minor, H. 40

SOURCES

Although it was composed in 1744, H. 40 was published only in 1761. The print, in the serialized anthology *Musikalisches Allerley* (MA), is listed in the *Nachlassverzeichnis*,[1] showing that Bach recognized it as an authorized issue of the work. The print is the only independent source of the final version and serves as the principal source for the present edition; all but two of the manuscript copies give an earlier version.

Although Bach was still resident in Berlin when the print appeared in that city, the print contains many errors, raising the question of whether Bach took an active role in the work's publication. Particularly problematical are two parallel passages in the first movement that had undergone revision (I. 16–19 and 71–3). To a considerable degree the print and the manuscripts agree on orthographic details such as beaming and the division of the notes between the staves, suggesting that all stem from a single autograph that was reworked at some point.

MA. *Musikalisches Allerley.* Print from movable type; part of a series containing various works by Bach and other composers.

Musikalisches Allerley was an anthology of keyboard and chamber works issued in weekly instalments from 22 November 1760 to 20 August 1763 by the Berlin music publisher Friedrich Wilhelm Birnstiel. Seventy-two issues appeared; most contained four pages, and every eight issues constituted a *Sammlung*, each with its own title page and table of contents. A single series of issue and page numbers runs through all seventy-two issues; the last numbered page is 270. (Title pages, each with table of contents on the reverse, were unnumbered.)

The following exemplars are known to exist. Of these, MA 4, 8, 9, 13, 14, and 15 were consulted for this edition.

MA 1. Vienna, Gesellschaft der Musikfreunde. Lacks *Sammlungen 5–9.*

MA 2. Vienna, Österreichische Nationalbibliothek. Lacks *Sammlung 9.*

MA 3. Brussels, Conservatoire Royal de Musique, Bibliothèque, 6313.

MA 4. Berlin, Deutsche Staatsbibliothek. In the first, second, fifth, seventh, and ninth *Sammlungen*, the names of some composers are followed by entries in an eighteenth-century English hand, such as after Agricola: 'Composer for the King at Berlin'. Names of composers also have been added to some of the tables of contents in the same hand. At the bottom of the title page for the seventh *Sammlung* appears the handwritten note: 'Ebeling geheftet in blaupapier.' The title page of the ninth *Sammlung* bears the signature A. Köhle. This is the only copy seen here to include handwritten corrections in the copy of H. 40; these occur in the third movement, bar 52.

MA 5. Bonn, Musikwissenschaftliches Seminar der Universität. Lacks *Sammlung 9.*

MA 6. Göttingen, Niedersächsische Staats- und Universitätsbibliothek. Lacks *Sammlungen 7–9.*

MA 7. Halle/Salle, Bibliothek des Musikwissenschaftlichen Instituts. First *Sammlung* only.

MA 8. Leipzig, Musikbibliothek der Stadt. The title page of the first *Sammlung* bears the signature 'Schich' [*sic*].

MA 9. Munich, Bayerische Staatsbibliothek. *Sammlungen 2–6* only.

---

[1] *Verzeichniss des musikalischen Nachlasses des verstorbenen Capellmeisters Carl Philipp Emanuel Bach* (Hamburg, 1790); facs. edn. annotated R. W. Wade as *The Catalog of Carl Philipp Emanuel Bach's Estate. A Facsimile of the Edition by Schniebes, Hamburg, 1790* (New York, 1981), p. 6. The *Nachlassverzeichnis* contains a listing of Bach's works, with incipits for instrumental works not issued in authorized prints in his lifetime. It is the source of the dates of composition given here.

MA 10.   Schwerin, Mecklenburgische Landesbibliothek.

MA 11.   Copenhagen, Det kongelige Bibliotek.
Sammlung 6 only.

MA 12.   London, Royal Academy of Music.

MA 13.   London, British Library. The title page
of the first *Sammlung* is signed 'H. E. D.
Biehl.'

MA 14.   The Hague, Gemeente Museum.

MA 15.   Ann Arbor, University of Michigan.
This copy lacks title pages to
Sammlungen 7 and 9; pages 269–70 are
also absent and have been replaced by a
modern manuscript copy from an
unstated source. The exemplar stems
from the Wagener collection, according
to the library catalogue card; a book-
plate on the inside of the cover reads
'Stellfeld Purchase 1954'.[2]

No editor is named, but a short note signed by
the publisher opens the first issue. Here Birnstiel
promises to provide experts and amateurs with 'the
newest musical essays by good composers in the
German, Italian, and French style'.[3] The series was
to be continued each Saturday. A note at the bottom of the first page announces that each issue costs
two Groschen.

The series was evidently planned with some care,
and the layout of music and of title pages and contents in the several *Sammlungen* is highly consist-
ent. The contents of each issue must have been
decided well in advance of publication; short keyboard dances and *Oden* occupying a single page (or
less) mingle with longer works, including chamber
sonatas and vocal ensembles in score. Sonatas and
other multi-movement works often extend over
two issues, the first issue sometimes breaking off in
the middle of a movement, but page-turns nearly
always occur at the ends of movements or sections.
Occasionally an issue or a page containing the end
of a long composition is padded out with one or
two short pieces, and two paired pieces (for exam-

ple, two minuets in the same key) are sometimes
separated by a longer movement occupying several
pages. If the dates of publication within the
Musikalisches Allerley are accurate, its issues usually appeared regularly every week for eight weeks,
but there were sometimes gaps of a few months
between collections, as can be seen in Table 1.[4]

Table 1: Publication History of the *Musikalisches Allerley*

Sammlung. Number	Issue Numbers	Dates of Issue (day. month. year)	Page Numbers
1	1–[8]	22.11.1760–[10.1.1761]	1–30
2	9–16	17.1.1761–7.3.61	31–60
3	17–24	14.3.61–2.5.61	61–90
4	25–32	9.5.61–4.7.61	91–120
5	33–40	11.7.61–29.8.61	121–50
6	41–8	28.11.61–16.1.1762	151–80
7	49–56	3.7.1762–21.8.62	181–210
8	57–64	1.1.1763–19.2.63	211–40
9	65–72	2.7.63–20.8.63	241–70

Virtually all of the composers were members of
what is loosely referred to as the Berlin school.
Kirnberger and Marpurg are represented by the
greatest number of pieces, although most of
Marpurg's contributions are *Oden* occurring in the
first three *Sammlungen*. The proportion of sonatas
to shorter pieces increases somewhat in the later
Sammlungen; Bach is represented by only eleven
pieces, including four entitled 'Claviersonate'
beginning in the fourth *Sammlung*.

The title page of the fifth *Sammlung*, in which H.
40 appears, reads: 'Musikalisches Allerley / von /
verschiedenen Tonkünstlern. / 5te Sammlung. /
Berlin, / bey Friedrich Wilhelm Birnstiel, Königl.
privilegirten Buchdrucker. 1761.' Overleaf appears
the 'Inhalt / der fünften Sammlung' listing the contents of issues 33–40 (11 July–29 August 1761)
without the names of the composers.

H. 40 occupies the whole of the '38tes' and '39tes
Stücke' (pages 141–8). The first movement occupies the '38tes Stück' (pages 141–4), whose initial
page bears the following title: 'Musikalisches
Allerley. / 38tes Stück. / Berlin, den 15ten August
1761.' The music follows beneath this, under the
heading: 'Claviersonate. / Vom Herrn Carl Philipp
Emanuel Bach.' At the bottom of the last page of
this issue is the notice: 'Die Fortsetzung im nächsten

[2]   H. 40 from exemplar MA 15 is reproduced in facsimile in D. Berg, ed., *The Collected Works for Solo Keyboard
by Carl Philipp Emanuel Bach 1714–1788* (New York,
1985), III, pp. 7–14.

[3]   'die neuesten musikalischen Versuche guter Ton-
meister . . . im deutschen, italienischen und französischen
Geschmack.' There appears to be no foundation for the
entry 'herausgegeben von Friedr. Wilh. Marpurg,' added by
hand to the title page of the first *Sammlung* in MA 14.

[4]   Table 1 has been supplied by R. W. Wade.

Stücke.' Issue 39 opens with a title similar to that of Issue 38, followed by the notice: 'Beschluß der Claviersonate. / Vom Herrn Carl Philipp Emanuel Bach.' At the conclusion of the last movement is the notice: 'Bey Friedrich Wilhelm Birnstiel zu haben.'

Only one variant occurs in H. 40 among the exemplars examined, and only in MA 15, in the passage in the first movement discussed below (bars 16–19). The passage is faulty in both readings, but the variant in all the other exemplars seen is musically nonsensical, and occurs in a passage that underwent revision. Hence it is likely to have been the result of a misreading of the score supplied by Bach, and to have been corrected by someone in the printer's shop before all the copies had been printed. But the many remaining errors make it doubtful that Bach himself was involved in the printing process. Despite the numerous mistakes in the print, only two handwritten corrections have been observed, both in bar 52 of the third movement in MA 4. The most common of these errors are the displacement or omission of accidentals (see below under 'Establishing the text') and the omission of slurs and ties.

B Br. Brussels, Bibliothèque Royale Albert I, II 4094 (fonds Fétis 2969). Contains twenty-five keyboard works by Emanuel Bach, copied from various printed anthologies by J. J. H. Westphal. Oblong format, 24.5 × 32 cm.

The Schwerin organist and collector J. J. H. Westphal (1756–1825), who assembled a nearly complete collection of Bach's instrumental music, was also responsible for an unpublished thematic catalogue of the composer's works now in the Bibliothèque Royale, Brussels (II 4104). This catalogue, in its final draft, was the source for various bibliographic entries made in the nineteenth century in manuscripts belonging to the Brussels and Berlin libraries. It also provided the basis for an unpublished nineteenth-century thematic catalogue in Berlin[5] and for the thematic catalogue by Alfred Wotquenne (1867–1939).[6]

II 4094 in the Bibliothèque Royale is a bound volume consisting of four originally separate manuscripts containing Westphal's copies of published works by C. P. E. Bach (W. 62/1–24 and H. 179 (W. 112/7)). The paper bears the Netherlands watermark BLAUW, implying a late-eighteenth-century date. Together with other sources from Westphal's collection, it was acquired by the Belgian musicologist François Joseph Fétis (1784–1871). At his death it was purchased from his estate by the Belgian government and deposited in the Bibliothèque Royale Albert I.[7]

The title page of part 3 (folio 29^r of the whole source), which is carefully laid out to resemble that of a printed edition, reads: 'Sechs Clavier Sonaten / von / dem Herrn Capellmeister Carl Philipp Emanuel Bach. / aus verschiedenen Sammlungen, worinnen sie einzeln / gedruckt stehen, zusammen getragen. / Dritte Sammlung. / Inhalt.' A thematic index of the contents follows in two columns. At the left of each column are Westphal's titles ('Sonata I', 'Sonata II', etc.) and the keys of the works; in the centre are the musical incipits; and to the right are bibliographic entries describing the printed sources of the works. The four 'sonatas' (the first is actually a suite) that appeared in *Musikalisches Allerley* are given first, in the same order as in the print (H. 66, 63, 40, 2). The two last works are H. 41 (W. 62/7) and 132 (W. 62/22).

In Westphal's thematic catalogue the works from *Musikalisches Allerley* are listed in group 11 of the sonatas published in anthologies. H. 40 is the third sonata listed in sub-group 'c', which evidently corresponds with the sonatas in 4094. The incipit in the catalogue is identical to the one on the title page of the copy.

H. 40 appears on folios 34^v–37^r of II 4094. The title 'Sonata. III' appears in the upper left of page 34.

The copy in II 4094 is probably a direct copy of Westphal's exemplar of *Musikalisches Allerley* B Bc 63/3. Like other copies by Westphal, it occasionally departs from its probable model, suggesting that Westphal himself may have edited the text (notably in I. 18–19). On the first page of the last movement, faint numbers have been added in a foreign hand beneath the lower stave: '2' (after bar 8), '4' (after bar 15), '6' (after bar 26), etc. These points corre-

---

[5] Now Mus. ms. theor. K. 490 in the Deutsche Staatsbibliothek, Berlin.

[6] On the various versions of Westphal's catalogue and its relationship to later catalogues, see R. W. Wade, *The Keyboard Concertos of Carl Philipp Emanuel Bach*, Studies in Musicology, no. 48 (Ann Arbor, 1981), pp. 7–14.

[7] On Fétis's acquisitions from Westphal's, see M. Terry, 'C. P. E. Bach and J. J. H. Westphal—A Clarification', *JAMS* 22 (1969), pp. 106–15, especially 115. Here and below, information about measurements, watermarks, and provenance has been kindly supplied by Ulrich Leisinger unless otherwise indicated.

spond with the ends of systems in the edition by Aristide Farrenc (1794–1865) in *Le Trésor des pianistes* (Paris, 1861–72). The copy in 4094 was evidently the source for Farrenc's edition, although the only source named there is *Musikalisches Allerley*.[8] At several points, notably bars 18–19 of the first movement, Farrenc's edition follows 4094 rather than *Musikalisches Allerley*, and the numbers added in 4094 suggest that it served as the printer's copy for at least the last movement in Farrenc's edition. Farrenc evidently had access to the Fétis collection, where 4094 was to be found in the 1860s.[9] But while he might have seen the exemplar of *Musikalisches Allerley* (MA 3) in the Brussels Conservatory, the few discrepancies between his edition and 4094 are probably editorial emendations or typographic errors. Thus Farrenc's edition itself has no value as a source.

P 790. Berlin, Staatsbibliothek Preußischer Kulturbesitz, Musikabteilung, Mus. ms. Bach P 790. Contains copies of keyboard sonatas by C. P. E. Bach by various unknown copyists. Oblong format.

P 790 contains copies of nine sonatas, one of them twice. Each has a separate title page. The manuscript belonged to the collector Aloys Fuchs (1799–1853) and the copies in it are the work of members of the group of the Viennese writers of around 1800 designated Su VI by Paul Kast.[10]

The copy of H. 40 in P 790 occupies pages 53–62. The title page (page 51) reads: 'Sonate / pour / Piano Forte / de / Charles P. E. Bach'. This is ornamented by an elaborate pattern of arcs and other designs. Added below in a foreign hand is an incipit on two staves giving bars 1–2 of the first movement. Other entries in other hands are: '5.' in the top centre, corresponding to the copy's place in P 790; 'C' in the lower left corner; and the following bibliographic entries in different hands across the bottom: 'Th Kat 59,1 = Nachl 6,40', '[Wotquenne 62,6]'.[11]

All pages, including the title page and pages 52 and 62 (which are otherwise blank), are ruled in ten staves. At several points missing dynamic indications have been inserted and at least one other correction made (III. 52), probably by a later hand.

H. 40 appears to have been copied from *Musikalisches Allerley*. But at several points it lacks accidentals, notably at bar 58 of the first movement. Since P 790 contains a number of probably careless omissions (for example, I. 41, 77), the variants involving accidentals are more likely to have resulted from carelessness than from editing by the copyist or dependence on some lost independent source.

P 367. Berlin, Staatsbibliothek Preußischer Kulturbesitz, Musikabteilung, Mus. ms. Bach P 367. A collection of keyboard and ensemble works by C. P. E. Bach, originally at least five separate manuscripts in various hands and of various sizes. Keyboard works in oblong format, 22 × 34 cm. (watermark: lily; countermark: IV).

P 367 as a whole bears no general title page or possessor's mark. Although a copy of H. 853 (Wq. n. v. 10) in the second section of the manuscript bears the signature 'Pölchau', that is, the collector Georg Pölchau (1773–1836), there appear to be no traces of his ownership in the section containing sonatas. The copy of H. 40 in P 367 is the fourth of six sonatas in the hand of Johann Gottfried Müthel (1728–88) that now occupy the last section of the collection, pages 126–46 as currently bound and paginated.[12]

The pagination is not original, but no earlier pagination or foliation was observed in the copy of H. 40, even though this section of the collection appears to have been bound or at least ruled and planned before the music was entered in. None of the pieces has a separate title page. On two ruled but otherwise blank pages (125 and 135) a later owner has added 'autogr v Müthel'. The (correct) attribution 'di C. P. E. Bach' on page 126, part of the heading of the copy of H. 59 (W. 62/10), has been crossed out.

The copy of H. 40 occupies pages 136–9. At the

[8] *Le Trésor des pianistes* was issued in instalments gathered into twenty-three volumes (Paris, 1861–72). The instalment containing H. 40 appeared in 1863.

[9] The edition of H. 47 (Paris, 1864) is 'd'après les manuscrits appartenants à Mr. F. J. Fétis.'

[10] For copyists and inventory, see P. Kast, *Die Bach-Handschriften der Berliner Staatsbibliothek*, Tübinger Bach-Studien, Heft 2/3 (Trossingen, 1958), pp. 47, 139.

[11] The last reference is to the Berlin copy of Westphal's catalogue, Mus. ms. theor. K. 490 in the Deutsche Staatsbibliothek; 'Nachl' is the *Nachlassverzeichnis*, which lists H. 40 as entry 40 on page 6.

[12] Complete inventory in Kast, p. 26.

top left of page 136 is the title: 'Sonata per il Cembalo Solo' and to the right of this the attribution 'di C. P. E. Bach'. Added in the centre in a later hand is: 'Them. Verz. 6,40', a reference to the Berlin copy of Westphal's catalogue (see note 11).

An idiosyncrasy in the copy of H. 40 in P 367 is the use of an ornament sign that resembles a turn in horizontal form with a vertical stroke through the middle. It usually occurs where other sources give a trill sign, and is readily distinguished from real turns since Müthel always draws these in the older upright form. The sign appears also in H. 18 (W. 65/9), but in none of the other sonatas in this section of P 367.

Müthel visited Bach at Berlin in 1751 during a journey that also included visits to Leipzig, Dresden, and Naumburg, all points of contact with members of the Bach circle. The two composers subsequently corresponded for twenty years, and Müthel eventually owned or copied a considerable number of works by Emanuel Bach.[13] The copy of H. 40 is accurate, and, except for the notation of ornaments, agrees closely with the copy in P 368.

P 368. Berlin, Staatsbibliothek Preußicher Kulturbesitz, Musikabteilung Mus. ms. Bach P 368. A collection of keyboard works of C. P. E. Bach, W. F. Bach, and at least one other composer, by various copyists.

The cover of P 368 bears the distinctive heart-shaped label of the Leipzig Thomaskantor Johann Gottfried Schicht (1753–1823). Several hands have added notations to the label, although it is difficult to determine precisely which markings are original. The complete inscription now reads: 'P 368 / No: 762.–785. / [crossed out:] Sonate / Divertimento. / per il / Cembalo, / del Sgr. C. P. E. Bach e / del Sgr. W. F. Bach. / Schicht. / 919 [?]'.

P 368 consists of nineteen fascicles on paper most likely from Dresden. Kast named Gottfried August Homilius (1714–85) and an unidentified eighteenth-century writer as copyists, but the copies assigned to Homilius show considerable differences in handwriting. Of several unattributed

pieces, two are known from other sources as works of Wagenseil. The only attribution to composers other than the Bach sons is that of one piece to 'Mons. Gronau', presumably the Danzig organist Daniel Magnus Gronau (d. 1747).[14]

Homilius was a student at the Leipzig university from 1735 until 1741 or 1742, when he was appointed organist at the Frauenkirche in Dresden. He later (1755) became music director of the city's three chief Protestant churches. While in Leipzig he studied with Sebastian Bach. In Dresden he might have exchanged music with Friedemann Bach, organist at the Sophienkirche 1733–46.[15]

The copies of works by C. P. E. Bach that have been assigned to Homilius are of the sonatas H. 16 (W. 65/7), H. 18 (W. 65/9), H. 19 (W. 65/10), H. 46 (W. 65/16), H. 51 (W. 65/20), and H. 56 (W. 65/22), and the variations H. 54 (W. 118/4). All of the sonatas are given in early versions, those of H. 16, H. 18, and H. 19 presumably predating the reworking of those works that occurred in 1743–4.[16] But as H. 56 was not composed until 1748, it is possible that certain copies were made after Bach had already revised at least some of the works. In that case the copyist is unlikely to have acquired his texts directly from Bach.

The second writer copied five works of Emanuel Bach: the sonatas H. 22 (W. 62/3), H. 23 (W. 65/12), H. 32.5 (W. 65/13), H. 39 (W. 62/5), and H. 40, all in early versions. These now fall within a single section of the manuscript (pages 54–103) measuring 33 × 20 cm. (watermark: crowned coat

[13] On Müthel's relationship to Bach, see R. G. Campbell, 'Johann Gottfried Müthel, 1728–1788' (Ph. D. diss., Indiana University, 1966), pp. 23–7; E. Kemmler, *Johann Gottfried Müthel (1728–1788) und das norddeutsche Musikleben seiner Zeit*, Wissenschaftliche Beiträge zur Geschichte und Landeskunde Ost-Mitteleuropas, no. 88 (Marburg/Lahn, 1970), 21–7; and Wade, *The Keyboard Concertos*, p. 42.

[14] U. Leisinger and P. Wollny, in '"Altes Zeug von mir": Carl Philipp Emanuel Bachs kompositorisches Schaffen vor 1740', *Bach-Jahrbuch* 79 (1993), p. 169, identify Kast's Inc. 67 and 72 in P 368 as movements from items 75 and 8, respectively, in H. Michelitsch, *Das Klavierwerk von Georg Christoph Wagenseil* (Vienna, 1966). The tenth movement of Inc. 68 is a version of the polonoise H. 340 (= Wq. n.v. 54) (ibid., p. 168). The source is described in P. Wollny, 'Studies in the Music of Wilhelm Friedemann Bach: Sources and Style' (diss., Harvard University, 1993, pp. 96–8), where it is dated 1748–50. P 368 is listed as item 919 in *Versteigerungs-Katalog der von dem verstorbenen Herrn J. G. Schicht, Cantor an der Thomasschule zu Leipzig hinterlassenen Büchersammlung* (Leipzig, 1832).

[15] W. Horn also notes the possibility that W. F. Bach might have provided music to Homilius, in *Carl Philipp Emanuel Bach: Frühe Klaviersonaten* (Hamburg, 1988), p. 260.

[16] Facsimiles of Homilius's copies of H. 16, H. 18 and H. 19 appear in Berg, ed., *The Collected Works*, III, pp. 196, 212, 222.

of arms). The works lack separate title pages, and in some cases (including H. 40) have no title or other heading at all. The handwriting is completely different from that of Homilius, and the two copyists may not have had anything to do with each other, although both copied early versions.

The copy of H. 40 occupies the pages of P 368 numbered (in a foreign hand) 88–95. There are several omissions and other errors but the text otherwise is very close to that of P 367.

D BNba. Bonn, Beethoven-Archiv, Sammlung Herbert Grundmann HM II. Copy of H. 40 by an unidentified copyist, oblong format (23 × 31 cm.).

This copy of H. 40 is from a *Konvolut* containing seventeen fascicles in which appear nineteen keyboard sonatas (mostly from W. 62) and the Simrock print of six fugues from W. 119. It is from the collection of Ludwig Scheibler (1848–1921), from which it passed through the estate of Erich Prieger (1849–1913) and the collections of Paul Mies and Herbert Grundmann before entering the Beethoven-Archiv.

H. 40 is in fascicle 6 and occupies pages 59–69. The copyist is the same as that of D KIl 52/5 (see below on H. 51). The cover bears the title: 'SONATA / per il Cembalo / dal Sigl. C. F. E. Bach / CB. lii [?]'. The original text is close to but independent of that of P 368; many additions in a later hand give readings of the later (printed) version.[17]

D KIl. Kiel, Schleswig-Holsteinische Landes-bibliothek, Mb 48/2. Unknown copyist.

Like the Kiel copies of H. 46–8 and H. 51, this one shows signs of having passed through several owners. But the handwriting and the various markings found here do not conform to the patterns described below for any of the other Kiel sources. Like the Bonn source, this manuscript was previously in the Scheibler and Prieger collections.

The copy of H. 40 is on eight unnumbered pages. The original title at the top of the first page reads: 'Sonata Per il Cembalo Solo.' The first word is offset to the left. In the upper right-hand corner, probably in the same hand, is the attribution 'dall Sigre. C. P. E. Bach'. Added at the top centre in a foreign

hand are the figures '1297–1926' (?), and to the right of the title appears an illegible entry in another hand, possibly beginning 'No.' The call number has been added by a third hand beneath the title, and at the bottom left of the page is a modern bibliographic entry, 'Wotquenne. Cat. them. Nr. 62,6.' An illegible entry, possibly a *volti* indication, occurs at the bottom right.

The text is clear and accurate, and lacks the error (subsequently corrected) found in the slow movement in the following two copies (bar 30). But the rest is lacking in the first bar of the slow movement; this reading in a common model might have given rise to the incorrect emendation found in P 365 and P 414. A few ornaments found nowhere else suggest that the writer of D KIl 48/2 was aware of the ornament tradition of Bach's *Versuch* and may occasionally have supplemented the original signs on his own.

P 365. Berlin, Deutsche Staatsbibliothek, Mus. ms. Bach P 365. A collection of keyboard works of C. P. E. and W. F. Bach by several unidentified Berlin copyists.

P 365, a *Konvolut* according to Kast, contains twenty-four pieces, mostly sonatas, by Emanuel Bach, together with two pieces by Friedemann.[18] Most of the pieces appeared in print during the eighteenth century, but the copy of H. 40 follows the manuscript tradition. The unidentified copyists of P 365 are those designated Anon. 302, Anon. 303, and members of the group known as Su III; some copies by Anon. 303 and 'Su III' were prepared for Bach.[19]

The copy of H. 40, on pages 66–79, is assigned to Su III but shows no sign of having been overseen by the composer. It lacks title page and attribution; the title at the top of page 66 is: 'Sonata'. The copy contains a greater number of small errors than either of the copies in P 367 and P 368, as well as several apparently arbitrary alterations, notably the unique version of the second ending at the end of the first movement (also found in D KIl, but with an apparent error). This is probably the copyist's

---

[17] U. Leisinger furnished the description of the Bonn source, a copy of which became available to the editor too late for its readings to be incorporated in the list of variant readings. Concerning Scheibler's collection, see U. Leisinger and P. Wollny, '"Altes Zeug von mir"', p. 130 n. 14.

[18] For inventory, see Kast, pp. 25–6.

[19] Designations are from Kast, pp. 25–6. The copyist of H. 40 in P 365 is not the same as the copyist also designated 'Su III' of H. 51 in P 359. In addition to the contents listed by Kast, the manuscript contains an incomplete copy of H. 61 (W. 65/25) in the same hand as the copy of H. 77 (W. 62/14).

own interpretation of the notation for the second ending employed in the earlier version of the sonata. Nevertheless this copy, together with the following one, confirms many readings of P 367 and P 368 for the earlier version.

P 414. Berlin, Staatsbibliothek Preußicher Kulturbesitz, Musikabteilung, Mus. ms. Bach P 414. Contains copies by the same scribe as P 365 of keyboard works by C. P. E. and J. S. Bach, Johann Gottlieb Goldberg, and at least one anonymous composer. Oblong format.

P 414 contains only two complete works by C. P. E. Bach, the organ sonatas H. 84 (W. 70/3) (in F) and H. 87 (W. 70/6).[20] Following H. 84, on pages 42–3, is a copy of the slow movement of H. 40. There is no title. The handwriting and text closely match those of P 365.[21] Both contain the same copying error and subsequent correction in bar 30, although an error in the following bar in P 414 was not corrected. The copy in P 414 is probably a direct copy from P 365; there is no evidence that Bach authorized the attachment of the slow movement of H. 40 to H. 84.

US NHu. New Haven, Yale University, Lowell Mason Collection, 5009. Keyboard works of C. P. E. Bach and Kirnberger by a copyist of the late eighteenth or early nineteenth century.

The Lowell Mason collection, better known for its sources of works by J. S. Bach, also contains a relatively small number of manuscript copies of music by C. P. E. Bach. The present manuscript, like many in the collection, was purchased in 1852 by Lowell Mason (1792–1872) from the estate of Johann Heinrich Christian Rinck (1770–1846). Mason's heirs presented the collection to Yale University in 1873.[22] Rinck had studied at Erfurt with Johann Christoph Kittel (1732–1809), one of the last students of J. S. Bach, but he is not known to have had any connection with Emanuel Bach or his heirs.

The cover bears a title in an eighteenth-century

German hand not recognizable elsewhere in the manuscript: '3. Sonaten / di / C. P. E. Bach.' The stamp of the Lowell Mason collection and the handwritten number 5009 (crossed out) appear in the upper right corner.

There are twenty-four pages, all but the first bearing music. The first is a title page reading: 'III. / SONATA / peril [*sic*; as if one word] / Cempalo [*sic*] Solo. / del Sigre. / C. P. E. Bach: / Poss. J: Ch: H: Rinck.' The Roman numeral III appears to be a later addition, suggesting that the three sections of the manuscript were originally separate. The possessor's mark, presumably in Rinck's hand, does not match lettering elsewhere in the manuscript, which was apparently copied by someone else.

The source includes a number of Bach's character pieces, but these are given as movements of a synthetic 'sonata', designated by tempo marks only, without their descriptive titles. The character pieces included are *La Prinzette*, H. 91 (W. 117/21), titled 'Allegretto' (fo. 7[r]); *L'Aly Rupalich*, H. 95 (W. 117/27), titled 'Allegro assai' (fos. 7[v]–8[v]); *La Gleim*, H. 89 (W. 117/19), titled 'Allegro grazioso' (fos. 8[v]–9[r]); *La Stahl*, H. 94 (W. 117/25), titled 'Grave' (fos. 9[v]–10[r]); *La Buchholz*, H. 93 (W. 117/24), titled 'Allegro' (fos. 10[v]–11[r]); *L'Herrmann*, H. 92 (W. 117/23), titled 'Allegro Moderato' (fos. 11[v]–12[r]). A single title is given for all six character pieces: 'Sonata / Petites / Pieces'. Evidently intended as part of the same synthetic 'sonata' is the last piece, on fo. 12[v], an Allegro bearing the further inscription 'fürs Klavier: von H. Kirnberger in Berlin'. The incipit corresponds to that of the Allegro in G, E. 18, published in *Musikalisches Vielerley* (Hamburg, 1770). The handwriting of this entry, in German script, does not appear to match anything elsewhere in the manuscript. The remainder of the manuscript consists of H. 40 (fos. 1[v]–5[r]) and the variations H. 54 (W. 118/4; fos. 5[v]–6[v]).

The title of H. 40 given at the upper left above the music (fo. 1[v]) is 'Sonata peril [*sic*] Cembalo Solo', and the attribution 'del Sigr. C. P. E. Bach' appears in the upper right corner.

The manuscript gives a somewhat inaccurate text of the early version, containing some careless errors (see, for example, variants listed for I. 3, 29, 40; omission of II. 33) and a small number of arbitrary additions (for example, trills on the dotted eighths in II. 20–1, *forte* on the chords in II. 45, 47). But certain details missing in other sources (for example, the flat in I. 27, the double-stemmed note

[20] Complete inventory in Kast, p. 29.

[21] In Kast, the copyist of P 414 is designated 'Su, um 1800'.

[22] G. Herz, *Bach Sources in America* (Kassel, 1984), pp. 210–11. See also H. C. Fall, 'A Critical-Bibliographical Study of the Rinck Collection', MA thesis, Yale University, 1958, which includes an inventory of the collection.

in I. 43) are present, suggesting that this is an independent copy of the earliest known version. Particularly notable is the frequent use of the abbreviation *tr* where other sources give specific ornament signs; since Bach himself rarely indicated specific ornament signs in the 1740s, it is possible that manuscript 5009 preserves the earliest readings at these points (for example, I. 8; II. 4, 5, 18).

D LEm. Leipzig, Musikbibliothek der Stadt, Sammlung Gorke Nr., 346 (since 1952 on permanent loan to Leipzig, Bach-Archiv). Unknown copyist.

The Gorke collection was assembled by the Eisenach banker Manfred Gorke (1897–1956) and donated to the city of Leipzig in 1935. The copyist and provenance of manuscript 346 are unknown, although one of two watermarks found in the copy includes the date 1751.[23]

The source gives the same early version of the text as P 368, D BNba, P 367, P 365, P 414, and D Mbs, but contains many unique errors and is of little value to the edition. At several points the writer appears to have attempted to edit the text, notably in bar 18 of the first movement, which shows two corrections. The readings both before and after correction may have arisen through attempts to solve the voice-leading problems in the passage.

D Mbs. Munich, Bayerische Staatsbibliothek, Mus. ms. 1795. Contains three copies of keyboard sonatas by C. P. E. Bach, all in the same unidentified hand and with separate title page. Copy of H. 40 employing soprano clef.

Manuscript 1795 consists of three originally separate manuscripts containing copies of H. 17 (W. 65/9), H. 87 (W. 70/6), and H. 40. There is no general title page, but the folios have been numbered in the upper right corner by a foreign hand. Just beneath the last folio number (16) are two initials ('J. J.'; Jesu juva?) followed by an illegible mark.

The copy of H. 40 occupies fos. 11ᵛ–16ʳ. The title page, on fo. 11ʳ, reads as follows: 'Sonate. ex F: mol. / à / Clavicembalo. Solo. / del Sigr: Carl Ph: Eman: Bach'. Added above the first line in a foreign hand is: 'No. 9'. In a second foreign hand is written

at the bottom: '9ᵇ/5'. At the top of the first page of music appears only the word 'Cembalo.'

Both music and verbal rubrics (for example, 'Secunda Parte / Vertat:' at the end of fo. 12ʳ) employ a style different from that used in Bach's own circle. In addition, the copy is the only one to give the upper stave in soprano clef, although no transposition errors are present. Nevertheless the text contains many unique errors as well as several apparently arbitrary alterations, such as the tempo (Allegro non molto) for the first movement. The copy is of little value except as evidence for the circulation of the early version beyond Bach's immediate circle.

Establishing the text
That the version of the manuscript tradition is earlier than the published one is clear from the additional embellishment of the slow movement in the print, which at many points substitutes explicit ornament signs for the vaguer indication *tr*. In addition, the print contains greater consistency in articulation and dynamics in parallel passages, although the discrepancies in the manuscript tradition may stem partly from copyist errors. Most of the errors in *Musikalisches Allerley* (MA) can be corrected by reference to the manuscripts, even though these are themselves often faulty. Only a few passages raise serious textual questions (I. 58, and the passages discussed below; II. 13–14). By the same token, the odd placement of the tempo mark 'Presto' between the staves at the beginning of the last movement suggests that it was a late addition to the autograph.[24]

Although P 367, P 368, D BNba, KIl, P 365, P 414, and US NHu form a group distinct from D LEm and D Mbs, there is little evidence that the distinctive readings of the latter two stem from the composer. The turns in D LEm and D Mbs in the slow movement (especially bars 2–5 and parallel passages) might conceivably belong to a transitional version. But these signs might equally well be arbitrary alterations. Within the first group, D KIl, P 365, P 414, and US NHu form a distinct subgrouping, within which D KIl is further distinguished by a few otherwise unattested ornament signs in the first two movements. But there is no reason to give these any special credence, although they are stylistically plausible.

[23] Watermark and date reported in H.-J. Schulze, ed., *Katalog der Sammlung Manfred Gorke: Bachiana und andere Handschriften und Drucke des 18. und frühen 19. Jahrhunderts*. Bibliographische Veröffentlichungen der Musikbibliothek der Stadt Leipzig, 8 (Leipzig, 1977), p. 84.

[24] The sources of the manuscript tradition confirm that both 'Presto' and 'e staccato' were originally absent.

The most important textual problem occurs in two parallel passages (I. 16–19 and I. 71–3) that underwent substantial revisions. Even after the correction made at bar 19 in MA 15 (the removal of an extraneous b♭ on the downbeat), a redundant natural (for d') remains on the third beat of the previous bar. The print also contains an inconsistency between the parallel bars 17 and 72 (bar 17 lacks the eighth-note d' on the third beat). B Br gives a

weak and apparently conjectural reading in bars 18–19. *Le Trésor des pianistes*, while following B Br at that point, indicates a crossing of voices in bar 72, upper stave. Voice crossing is in fact implied in both bars 17 and 72. While the print omits the note d' on the third beat of bar 17, it is present in the manuscript tradition and has been retained in the edition.

LIST OF VARIANT READINGS

(Music examples can be found on pp. 74–6)

bar / stave / note-and-rest no.	source: remark	bar / stave / note-and-rest no.	source: remark
First Movement		16–17	P 367, P 368, D KIl, P 365, US NHu, D LEm, D Mbs: as Ex. 1a except as noted below; MA, B Br: as Ex. 1b (=*CPEBE*)
—	P 367, P 368, D KIl, P 365: no tempo mark		
	D Mbs: Allegro non molto		
—	P 368, D Mbs: time signature: ¢	16 / top / 1	D LEm, D Mbs: no rest
3 / bottom / 8	US NHu: g not f	17 / top / 5	d' from P 367, P 368, D KIl, P 365, D LEm, D Mbs
5 / top / 7	P 367, P 368, D KIl, P 365: no ♭		
5 / bottom / 4	P 367, P 368, US NHu, D LEm: tr not ⌇⌇⌇	17 / bottom / 1	P 368, D LEm: no rest
	D Mbs: ⌇?	18–19	P 367, P 368, D KIl, P 365, US NHu, D LEm, D Mbs: as Ex. 2a except as noted below; *CPEBE* as Ex. 2b; MA, P 790: as Ex. 15a (MA 15 lacks ♭ in bar 19); B Br: as Ex. 15b
6 / top / 9	US NHu: no n		
8 / top / 1–2	P 367, P 368, P 365, D LEm, D Mbs: no slur on f'–e'		
	P 368: nor on b–c'		
8 / top / 2	P 367, P 368, P 365: ⌇ on g'	18 / 1	D LEm: orig. F/d/b/d', top note erased
	US NHu: tr on g'		
	D LEm: ⌇ on g'	18 / top / 8	P 365: no e♭'
	D KIl: ⌇ on e'	18 / bottom / 2–3	US NHu: no a♭, no a♮
8 / bottom / 1–2	D KIl, P 365: slur	18 / downstem / 5	D LEm: as Ex. 2a but orig. d not D (?), erased
11 / top / 3	P 368, D LEm: no rest		
11	D LEm: as Ex. 14a; D Mbs: as Ex. 14b; remaining sources as Ex. 14c (=*CPEBE*)	19 / top / 1	P 367: as Ex. 2a but no ♮ before b
			US NHu: no b♮
13 / top / 1	US NHu: The g is separately stemmed and followed by 8th rest, quarter rest	21 / top / 1–2	D Mbs: no chord, no rest
		21 / bottom, upstem / 1	P 367, P 368, D KIl, P 365: quarter note, not 8th-note
15 / middle part	D KIl, P 365, US NHu: following downbeat: 8th rest, quarter rest		US NHu: no c
		22, 23 / bottom / 2	D Mbs: no f', e♭'
15 / bottom / 2–4	D LEm: no rests	23 / top / 6	MA, B Br, P 790: ♮ on 6 not 7
15 / bottom / 3	D Mbs: two 8th rests		

bar / stave / note-and-rest no.	source: remark
24 / top / 8	P 367, P 368, D KIl, P 365: tr not 𝆗
	US NHu: 𝆗
	D LEm, D Mbs: no orn.
24 / bottom / 1	P 367, P 368, D LEm: preceded by ♮
24 / bottom / 2–3	D Mbs: no tie
24 / bottom / 9	MA, B Br, P 790: ♮ on 9 not 10
25 / top / 1–2	D Mbs: no tie
27 / bottom / 8	MA, B Br, P 790, D KIl, P 365, D Mbs: no ♭
	D KIl: ♭ inserted (foreign hand?)
28 / top, upstem / 14	MA, B Br: ♮
28 / top, upstem / 15	P 367, P 368, D KIl, P 365: no ♮
29 / top / 9	P 367, P 368, D KIl, P 365, US NHu, D LEm (?), D Mbs: 1-flag app.
	D LEm: 2-flag app.?
29 / top / 10	P 367, P 368, US NHu, D Mbs: tr not ≈
	D KIl, P 365, D LEm: no orn.
29 / bottom / 3	US NHu: g not f
30	P 367, P 368, D KIl, P 365, US NHu, D LEm: no second ending; indicated by fermata over third beat
30 / bottom / 7	D KIl, P 365: no ♮
30b / bottom	D Mbs: as Ex. 16
35–8 / bottom / 4	P 367, P 368, US NHu, D LEm: tr not 𝆗
	D Mbs: 𝆗
36 / top / 6–7	P 367, P 368, D LEm: no tie
39 / bottom / 2	P 367, P 368, D LEm: no c'
40 / top / 12–14	MA, P 790: 8th-note, two 16th-notes
40 / top, downstem / 2	US NHu, P 790: no g'
41–2 / top	P 367: each orn.: 𝆕 not 𝆗
41 / top / 8	US NHu, D LEm, D Mbs: no 𝆗
41 / bottom, upstem / 1	MA, B Br, P 790, D Mbs: no rest
41 / bottom, upstem / 2	P 790: no f'
42 / top / 1, 9	D Mbs: tr not 𝆗

bar / stave / note-and-rest no.	source: remark
	US NHu, D LEm: no orn.
43 / bottom / 1	P 367, P 368, D KIl, P 365, D LEm, D Mbs: no upward stem
	D KIl, P 365: half rest between staves
44 / top / 1	D KIl, P 365, D LEm, D Mbs: no rest
44 / top / 4	D LEm: no eb'
45 / bottom, upstem / 1	P 367, P 368, D KIl, P 365, US NHu, D LEm, D Mbs: no bb
45 / bottom / 4	US NHu: Ab not c
47 / top / 1–3	D Mbs: no chord, no rests
47 / bottom, upstem /2–4	MA, B Br, P 790, P 367, P 368, US NHu, D LEm: no rests (but all stems in bass are downward in MA, B Br, P 790, P 368)
51 / top / 9	P 367, P 368, D KIl, P 365, D Mbs: 1-flag app.
51 / top / 10	P 367, P 368, D KIl, P 365: no ≈
	US NHu, D LEm, D Mbs: tr
54 / top / 3	D KIl, P 365: no ♮
54 / bottom	US NHu: ♭ on 9 (A) not 10 (G)
58 / top / 9	P 367, P 368, P 365, US NHu, D KIl, D LEm, D Mbs and P 790: no ♮. Compare with the next variant; both are plausible early readings.
58 / bottom / 3	P 367, P 368, D KIl, P 365, US NHu, D LEm, D Mbs: ♮
59 / top / 1–3	D Mbs: 16th-note, 16th-note, 8th-note
59 / top / 8	P 367, P 368, D LEm: tr not 𝆗
	D KIl: ≈
	US NHu: 𝆗
	D Mbs: no orn.
60 / top / 14	P 367, P 368, D KIl, P 365, US NHu, D LEm, D Mbs: no ♮
60 / top / 15	MA, B Br, P 790: ♮ on 15, not 14
60 / bottom / 3	P 367, P 368: no ♮
61 / top, downstem / 1	D KIl, P 365: followed by 8th rest, quarter rest

bar / stave / note-and-rest no.	source: remark
62–3 / top, upstem	D LEm, D Mbs: no tie
62 / bottom	D KIl, P 365: whole rest
64 / top / 7	P 367, P 368, D KIl, P 365: no ♮
64 / bottom / 1	P 367, P 368, D KIl, P 365, US NHu, D LEm, D Mbs: no g'
69	P 367, P 368, D KIl, P 365, US NHu, D LEm, D Mbs: as Ex. 3a; remaining sources as Ex. 3b (=CPEBE)
70 / top	D KIl, P 365: rests in middle part as in bar 15
	US NHu: 8th rest above 1
70 / bottom / 3	US NHu: no quarter rest
70 / bottom / 4	US NHu, D LEm: no half rest
71–3	P 367, P 368, D KIl, P 365, US NHu, D LEm, D Mbs: as Ex. 4a except as noted below; remaining sources as Ex. 4b
71 / top / 1	D LEm, D Mbs: no rest
71 / bottom / 1–2	D LEm: no rests
72 / top	D KIl, P 365: above 6–8: 8th rest, quarter rest
72 / top / 4	US NHu: two stems, upward and downward
72 / bottom / 1	D LEm, D Mbs: no rest
72 / bottom / 5	D LEm: no rest
72 / bottom / 5–8	US NHu: no g–g–g–f
73 / top / 1	P 367 (?), P 368, D KIl, P 365, US NHu: no rest
74 / top / 9	P 367, P 368, D KIl, P 365: 1-flag app.
	D Mbs: 2-flag app.
74 / top / 10	P 367, P 368, US NHu, D LEm, D Mbs: tr not ≈
	D KIl, P 365: no orn.
77 / top, downstem	P 790: no ab'
77–8 / top	D LEm: no tie
78 / top / 8	B Br, P 367, P 368, US NHu, D LEm: tr not ⌇
	D KIl: ⌒⌇
	D Mbs: no orn.

bar / stave / note-and-rest no.	source: remark
81 / top / 2–3	P 367, D LEm, D Mbs: no tie
82 / top / 1	D KIl, P 365: no ♮
83 / top / 9	P 367, P 368, D KIl, P 365: 1-flag app.
	D Mbs: 2-flag app.
83 / top / 10	P 367, US NHu, D Mbs: tr not ≈
	D LEm: ⌇
	P 368, D KIl, P 365: no orn.
84	P 367, P 368, US NHu, D LEm, D Mbs: second ending indicated by fermata as in bar 30
84a / top, upstem / 7	D KIl, P365: f' not eb'
84a / bottom / 10	P 365: f' not eb'
84a / top / 7	P 367, P 368, US NHu, D LEm, D Mbs: no ♭
84b / top, bottom / 5	D KIl, P 365: quarter-note, instead of 8th-note, 8th rest

Second Movement

bar / stave / note-and-rest no.	source: remark
1 / bottom / 1–2	P 365: dotted half (no rest). Possibly a conjecture by a copyist working from a source such as D KIl, which has a half-note and no rest
2–3	P 367, P 368, P 365, P 414, US NHu, D KIl, D LEm, D Mbs: as Ex. 5a except as noted below; remaining sources as Ex. 5b (=CPEBE)
2 / top, upstem / 1 (Ex. 5a)	D LEm: ∞
3 / bottom / 1 (Ex. 5a)	D LEm: ∞
4 / top / 1	P 367, P 368, P 365, P 414, US NHu, D KIl, D LEm, D Mbs: no app.
4 / top, upstem / 2	P 367: ⌀♭ not ≈
	P 368, D LEm: ∞
	P 365, P 414, D KIl: ⌇
	US NHu: tr
	D Mbs: ⌇
5 / bottom / 1	P 367, P 368, P 365, P 414, US NHu, D KIl, D LEm, D Mbs: no app.
5 / bottom / 2	P 367: ⌀♭ not ≈
	P 368, D LEm: ∞

bar / stave / note-and-rest no.	source: remark
	P 365, P 414, D KIl: ∿
	US NHu: tr
5, 6 / top / 2–3	P 367, P 368, P 365, P 414, US NHu, D KIl: no slur
6–7 / bottom / 1–2	P 367, P 368, P 365, P 414, US NHu, D KIl, D LEm, D Mbs: no slur
10 / bottom, upstem / 1	P 367, 368, P 365, P 414, US NHu, D KIl, D LEm, D Mbs: quarter-note not 8th-note
11 / top, upstem / 3, 5	US NHu: 1-flag apps.
12 / top / 1–2	P 365, D LEm: no slur
12 / top / 1	P 367, P 368, P 365, P 414, US NHu, D KIl, D LEm, D Mbs: no d'
12 / bottom / 3, 5	US NHu: 1-flag apps.
13–14 / top	MA, B Br, P 790: no inner voice (but notes present are all upstem)
13 / bottom / 1–2	US NHu, D LEm: no slur
14 / top / 2	rest only in D LEm
14 / bottom / 4	D LEm, D Mbs: no ∞
15–16 / bottom	P 414: no tie
15 / top, downstem / 1–2	P 367, P 368, P 365, P 414, US NHu, D KIl, D LEm, D Mbs: no rests
16 / top, upstem / 1	P 367, P 368, D KIl, P 365, P 414, US NHu, D LEm, D Mbs: no app.
18 / top / 1	P 367, D KIl, P 365, P 414, US NHu: ∞; intended to fall between 1 and 2?
18 / top / 3–4	P 367, P 368, D KIl, P 365, P 414, US NHu, D LEm, D Mbs: no slur
18 / top / 4	P 367: ⌐♭ not ∿
	P 368, D LEm: no orn.
	US NHu: tr
	D Mbs: ∿
19 / top, upper voice / 1–3	US NHu: 8th-note, quarter note, 8th-note (app. written as regular note)
21–2 / top	D LEm: e'' tied over barline
21 / bottom / 6	D LEm: ∿
22 / top, downstem / 1	US NHu: no e''
23 / top, downstem / 3	D KIl, P 365, P 414, D Mbs: no rest
24–5 / top, downstem	D LEm, D Mbs: g' tied over barline
24 / top, downstem	D KIl, P 365, P 414, US NHu: a' (quarter) on downbeat
26 / top, upstem / 3–4	P 367, P 368, D KIl, P 365, P 414, US NHu, D LEm, D Mbs: no slur
26 / top / 4	P 367: ⌐♭ not ∿
	P 368, D LEm: ∞
	D KIl, P 365, P 414, US NHu: tr
	D Mbs: ∿
27	P 367, P 368, D KIl, P 365, P 414, US NHu: pp not p
	D KIl, P 365, P 414: pp also beneath lower stave
	D Mbs: no dyn.
	P 790: dyn. in later hand?
27 / top / 1	P 790: followed by 8th rest, quarter rest, quarter rest
27 / bottom, upstem / 3	P 367: ⌐♭ not ∿
	P 368, D KIl, P 365, P 414, US NHu: no orn.
	D LEm: ∞
	D Mbs: ∿
28 / 1	P 367, P 368, D KIl, P 365, P 414, D Mbs: no f
	P 790: dyn. in later hand?
28 / bottom, upstem / 2–3	D KIl, P 365, P 414: no rests
28 / bottom, downstem / 1	D KIl, P 365, P 414: quarter-note, quarter rest
29–30	P 367, P 368, D KIl, P 365, P 414, D LEm, D Mbs: as Ex. 6a except as noted below; remaining sources as Ex. 6b (=CPEBE)
29 / top, upstem / 1 (Ex. 6a)	D LEm: ∞
30	P 365, P 414: first beat initially om., later inserted

bar / stave / note-and-rest no.	source: remark
31 / top / 1	P 367, P 368, D KIl, P 365, P 414, US NHu, D LEm, D Mbs: no app.
31 / top, upstem / 2	P 367: ⌀ not ≋ P 368, D LEm: ∞ D KIl, P 365, P 414: ⌇ US NHu: tr D Mbs: ↝
31 / bottom / 3	P 414: *d♭'* not *b♭*
32 / top, upstem / 3	P 368: ♯
32 / bottom / 1	P 367, P 368, D KIl, P 365, P 414, US NHu, D LEm, D Mbs: no app.
32 / bottom / 2	P 367: ⌀ not ≋ P 368, D LEm: ∞ D KIl, P 365, P 414: ⌇ US NHu: tr D Mbs: ↝
32, 33 / top, upstem / 2–3	P 367, P 368, D KIl, P 365, P 414, US NHu, D LEm, D Mbs: no slur
33–8 / bottom / 1–2	P 367, P 368, D KIl, P 365, P 414, US NHu, D LEm, D Mbs: no slurs
33	US NHu: this bar om.
33–4 / top, downstem	MA, B Br, P 790, D LEm: no tie
34 / top, upstem / 1–2	P 367, P 368, D KIl, P 365, P 414, US NHu: dotted half not quarter, half
36 / top, downstem / 2	D LEm: *b♮'*
38–9	P 367, P 368, D KIl, P 365, P 414, US NHu, D Mbs: as Ex. 7a except as noted below; D LEm: as Ex. 17; remaining sources as Ex. 7b (=*CPEBE*)
39 / top / 1	P 367, P 368, US NHu, D Mbs: as Ex. 7a but with a different ornament: P 367, ⌀; P 368, ∞; US NHu, tr; D Mbs, ↝
39 / top, downstem/ 1 (Ex. 7a)	P 368: *a'* (quarter) not *a'* (8th), 8th-rest
39 / top, downstem/ 2–4 (Ex. 7a)	P 367, P 368, D Mbs: no rests
43 / top / 6	D KIl, P 365: no ♮ P 365: ♮ inserted (foreign hand)
43 / bottom / 6	P 367, P 368, D KIl, P 365, P 414, US NHu, D LEm, D Mbs: *a* not *c♯'*
44 / top / 3–4	P 367, P 368, D KIl, P 365, P 414, US NHu, D LEm, D Mbs: no slur
44 / top / 4	P 367: ⌀ not ≋ P 368, D LEm: ∞ D KIl, P 365, P 414: ⌇ US NHu: tr D Mbs: ↝
46 / top / 5	P 367, P 368, D KIl, P 365, P 414, D LEm, D Mbs: no ∞
48 / bottom / 1	P 367, D KIl, P 365, P 414: two tied quarter-notes
49 / top, both / 1	P 367, P 368, D KIl, P 365, P 414, US NHu, D LEm, D Mbs: no apps.
49 / top, downstem / 2	D Mbs: no *f'*
50 / bottom / 1	P 367, P 368, D KIl, P 365, P 414: two tied quarter-notes
51 / bottom	P 367, P 368, D KIl, P 365, P 414, D LEm, D Mbs: as Ex. 8a; remaining sources as Ex. 8b (=*CPEBE*)
52 / top / 1	P 367: ⌀ not ↝ P 368: no orn. D KIl: ⌇ [*sic*] US NHu, D LEm: tr D Mbs: ↝
54–5	P 367, P 368, D KIl, P 365, P 414, US NHu, D LEm, D Mbs: as Ex. 9a except as noted below; remaining sources as Ex. 9b (=*CPEBE*)
54 / top, upstem / 1	D LEm: as Ex. 9a but with ∞
55 / bottom / 1	D LEm: as Ex. 9a but with ∞
56 / top / 1	P 367, P 368, D KIl, P 365, P 414, D LEm, D Mbs: no app.
56 / top / 2	P 367: ⌀ not ≋ P 368, D LEm: ∞ D KIl, P 365, P 414: ↝ US NHu: tr D Mbs: no orn.

bar / stave / note-and-rest no.	source: remark
57–61	P 367, P 368, D KIl, P 365, P 414, US NHu, D LEm, D Mbs: as Ex. 10a except as noted below; remaining sources as Ex. 10b (=*CPEBE*)
57 / bottom / 1	P 367, P 368, US NHu, D LEm, D Mbs: as Ex. 10a but with a different ornament; P 367, ∾; P 368, D LEm, ∾; US NHu, tr; D Mbs, ⤳
59 / top / 1–2	D KIl, P 365, P 414: regular notes: 8th, quarter
59 / top / 2	P 367, P 368, D Mbs: as Ex. 10a but with a different ornament; P 367, ∾; P 368, tr; D Mbs, ⤳ US NHu: as Ex. 10a but no orn.
60 / bottom / 1	P 790: *c* (half) directly beneath *c'* (quarter)
60 (Ex. 10a)	P 368, D KIl: no *pp* D LEm, D Mbs: *p* not *pp*
60 / top / 1	P 367, P 368, D Mbs, D LEm: as Ex. 10a but with a different ornament; P 367, ∾; P 368, D LEm, ∾; D Mbs, ⤳
60–1 / bottom (Ex. 10a)	D LEm, D Mbs: no tie
60 / bottom, downstem / last	D LEm: as Ex. 10a, but no *f*
61 (Ex. 10a)	D KIl: 'piano' between *C* and *F*
61 / bottom, upstem / 1	D LEm, D Mbs: 2-flag app. US NHu: also a 1-flag app. *g*
61 / bottom, downstem / 2	D LEm: as Ex. 10a, but no *e*
61 / bottom, downstem / 1	P 365, P 414: half-note *C* (no dot)
62	P 367, P 368, D KIl, P 365, P 414, US NHu, D LEm: no *f*
63 / bottom	P 367, P 368, D KIl, P 365, P 414, US NHu, D LEm, D Mbs: no *f*
63–4 / top, upstem	MA, B Br, P 790, D Mbs: no tie (MA, B Br: bar 63 = end of system)

bar / stave / note-and-rest no.	source: remark
63 / bottom / 7	US NHu: no ♯
64 / top, upstem / 2	MA: 8th (*sic*) P 790: 16th (!)
65 / top, upstem / 1	US NHu: no ∾
66 / top, downstem	D KIl, P 365, P 414: preceded by two quarter rests
66–7 / top, downstem	US NHu: tie
67–8 / top, downstem	US NHu, D LEm: no tie
68 / top, upstem / 2	P 367, US NHu, D LEm: tr not ⤳ P 368: illegible mark, possibly ⤳ D KIl, P 365, P 414: no orn. D Mbs: ⤳
68 / bottom / 3	fermata only in D KIl, P 365, P 414
69 / top / 1	P 790, P 368, D LEm, D Mbs: no downward stem
Third Movement	
—	MA, B Br: 'stacato' [*sic*] P 367, P 368, P 365, US NHu, D LEm: 'Spirituoso' D KIl: 'Spirituoso mà presto' D Mbs: 'Spirituoso è Staccato'
6, 8 / bottom / 3	P 367, P 368, D KIl, P 365, US NHu, D LEm, D Mbs: 8th-note, 8th rest not quarter-note
12	P 367, P 368: as Ex. 18a (in P 368 bass *c'* is set directly beneath treble *d'*); P 365, D LEm: as Ex. 18b except as noted below; remaining sources as Ex. 18c (=*CPEBE*) except as noted below
12 / top / 1–3	D KIl, D Mbs: no '3' over triplet
12 / top / 1 (Ex. 18b)	D LEm: no ⤳
12 / top / 1	D KIl: ⤳
12 / top / 2	D LEm: ♮ before *d'*
13–14 / bottom	strokes in P 368, D KIl, P 365 only; in bar 13 also in D LEm, D Mbs

bar / stave / note-and-rest no.	source: remark
14 / top / 3	P 367, D Mbs: no stroke
15–16, 20–2 / top	P 367: no strokes
19–20 / bottom	P 367: no strokes
20 / bottom / 3	P 367, P 368, D KIl, P 365, US NHu: no ♭
23 / top / 3	MA, B Br, P 790: e♭'' not d♭''
26 / top / 1–2	P 367, P 368, P 365, D LEm, D Mbs: no slur
26 / bottom / 3	P 367, P 365: no stroke
28 / bottom / 3	P 367, US NHu, D LEm, D Mbs: no stroke
31 / top / 1	P 367, P 368, D KIl, P 365, US NHu, D LEm: tr not ⁓ D Mbs: ⁓
34–5	D Mbs: these bars absent
39 / top / 1	MA, B Br, P 790, P 367, P 368, D KIl, P 365, D LEm: no ♮ B Br: ♮ added lightly?
39 / top / 3	MA, B Br, P 790, D Mbs: fermata on 3 not 4 US NHu: fermata was on 3, but was then redrawn to appear on 4
39 / bottom / 1–2	P 368, US NHu, D LEm, D Mbs: no slur
39 / bottom / 3	fermata in D KIl, P 365, D LEm only
41, 43 / top / 3	P 367: ⁓
44	P 367, P 368: no *p* P 790: inserted in later hand?
48	US NHu: no *f*
48–9 / bottom	MA, B Br, P 790: no tie MA, B Br, P 790, P 368: accidental repeated in bar 49 (P 368: new system)
51 / top / 4	P 367, P 368, D KIl, P 365: no ♮
51 / bottom / 3	P 367, P 368, D KIl, P 365: no ♮
52	D LEm: *p* not *pp*
52 / top	D KIl, P 365: *pp* repeated above top stave
52 / top / 2	MA, P 790: ♮ not ♭ MA 4: ♮ altered by hand to ♭ P 790: corr. (in foreign hand?)
52 / bottom / 3	MA: no *e'* (but tie to next bar is present) MA 4: notehead entered by hand
54	B Br, P 790: no *f* D KIl, P 365: *f* repeated beneath lower voice (on upper stave)
54 / top / 2	MA: 8th-note (*sic*)
58 / bottom, downstem / 1	P 367, P 368, D KIl, P 365, D LEm, US NHu, D Mbs: as Ex. 11a; remaining sources as Ex. 11b (=CPEBE)
59 / bottom, upstem / 1	P 367, P 368, D KIl, P 365: 1-flag app. D Mbs: 2-flag app.
59 / bottom, upstem / 2	US NHu, P 790: no tr
68 / bottom / 3–4	P 367, P 368, D KIl, P 365, US NHu, D LEm: quarter-note not 8th-note, 8th rest; also, this quarter-note has a stroke except in P 368 and D LEm
77 / bottom / 2	P 367: *a♭* (8th, with stroke) written as correction over rest
85 / top / 2	MA, B Br, P 790: *b♭''* not *c'''*; CPEBE = P 367, P 368, D KIl, P 365, D LEm, D Mbs (cf. bars 77, 81)
90 / top / 3	P 367: ⚬♭ not ⁓ P 368: ∾ D KIl, P 365, US NHu: tr D LEm: no orn. D Mbs: ⁓
91 / top / 1	MA, B Br, P 368, D KIl, P 365: stroke
96 / bottom / 1	P 790, P 368, D LEm, D Mbs: no stroke
98 / bottom / 1	P 790, P 367, P 368, D KIl, P 365, US NHu, D LEm, D Mbs: no stroke
99 / top / 3	US NHu: *d♭'* not *c'*
101 / bottom	P 367, P 368, D KIl, P 365, US NHu, D LEm, D Mbs: as Ex.

bar / stave / note-and-rest no.	source: remark	bar / stave / note-and-rest no.	source: remark
	12a; remaining sources as Ex. 12b (=*CPEBE*)	129 / top / 2	stroke in D KIl, P 365
103 / top / 1–2	P 790, P 367, P 368, D KIl, P 365, US NHu, D LEm, D Mbs: no slur	130 / top / 2	only US NHu gives a stroke here
		133, 135, 137 / top / 3	P 367: ⤳
103 / top / 2	P 367: ⟳ not tr	136	P 367, P 368, P 365: *p* on second beat
	P 368: ∞		D KIl, P 365: *p* repeated beneath lower stave
	D LEm: no orn.		
104 / top / 1	P 368: *eb'* not *ab*		D Mbs: *p* on downbeat
106 / second beat	MA, B Br, P 790, P 367, P 368, US NHu, D Mbs: fermatas on note not rest		P 790: *p* in foreign hand?
		140–1 / bottom	MA, B Br, P 709, D LEm: no tie
106 / top / 1–2	P 368, D Mbs: no slur		
112 / bottom / 2	P 368, D KIl, P 365, US NHu, D LEm: no stroke	140	P 367, D LEm, D Mbs: *f* on downbeat
			P 790: *f* in foreign hand?
113, 115 / bottom / 3	P 367, P 368, D KIl, P 365, US NHu, D LEm, D Mbs: 8th-note, 8th rest not quarter-note	144 / top	D LEm: *p* on second beat
			D Mbs: *pp* on downbeat
114 / bottom / 2	P 367, P 368, D KIl, P 365, US NHu, D LEm: no stroke		P 790: *pp* in foreign hand?
		146 / top	P 790, D KIl, P 365, D LEm: no *f*
119 / top / 3	stroke in P 367, P 368, D KIl, P 365		D Mbs: *f* on second beat
123 / top / 3	stroke in P 367, P 368, D KIl, P 365, P 709, D LEm, D Mbs	150 / bottom	P 367, P 368, D KIl, P 365, US NHu, D LEm, D Mbs: as Ex. 13a; remaining sources as Ex. 13b (=*CPEBE*)
123 / bottom / 3	P 367, P 368, D KIl, P 365: no ♭		
124–5 / top / 2	stroke in P 367, P 368, D KIl, P 365, P 709, D LEm, D Mbs	151 / bottom, upstem / 1	P 367, P 368: 1-flag app.
			D Mbs: 2-flag app.
127 / top, upstem / 1	stroke in P 367, P 368, D KIl, P 365	152 / bottom, downstem / 2	P 367, P 368: no dot
128 / top, upstem / 2	stroke in P 367, D KIl, P 365		

MUSIC EXAMPLES

Authentic Early Readings (Examples 1–13)

Ex. 1: H. 40, I. 16–17

Ex. 2: H. 40, I. 18–19

Ex. 3: H. 40, I. 69

Ex. 4: H. 40, I. 71–3

Ex. 5: H. 40, II. 2–3

Ex. 6: H. 40, II. 29–30

Ex. 7: H. 40, II. 38–9

Ex. 8: H. 40, II. 51

Ex. 9: H. 40, II. 54–5

Ex. 10: H. 40, II. 57–61

Ex. 11: H. 40, III. 58

Ex. 12: H. 40, III. 101

Ex. 13: H. 40, III. 150

Other Variant Readings (Examples 14–18)

Ex. 14: H. 40, I. 11

Ex. 15: H. 40, I. 18–19

Ex. 16: H. 40, I. 30b

Ex. 18: H. 40, III. 12

Ex. 17: H. 40, II. 38–9

SOURCES

H. 43 exists in two versions. The differences are greatest in the first movement, of which the earlier version is edited separately. Variants in this version of the first movement are noted in a separate listing following the main list of variant readings. The principal source for both versions is the copy in P 775, which originally gave the earlier version and was altered by Bach to give the later one.

Despite the existence of two distinct versions, the *Nachlassverzeichnis* gives only one date of composition—1745. Particularly in the earlier version, the sonata is strikingly simple in style by comparison with H. 40 and 46, the previous and following sonatas. Yet there is no reason to assume that the date given in the *Nachlassverzeichnis* is actually that of the revised version. The style of the sonata must be judged the result of a conscious effort to write in the simple, fashionable manner now usually termed *galant*.

P 775. Berlin, Musikabteilung, Mus. ms. Bach P 775. Manuscript copy of H. 43 by Bach's copyist Anon. 301 using soprano clef,[25] with autograph markings, 34.5 × 21.5 cm. (watermark: crowned eagle with breastplate 'Z' = 'Zittau eagle').

This collection of twenty-three sonatas (one of which appears twice) seems to have been drawn in large part from the composer's personal set of archival or reference copies.[26] Several other manuscripts in Berlin, Staatsbibliothek Preußischer Kulturbesitz (Mus. mss. Bach P 772 and P 776), and in Kraków, Biblioteka Jagiellońska (Mus. ms. Bach P 771) are similar in nature. The paper and orthographic style vary between copies, even those in a single hand. A few copies have their own title pages and some were originally paginated as individual manuscripts. Some also bear one or two numbers possibly in the composer's hand on the title page (if present) or at the top of the first page of music; these apparently served to keep the collection in order. Although most of the works in P 775 are relatively early and fall in partially chronological order, the present ordering of the copies does not consistently respect the numbering added to the titles.

The copy of H. 43 is by the unidentified copyist designated Anon. 301.[27] It occupies pages 133–40 (two sheets). There is no title page. All but the first of the eight pages are numbered in small underlined figures, possibly autograph, in the upper right and left corners. The title, entered by Anon. 301 at the top of the first page, reads: 'SONATA. per il Cembalo Solo. di C. P. E. Bach.' To the left of this appears in small figures: 'No. 44. / (42.)'. The lower number is on the same line as the title and the parentheses nearly encircle it. The second digit of the upper number has been altered, either from or to '2'. The upper number could be autograph, but this is far from certain.

No complete explanation has yet been offered for index numbers of these two types.[28] The number '42' corresponds with the number assigned to the sonata in the list of solo keyboard works in the *Nachlassverzeichnis*, but the fact that neither number was entirely cancelled suggests that both served some purpose to the composer or later owners of the manuscript; it seems unlikely that one is merely a correction of the other, especially as one of the existing numbers has itself been altered. It is conceivable that the presence of both figures is related to Bach's having checked or revised the copy.[29]

Later entries in various hands appear across the top of the page, above the earlier entries: 'Nr. 19', 'Th. Kat. 63,15 = Nachl [illegible]', and '[Wotquenne 65,15]'. The figure 19 is probably a reference to the place of the copy of H. 43 within P 775, although H. 43 is now actually the twentieth distinct work.[30] The thematic catalogue referred to is the unpublished Berlin version of Westphal's

[25] Facsimile in Berg, ed., *The Collected Works*, III, p. 275–82 (copyist identified as Michel, p. xxiv, but see above).

[26] Inventory in Kast, p. 46.

[27] Kast, p. 139.

[28] See D. Berg, 'Towards a Catalog of the Keyboard Sonatas of C. P. E. Bach', *JAMS* 32 (1979), pp. 276–303, especially 280–5. A thorough consideration by U. Leisinger and P. Wollny of these numbers is to appear in the 1995 *Bach-Jahrbuch*.

[29] See the discussion below of the copy in P 775 of H. 46. Some errors remain even in copies bearing both numbers.

[30] H. 11 (W. 65/5) occurs twice, as does the first movement of H. 16 (W. 65/7), making the copy of H. 43 the twenty-second distinct copy in P 775.

catalogue.[31] Similar entries, noting concordances between that catalogue and the *Nachlassverzeichnis* ('Nachl.'), appear in many Berlin manuscripts.[32] The single letter 'C' appears in the bottom left-hand corner of the page, as in other copies of Bach's works in P 775 and elsewhere (for example, the copy in P 790 of H. 40).

Anon. 301 must have worked for Bach in Berlin, to judge from the paper used and the absence of copies by him of works composed after Bach had left Berlin. H. 43 is the only copy by Anon. 301 in P 775. His association with Bach is, however, further demonstrated by copies of other works owned by the composer.[33] Since Anon. 301 copied a part[34] for the concerto H. 446 (W. 36), which dates from 1762, his copy of H. 43 might have originated as late as the 1750s or 1760s, and the autograph revisions in it could be even later.

Bach's alterations were made by erasing the original readings and inserting new ones. Where the revisions involved the addition of notes to the existing text, it is usually clear that the new readings were inserted between the existing notes. But the writing of the revisions is cramped even where lack of space did not demand it; noteheads are often somewhat irregularly spaced and sized, stems short, ornaments small, slurs unsteady. While these are all characteristics of Bach's later hand, the writing lacks the extreme unsteadiness of some of the late autographs and cannot yet be dated with precision.[35] Though extensive, the revisions are generally quite legible, and only in two, possibly three places was it necessary to supplement them with letters (I. 54, 56, 101). Although it is not usually possible from handwriting alone to determine whether the smaller additions, such as staccato strokes, are autograph, the fact that such markings recur (together with the more extensive revisions)

in all five copies based on P 775 indicates that they were probably Bach's, and they have been accepted as autograph for the purposes of the edition.

Most, but not all, of the alterations were probably carried out as part of a single thoroughgoing revision. In the first movement the alteration of the penultimate note in bar 94 (but not in bar 92) may have occurred at a relatively early date, as it already occurs in 43753, though not in US Wc. The same is true in bar 84, where the common model—probably the lost autograph—for all three sources of the early version evidently was unclear, as US Wc also shows a correction at that point. The original reading in US Wc and P 775 (given in the List of Variant Readings) was probably erroneous; 43753 shows what was surely the correct reading, one that forms a precise parallel with bar 88. Perhaps in the composing score Bach had made the correction in bar 84 only after writing bar 88; this must have preceded the addition of a sharp in the same bar on *d'*, which occurs only in the sources of the later version.

The sequence of events is more difficult to reconstruct in bar 88, where two of Michel's copies (P 359 and B Bc) have a sharp before the note *e'*. It is possible that the accidental was also present at one time in P 775, where the bottom line of the top stave appears to be broken in bar 88 by a small erasure. P 359 has a sharp at precisely the same point, although in both P 775 and P 359 the note itself appears on the second line of the stave, since both copies use soprano clef. If, however, the sharp was a later insertion, as it appears to have been, then such inaccurate placement might be expected; in P 775 the sharp present in bar 84 is similarly displaced.

The sharp in bar 88 is present in the normal position in B Bc, but it is absent from Michel's other copy, 43753, and from P 369. If in fact the sharp was present at one time but then erased in P 775, it is impossible to determine who did this and for what reason. The sharp appears to give a stronger reading, more closely parallel with bar 84. In both bars 84 and 88 the sharp creates a chord of the augmented sixth; it would seem anticlimactic if this unusual harmony were present only in the first of two otherwise identical phrases of a sequence. Since the accidental is present in two sources of good provenance it has been included in the edition within parentheses.

The text of P 775 *ante correcturam* is treated as a distinct source in the List of Variant Readings.

---

[31] Mus. ms. theor. K. 490 in the Deutsche Staatsbibliothek.

[32] The reading of the entry after 'Nachl.' is illegible, but most likely continued '6,42', a reference to page 6, entry 42, in the *Nachlassverzeichnis*.

[33] For example, the sonata H. 57 (W. 65/23) in Mus. ms. Bach P 371 in the Deutsche Staatsbibliothek, Berlin, which has an autograph title page.

[34] In Mus. ms. Bach St 530 in the Staatsbibliothek Preußischer Kulturbesitz, Berlin.

[35] I am grateful to Pamela Fox for the information that the rest added by Bach in bar 50 of the third movement can be dated with certainty to 'after 1780'.

Although the original readings are not always legible, most can be reconstructed with confidence from US Wc and 43753. While it is not always possible to tell whether slurs, ornaments, appoggiaturas, and other indications absent from US Wc and 43753 were also absent from P 775 *ante correcturam*, in most cases distinctions in handwriting or in the form of the entries strongly suggest that this is the case. Thus, in the absence of evidence to the contrary, it has been assumed that the readings of US Wc and 43753 were also readings of P 775 *ante correcturam*, and that all alterations in P 775 are autograph.

P 359. Berlin, Staatsbibliothek Preußischer Kulturbesitz, Musikabteilung, Mus. ms. Bach P 359. A collection of works for solo keyboard by C. P. E. Bach in various hands, including Bach's. Copy of H. 43 by Michel, using soprano clef (34 × 21.5 cm., no watermark).

P 359 contains copies of twenty-five works (mostly sonatas from W. 65), as well as the autographs of the fantasia H. 300 (W. 67) and the partial autograph of the sonata H. 32.5 (W. 65/13).[36] All of the copyists represented are known to have worked in conjunction with Bach, though not necessarily on these copies.[37] Each copy appears to have originally been a separate manuscript; several copies bear their own title pages, and it cannot be assumed that all were prepared under Bach's supervision. P 359 later belonged to the collector Georg Pölchau (1773–1836), whose name ('G Poelchau') appears on the inside of the cover.

The first (unnumbered) page serves as general title page for the collection and includes an index to the contents:

Sieben und Zwanzig noch ungedruckte / Clavier-Sonaten / von / Carl Philipp Emanuel Bach / aus seinem musical. Nachlass. / Die erste (H m) und letzte (Fis m) ist von seiner / eigenen Hand / (53 Bg) / Nach dem bekannten gedruckten Verzeichnisse der Bachschen / Nachlasses (Hamburg 1790 bey Schniebes) enthält dieser Band / folgende

Nummern: 32. 42. 46. 49. 52. 59. 61. / 76. 81. 86. 114. 128. 131. 118. 133. 148. 151. 152. 155. / 174. 176. 187. 190. 195. 205. 206. 210.

A series of numbers that seems to represent a preliminary draft of the list transcribed above appears lightly across the very top of the page. Many of the scores comprising the manuscript contain faint numbers on the title page or first page that correspond to the numbers of the works in the *Nachlassverzeichnis*, and which might have been entered when the title page was drawn up.

The copy of H. 43 contains neither possessor's mark nor any autograph entries. Its eight pages bear original pagination in small figures in the upper right or left corners. Beside each of these figures has been entered the running pagination for P 359 as a whole, of which the copy of H. 43 occupies pages 9–16 (two sheets). The title, written across the top, reads: 'SONATA per il Cembalo Solo. di C P E Bach.' Added in a foreign hand beneath the composer's name are the date and place of composition as given in the *Nachlassverzeichnis*: 'Berlin 1745'.

The writer of the copy of H. 43, known only as Michel, was also responsible for two other copies of the sonata. A tenor under Bach at Hamburg and Bach's chief Hamburg copyist, he produced a large number of generally accurate, neat manuscripts of music by Bach and his father.[38] It is likely that some of these were written after Bach's death, since Michel appears later to have worked alongside Johann Christian Kittel (1732–1809), one of Sebastian's last students, who visited Hamburg only in 1800.[39]

It is not possible, from the sources described in this volume, to reach firm conclusions about the chronology of Michel's copies. The few variants distinguishing his three copies of H. 43 provide insufficient evidence to serve as criteria for relative dating. However, another of his copies in P 359,

---

[36] The latter was completed by one of the copyists designated Su in Kast, p. 25, which includes the complete inventory.

[37] The copy of H. 83 (W. 65/29), assigned to Anon. 306 by Kast, has been recognized by Yoshitake Kobayashi as the work of Anon. 301, according to the list of errata supplied by the publisher to Berg, ed., *The Collected Works*.

[38] Michel has been identified through remarks in several of Pölchau's manuscripts; see Wade, *The Keyboard Concertos*, p. 26, and G. v. Dadelsen, *Bemerkungen zur Handschrift Johann Sebastian Bachs, seiner Familie und seines Kreises*, Tübinger Bach-Studien, Heft 1 (Trossingen, 1957), p. 24.

[39] Michel completed a copy of J. S. Bach's English Suites that Kittel had begun and afterwards corrected (Mus. ms. Bach P 419 in the Staatsbibliothek Preußischer Kulturbesitz, Berlin). See *J. S. Bach: Neue Ausgabe sämtlicher Werke*, V/7, *Kritischer Bericht* by A. Dürr (Leipzig, 1979), pp. 35–6.

that of H. 47, gives a relatively early text, and is similar in orthographic style (lettering, ornamental designs at ends of movements, etc.) to the copy of H. 43. This style, evidently the product of close imitation of earlier copies, such as P 775—note the precise identity in title—suggests that the copy of H. 43 dates from a time when Michel had yet to establish his own manuscript style. The copy of H. 48 in A Wgm 3872/14 shows a similar relationship to its model (the copy by Anon. 303 in P 775).

Also suggesting a relatively early date is an uncharacteristic error in the first movement, where bar 49 was entered twice, the second entry subsequently having been crossed out. Although the same passage contains two other small errors of omission (in bars 47 and 50), all must be ascribed to carelessness, as P 775 is clear in this passage and was almost certainly the model for the copy in P 359. All page breaks and most line breaks occur at the same points in both copies, and such details as the placement and orthography of verbal entries, even ornamental designs at the ends of movements, are similar.

B Bc. Brussels, Bibliothèque du Conservatoire Royal de Musique, ms. 5883. A collection of fifty sonatas by C. P. E. Bach in various hands. Copy of H. 43 by Michel, using soprano clef.

Under the number 5883 in the Conservatoire Royal, Brussels, is J. J. H. Westphal's collection of fifty keyboard sonatas not issued in authorized prints during Bach's lifetime. It was subsequently acquired by Fétis and later by the Brussels Conservatory.[40] Each of the individual copies bears a note in a foreign hand giving the number assigned to the work in Westphal's catalogue; all fall within group 15. In Wotquenne's thematic catalogue the collection is designated as item 65. The collection excludes the six sonatas identified in some sources as for organ and the six sonatinas H. 7–12 (W. 64); it includes one suite, H. 6 (65/4).

The copies are mostly by Michel; the following exceptions have been observed:[41] by Westphal: H. 19 (W. 65/10) and H. 21 (W. 65/11), each with an alternative movement copied by Michel; H. 48 (W. 65/18); H. 56 (W. 65/22); and H. 143 (W.

65/33). By an unidentified copyist: H. 16 (W. 65/7). By Anon. 305: H. 49 (W. 65/19), H. 211–13 (W. 65/44–6), H. 248 (W. 65/47), and H. 298 (W. 65/49). Autograph entries appear in at least two of Michel's copies, those of H. 46 and H. 51 (see the respective critical reports below). Regardless of copyist, the scores are in a distinctive format that Westphal may have specially requested, as he evidently did in ordering some copies from the Hamburg publisher J. C. Westphal.[42]

As Wade has shown, the section of Westphal's thematic catalogue listing the keyboard sonatas dates from the period 1792–1802, and the incipits in it were based on copies in his own possession and were not merely copied from the *Nachlassverzeichnis*.[43] Indeed, while the incipits in Westphal's catalogue closely match the openings of the six sonatas from 5883 edited in this volume,[44] the *Nachlassverzeichnis* gives a different reading for H. 49.[45] Westphal began acquiring music from Bach no later than January 1787, when the first surviving letter from Bach to Westphal was written.[46] As in most, if not all, of Westphal's copies of Bach's music, the works appear in the latest known versions. Michel's copies are always very accurate, the others somewhat less so, at least for H. 48–9 (see the critical commentaries below). The implication, then, is that Westphal acquired Michel's copies either directly from Bach during the composer's last years, or from Bach's widow.

The copy of H. 43 consists of eight pages on two sheets (watermark unclear); there is no title page, and no pagination was observed. The first page bears markings such as occur in other copies in the set. The original title, written across the top, is: 'Sonata. per il Cembalo solo. da C.P.E. Bach.' Just below this, at the left edge, is the number '15' and at the centre, in another hand, '15e. Sonate du No. 15 de Westphal'. A large number '24' is stamped at the

---

[40] For more on Westphal and his collection, see under B Br in the critical commentary for H. 40.

[41] This list supplements the handwriting identifications in Berg, ed., *The Collected Works*.

[42] See the letter quoted by Terry, *JAMS* 22 (1969), p. 11, reprinted in Rudolph Angermüller, 'Carl Philipp Emanuel Bachiana: Briefe, die bei Ernst Suchalla nicht veröffentlicht wurden', *Jahrbuch des Staatlichen Instituts für Musikforschung Preußischer Kulturbesitz 1985/86*.

[43] *The Keyboard Concertos*, p. 1.

[44] An ornament sign is omitted in the incipit for H. 46, and a rest in the accompaniment in that for H. 51.

[45] The slur in Westphal's copy and in his catalogue covers only notes 2–3 of bar 1.

[46] Translated by Terry in *JAMS* 22 (1969), p. 108.

bottom left, and a faint cursive inscription, 'Ms Michel', appears at the lower right.

The copy of H. 43 in 5883 exactly parallels the copy of the same work in P 775 in the placement of page breaks, though not of every line break, and except for two errors (one corrected) is an exact, finely written copy of the revised version. The only addition to the text is a necessary sharp entered in a foreign hand, possibly autograph, in bar 53 of the third movement.

3872/2. Vienna, Gesellschaft der Musikfreunde, VII 3872/2. Copy of H. 43 by Michel using soprano clef.

The source 3872 consists of at least seventeen separate copies by Michel of keyboard sonatas by C. P. E. Bach from the unpublished groups of works listed by Wotquenne as items 64 and 65. Similarities in format and verbal entries suggest that all were prepared at about the same time for a single owner.

The copy of H. 43 in this source bears the number 3872/2 and consists of twelve unnumbered pages. The music appears on pages 3–12, which are ruled in eight to twelve staves each. The title page reads: 'Sonata / per il / Cembalo solo. / da. / C. P. E. Bach'. Each word is underlined. An additional ornamental underline occurs beneath the composer's name; there is a similar mark in Michel's copy of H. 47 in P 775. Also present are 'N°: 2' in the upper right and various library markings and stamps, including the pencil entries 'Samml. Westphal / Wq. 65,15'. The first page of music bears the title 'Sonata. Cembalo. solo.'

A Wgm 3872/2 is a slightly less careful copy than B Bc, and it contains no autograph entries or other corrections. The text is that of P 775 *post correcturam*, but, except in the second half of the first movement, the format of the copy is distinct, with page breaks at different points. Nevertheless a few peculiarities of orthography, such as the beaming together of all of the sixteenths in bars 102 and 104 of the first movement, confirm that it stems from P 775 *post correcturam*. (Since the beaming was an artifact of Bach's manner of entering the revised readings in these bars, the beaming is not retained in this edition.)

P 369. Berlin, Deutsche Staatsbibliothek, Mus. ms. Bach P 369. A manuscript by a single unidentified copyist of thirty-six keyboard works by C. P. E. Bach, in oblong format (37 × 26.5 cm.). The copy of H. 43 uses soprano clef.

This source was prepared for the Hamburg music publishing firm founded by Johann Christian Westphal (?1727–99), according to Yoshitake Kobayashi.[47] The publisher J. C. Westphal was unrelated to the Schwerin organist and collector J. J. H. Westphal, with whom he corresponded. It has been suggested that J. C. Westphal competed with Bach in the sale of manuscripts by Bach and his father, and that the relations between Bach and publisher were 'friendly, but businesslike'.[48]

The present cover bears a label with the inscription 'XXXVI CLAVIER SONATEN von Carl Phil. Em. Bach, die nicht öffentlich erschienen sind'. The watermark reads 'D & C BLAUW' with a coat of arms including DXC, an Amsterdam mark of the eighteenth and early nineteenth centuries.[49] The thirty-six pieces include several works not ordinarily regarded as sonatas today.[50] The pages are ruled uniformly in twelve staves each, and numbered in the upper right or left corners. The first leaf is unpaginated, and its recto side contains a table of contents with musical incipits and rubrics in the same hand as the rest of the manuscript. (The reverse is blank.) The incipits are numbered 1–36, corresponding with the works in the manuscript, but the incipits agree with the *Nachlassverzeichnis* rather than with the following copies.[51] In three cases the incipits in P 369 omit slurs, ties, or staccato strokes, but otherwise they are identical to those in the *Nachlassverzeichnis*.[52]

One incipit, that for H. 22 (W. 62/3), was omitted, as it was in the *Nachlassverzeichnis*, since the work was published in 1763. But a space was left

[47] Cited in Berg, *The Collected Works*, VI, p. xiii (note 7), which contains several facsimiles from this source, though not of the copy of H. 43.

[48] Wade, *The Keyboard Concertos*, pp. 19, 30.

[49] Title as transcribed by Horn, p. 174. I am grateful to Pamela Fox for the information about the watermark.

[50] Inventory in Kast, p. 26.

[51] Discrepancies between the incipits and the copies were observed in the time signature of H. 5 (W. 65/3; item 4 in the *Nachlassverzeichnis*), in the placement of the tie in H. 43 (item 42), and in the presence of the arpeggio sign in the copy of H. 57 (W. 65/23; item 56).

[52] The incipit for H. 211 (W. 65/44; item 151) misplaces the trill in bar 1, whose location between notes 11–12 is ambiguous in the *Nachlassverzeichnis*.

for it, and item and page numbers were entered above the space. On the other hand, two of the last three incipits are present even though they do not occur in the *Nachlassverzeichnis*. Third from the end is the incipit for the sonata H. 135, which is given here not in the version published in 1762–3 (=W. 65/32) but in the latest version (=W. 70/1).[53] Next comes the incipit for H. 209 (W. 60), composed in 1766 but published only in 1785 by Breitkopf. Late revisions in both works might explain their position in the manuscript, but the very last work in P 369, H. 68 (W. 65/27), was never published and seems never to have been substantially revised.

As all but the last three pieces are in the order given in the *Nachlassverzeichnis*, the copyist must have had access to either the *Nachlassverzeichnis* or another accurate list of Bach's works.[54] Moreover, P 369 in general contains accurate copies of the latest versions of all thirty-six works. The copies were entered one after another, often following the previous piece in the middle of a page, so that there is no question of the copies having been entered out of order at different times. The collection includes mostly works from early and late in Bach's career—items that would probably have been relatively difficult to obtain in accurate copies except from Bach (or his widow). It is conceivable that the table of contents might have been drawn up first, on the basis of the *Nachlassverzeichnis*, to aid the copyist in finding among Bach's own separate manuscripts (now gathered together in P 775 *et al.*) those works which the publisher Westphal was lacking.

Because page-turns do not always appear in convenient locations, P 369 may have been meant to serve the firm of J. C. Westphal as an archival copy, not one for practical use. The copy of H. 43, on pages 66–71, is well laid out for performance, but the same is not true of the following work, the symphony H. 45 (W. 122/1), which begins on the third system of page 71 immediately following the completion of H. 43.

The title for H. 43, in the upper left of page 66, is simply 'Sonate 18'. This is followed by bibliographic additions in two different hands: 'Nachl Verz N. 42' and '[Wotquenne 65,15]'. The copy in

P 369 is probably a direct copy of P 775 *post correcturam*; an erroneous g♯' in bar 87 of the last movement probably arose because in P 775 the bar is the first of a new line and the note g' is written very close to the key signature (a sharp on the second space from the bottom).[55] The copy contains few other inadvertent errors, but the copyist consistently altered the placement of the tie in the opening theme of the first movement, changed the value of appoggiaturas, and added slurs to the second of two parts moving in parallel or contrary motion. Hence the chief value of the source is for the evidence it may provide regarding the relationship between Bach and J. C. Westphal.

US Wc. Washington, DC, Library of Congress, Music Division, M23.B13.W65(15)(case). Copy by Anon. 303 of the earlier version of H. 43, using soprano clef. In wrapper bearing titles in modern hand.

The Library of Congress houses a considerable number of separate manuscript copies of sonatas by C. P. E. Bach, the majority of them unpublished works in early versions. The catalogue cards for these copies bear the entry 'From the collection of Erich Prieger'. Four, including the copy of H. 43, are by the copyist designated Anon. 303.[56] His association with Bach is demonstrated by autograph entries in various copies, for example, that in P 775 of H. 48. Anon. 303 must have worked for Bach at a relatively early date, since the four copies in US Wc give early versions not only for the sonatas edited in this volume but for the two others; all appear to have belonged at one time to a collection now in Kiel (see below). He probably worked before or during the period of Anon. 301, since their copies of the early version of H. 43 are independent of one another. But not all of the copies of Anon. 303 were necessarily made under the composer's supervision, and the copyist may have introduced textual changes in copies not made for Bach (see below). Since autograph entries have not been found in any of the copies in the Library of Congress, variants in these sources cannot enjoy any special authority. Some copies in the Library of Congress include extensive notations by later owners, who sometimes entered the readings of the revised versions. While readings of revised versions

---

[53] According to Berg, *The Collected Works*, VI, p. xix.

[54] On catalogues possibly prepared by Bach before his death, see Berg, 'Towards a Catalogue', pp. 277–8, and Wade, *The Keyboard Concertos*, pp. 5–8.

[55] The same error may have occurred in P 359, but if so it has been erased.

[56] By Kast, p. x.

are not entered into the copies by Anon. 303, that of H. 43 does contain other kinds of alterations likely to have been added by a later hand.

The copy of H. 43 is in a wrapper bearing the following entries: 'Bach [underlined], Carl Philipp Emanuel. / Klaviersonate G-dur. / Komp. Berlin 1745. / Nachlass-Verz. S. 6 No. 42. Wotquenne, them. Verz. / No. 65/15. Ungedruckt. / Zeitgenöss. Abschrift.' Beneath this, in a different hand and in pencil is '7 S. Hochf.' [7 *Seiten Hochformat*]. At the lower right-hand corner is the pencilled entry: 'Wotqu. S. 21 / (No. 65/15)'. The last number has been added later, in the same hand. Another pencilled entry at the very top centre, the number '205' within a box, has either almost entirely faded or been erased. Similar entries in the same hands appear on the wrappers for H. 46 and H. 48.

The manuscript itself consists of eight unnumbered pages, stitched together but not bound. The last is blank except for the stamped number 603053 and an indecipherable two-word inscription in the upper right. At the centre top of the first page is the title: 'Sonata / per il Cembalo Solo.' with the attribution to the right: 'dell Sigl. C. P. E. / Bach.' In the upper left is a probably later entry: 'N. 5.' This corresponds with the number of the incipit for the work in the Kiel manuscript described below. Entries of this type occur also in copies of Bach's concertos from the Lasserre collection,[57] and in the three other copies of Bach sonatas by Anon. 303 in the Library of Congress. At the bottom left of page 2 is the present call number, and in the centre the figures 344325 / '25, which appear also in the copies of H. 46 and H. 48. One passage (I. 110–12, bottom stave) appears to have been left blank and the notes entered later in another hand; the ink used here is brown, not black, and has eaten into the page. The same ink was used in entering corrections at several other points as well; similar entries appear in the three other copies by Anon. 303 in the same library.

The copy is clear and generally accurate, usually agreeing with P 775 *ante correcturam* except where the copyist appears to have substituted ornament signs of his own for the original indications *t* or *tr*.[58] The ornaments unique to US Wc are not always stylistically probable. For example, the mordent in

bar 100 of the first movement precedes a descending half-step, a configuration proscribed by Bach.[59] In the slow movement, the additions in lighter ink include unwarranted alterations to the text in bars 19–20; erasures occur in bar 25, which originally agreed with P 775 *ante correcturam*. Where P 775 *ante correcturam* gives turns, US Wc is in agreement, but the signs in US Wc are drawn in horizontal form, suggesting that US Wc is of somewhat later origin. US Wc also agrees with P 775 *ante correcturam* in the placement of page and line breaks in the first movement, but afterwards diverges in order to fit the sonata onto seven instead of eight pages.

US Wc appears to be one of fourteen manuscripts whose incipits are entered on the single sheet that constitutes the manuscript Mb 61/2 in the Schleswig-Holsteinische Landesbibliothek, Kiel (pages 9–10 of Mb 61). The recto side of the leaf bears the heading '*Catalogus* der *Sonaten* von H. Bach' followed by thirteen numbered incipits, each written on one staff. The numbering then begins anew for a single additional item labeled '1. [illegible] *Allegretto*, vermutlich Verfasser [illegible] Bach.'

A modern hand has added Wotquenne numbers identifying some of the incipits. In fact all belong to works elsewhere attributed to C. P. E. Bach: (1) H. 48; (2) H. 143; (3) H. 351 (here designated '*Allegro variiert*'); (4) H. 58; (5) H. 43; (6) H. 7; (7) H. 12; (8) H. 42; (9) H. 10; (10) H. 56; (11) H. 15; (12) H. 105; (13) H. 116; (1) H. 139. The numbering of each incipit takes the form 'N. 5', much as in the title of H. 43 in US Wc. Matching numeration also appears on the title pages of the other works in the Library of Congress that, like H. 43, were copied by Anon. 303: H. 15 (W. 65/6 = 'N. 11' in Mb 61/2), H. 42 (W. 65/14 = 'N. 8'), and H. 48 (W. 65/18 = 'N. 1'). A faded pencil entry on the wrapper of the copy of H. 42 in the Library of Congress ('2 Kopie . . .' [?]) appears to indicate that this, like the Library of Congresss copy of H. 48, was a duplicate copy from the collection now in Kiel.

The incipit for H. 43 agrees with that of the early version (I. 0–4) save for the presence of a small mark, possibly an appoggiatura on f♯", preceding note 1 of bar 2. This also confirms that the Library

---

[57] See Wade, *The Keyboard Concertos*, pp. 45–7.

[58] Similar substitutions occur in one of Anon. 303's copies of H. 48 (Mb 53 in the Schleswig-Holsteinische Landesbibliothek, Kiel); see the description of that source and the discussion of ornaments in H. 48.

[59] C. P. E. Bach, *Versuch über die wahre Art, das Clavier zu spielen*, facs. edn., ed. L. Hoffmann-Erbrecht, 4. Auflage (Leipzig, 1978), I, p. 102 (mispaginated as 84; Theil I, Das zweyte Hauptstück, fünfte Abteilung, 14); trans. as *Essay on the True Art of Playing Keyboard Instruments* by W. Mitchell (New York, 1949), p. 131.

of Congress copy once belonged to the collection indexed in Kiel, since the latter gives early versions as well for H. 48 and three of the sonatinas H. 7–12 (W. 64).

43753. Vienna, Gesellschaft der Musikfreunde, VII 43753, also known as Q 11696. A copy of H. 43 by an unknown copyist, in oblong format using soprano clef.

The eight unnumbered pages comprising this copy are each ruled in ten staves. The title across the top of page 1 reads: 'Sonata per Cembalo Solo di C. F. Em. Bach.' The page bears stamps and handwritten markings added at various times. Handwritten at the top are 'W 65, 15'; '1745'; and the shelf mark 'VII 43753'. Stamps include the possessor's mark of Anthony van Hoboken ('A. v. Hoboken' beneath a sailing ship), another of the 'Gesellschaft / der Musikfreunde / in Wien', and above that 'Revision 1965' and the shelf mark 'Q 11696'. At the bottom is the stamp 'Geschenk / HOBOKEN / 1932' and three entries in different hands, 'W. S. 21 No 65', '13', and 'Ungedruckt'. In the lower right-hand corner is what appears to be a small handwritten star or asterisk.

The copy is fairly neat and accurate, but contains arbitrary additions, such as the rests in the first movement, bars 83–4, and slurs in the third movement, bars 77–8. The handwriting resembles that of Schlichting in the distinctive form of the bass clef. But in other points, such as the presence of 'volti' indications and the ornamental designs at double bars, the copy differs from the Schlichting copies that were available for comparison.[60] Schlichting seems most likely to have worked for Bach at Berlin; hence it would not be surprising to find a copy of the early version of H. 43 in his hand or that of a close associate.[61]

Establishing the text
P 775 *post correcturam* is probably the sole inde-

pendent source for the later version.[62] But the three sources of the earlier version (including P 775 *ante correcturam*) are independent of one another; each probably stems, directly or indirectly, from the lost autograph, which might have undergone small revisions prior to the thoroughgoing revision carried out in P 775. It is unclear which of the copies gives the earliest readings. 43753 is probably closer to the original at two points in the last movement (bars 38 and 46) and, perhaps, in the use of *tr* instead of more specific symbols for some of the ornaments (for example, in II. 33–6). On the other hand, 43753 agrees with the later version at bar 94 of the first movement.

That P 775 *ante correcturam* is independent of US Wc is clear from the readings at bar 112 of the first movement. In US Wc, the notes in the lower stave of bars 110–12 all appear to have been entered only in a later, foreign hand. The first note in bar 112 is *g*, which is otherwise unattested at this point. While seemingly more correct (following *f♯*) than the *G* of the other sources, the reading of the latter is to be preferred as the less obvious one. (The corresponding passage in I. 25–6 is not precisely parallel and therefore offers no ground for determining the correct reading.) It is conceivable, however, that Bach would have overlooked an error at this point while reviewing P 775 *ante correcturam*, as it occurs in a passage that was not revised.

Ornament signs
As noted in the preface, the cross or 'plus' sign is apparently synonymous with *t* or *tr*; indeed, at least some of the signs indicated in the edition as + may actually be versions of the letter 't'. In P 775, the ornament indicated in the edition as *tr* actually appears as a cross to which a squiggle—rarely if ever a distinct letter 'r'—has been added, possibly at a later date. All but one of the work's ornaments (that in III. 62) appears as 't.' (followed by a full stop) in the copy of the early version in 43753, which in this regard is likely to reflect the earliest state of the work. For this reason, all such signs appear as + in the edition of the early version of the first movement. Because of the difficulty in distinguishing *t* from + in some copies, the two signs have been treated as identical in the List of Variant Readings.

[60] Seen here were the copies of H. 23 (W. 65/12) and 53 (W. 69) reproduced in Berg, ed., *The Collected Works*, iii, p. 251, and iii, p. 319.

[61] Schlichting appears to have copied no works composed after Bach's departure for Hamburg. Although he has been placed in Hamburg—see H.-J. Schulze, *Studien zur Bach-Überlieferung im 18. Jahrhundert* (Leipzig, 1984), p. 118—arguments placing him in Berlin have been presented in Wade, *The Keyboard Concertos*, pp. 26f, and in J. Rifkin, ' ". . . Wobey aber die Singstimmen hinlänglich besetzt seyn müssen . . .": Zum Credo der h-Moll-Messe in der Aufführung Carl Philipp Emanuel Bachs', *Basler Jahrbuch für historische Musikpraxis*, 9 (1985), p. 106 n. 9.

[62] The *Nachlassverzeichnis* is an additional source for the incipit of the first movement; it confirms that the reading adopted here was that authorized by Bach at the end of his career.

LIST OF VARIANT READINGS

bar / stave / note-and-rest no.	source: remark
First Movement	
—	P 775 p. corr.: tempo: 'Allegro'; no trace of an earlier reading 'Allegretto' (=US Wc)
0–1 / top	P 369: tie in upper not middle voice
0–1, 2–3 / top, upstem	P 775 p. corr.: tie erased
2–3 / top, downstem	P 775 p. corr.: tie erased
8 / top / 1	P 359, B Bc: tr not + / 3872/2: ⁓ (t?) / P 369: tr (t?)
13 / top / 1	P 359, 3872/2: tr not +
34–5 / top	P 369: tie in upper not middle voice
34–5, 36–7 / top, upstem	P 775 p. corr.: tie erased
36–7 / top, downstem	P 775 p. corr.: tie erased
45 / top / 1	P 359, B Bc, 3872/2, P 369: tr not +
47 / top, upstem / 1–2	P 359: no slur
48, 50 / top, upstem / 1	P 359, B Bc, 3872/2, P 369: tr not +
49	P 359: this bar repeated, second entry crossed out 3872/2: no slur
49 / top / 1–2	P 775 p. corr.: slur added? (present in US Wc)
50	P 359: no f
54 / bottom	P 775 p. corr.: 'f.' added (autograph); conceivably indicating pitch (not dynamics), since placed beneath 2 (compare bar 56). But followed by period, and the revision of the notes is easily legible. Present as dyn. in P 359, B Bc, 3872/2, P 369
56	P 775 p. corr.: letters 'f e' added (autograph) beneath 3–4, which are interpolations and almost illegible. First letter perhaps initially 'c', altered to 'f'; any corresponding alteration in the notes illegible
67–8 / top, upstem	P 775 p. corr.: tie erased P 369: orig. no tie, added lightly
69 / top / 1–2	P775 p. corr. P359 (?), 3872/2, P 369: small 16ths not 32nds
69 / top / 2	P369: no ♭
80 / top / 1	P 359, B Bc, 3872/2, P 369: tr not +
84	P 775 p. corr.: added: f♮, rest, ♯. Antepenult orig. f, changed to a. Erasures in lower stave suggest that other changes were made, but orig. reading is illegible.
88 / top / 6	♯ in P 359, B Bc P 775 p. corr.: erasure
90 / bottom / 4	♯ only in P 369, added lightly
101 / top	P 775 p. corr.: 'fis' over 2–3
112 / bottom / 1	US Wc: g
Second Movement	
1 / top / 2–6	P 775 a. corr., US Wc, 43753: no slur
1 / top / 5	P 775 a. corr., US Wc, 43753: no ⁓
1 / bottom	US Wc, 43753: half-note, quarter rest
2 / top / 1	3872/2: t not tr US Wc: ⁓
2 / bottom / 3	P 775 a. corr., US Wc, 43753: no app.
3 / top / 1	43753: no ♯ (on turn)
4 / top	P 775 a. corr., US Wc, 43753: as Ex. 19a; remaining sources as Ex. 19b (=CPEBE)

Ex. 19

a   b

bar / stave / note-and-rest·no.	source: remark	bar / stave / note-and-rest no.	source: remark
5–10	P 775 a. corr., US Wc, 43753: no slurs	23–5	P 775 a. corr., US Wc, 43753: no slurs
7 / top / 1	P 359: orn. unclear; perhaps ⁓ P 775 a. corr. (?), 43753: t not c⁓	23 / top / 1–3	P 775 a. corr., US Wc, 43753: same pitches, but rhythm is two 16th-notes, an 8th-note, a quarter-note, and a quarter rest
9 / bottom / 2, 5	P 775 a. corr., US Wc, 43753: no ♯, no ♮		
11 / top / 1–4	slur in all sources except US Wc, 43753	25 / bottom / 4, 6, 8	US Wc: apps. erased (!)
11 / bottom / 2	B Bc: ♮ (!)	27 / top / 2–6	P 775 a. corr., US Wc, 43753: no slur
11 / bottom / 2–6	P 775 a. corr., P 359, US Wc, 43753: no slur	31 / top / 1	P 775 a. corr. (?), 43753: t not tr US Wc: c⁓
12 / top / 1	US Wc: ⁓ not tr 43753: t	32 / top	P 775 a. corr., US Wc, 43753: no slur, no ⁓
13, 16	P 775 a. corr., US Wc, 43753: no dyns.	33–6 / top	43753: each orn.: t not c⁓
13 / top / 2–6	P 775 a corr., US Wc, 43753: no slur	33–6 / bottom	P 775 a corr., US Wc, 43753: no slurs, no c⁓
13 / top / 5	P 775 a. corr., US Wc, 43753: no ⁓	40 / top / 5–6	P 775 a . corr., US Wc, 43753: no slur
13 / bottom (both voices)	P 775 a. corr., US Wc, 43753: three quarter-notes not six 8th-notes	40 / top / 6	P 775 a. corr. (?), 43753: t not tr US Wc: ⁓
15 / top / 1–2	P 775 a. corr., US Wc, 43753: no slur	40 / bottom / 1–3	P 775 a. corr., US Wc, 43753: Instead of *g–e♭–C*, these sources have *g–C* as two 8th-notes.
15 / top / 5	B Bc, 3872/2, P 369: tr not + US Wc: ⁓ P 359: t (tr?)		
16 / top / 1–2	P 775 a. corr., US Wc, 43753: no ∞	41–5 / 2–6	P 775 a. corr., US Wc, 43753: no slurs
17 / top / 1–2	P 775 a. corr., US Wc, 43753: no slur	41 / top / 1	US Wc: ∞
18 / top / 1–2; 2–3	43753: no slur; dotted 16th, 32nd	41 / top / 2	P 775 a. corr., US Wc, 43753: no c⁓
18 / top / 8	P 775 a. corr. (?), 43753: t not tr US Wc: ⁓	43 / top / 1	P 775 a. corr. (?), US Wc: ⁓ not c⁓ 43753: t
19–20	P 775 a. corr., US Wc, 43753: no slurs	45 / bottom / 2, 5	P 775 a. corr., US Wc, 43753: no ♯, no ♮
19	P 775 a. corr., US Wc, 43753: no *f*	46 / bottom / 3–4	43753: 8th rest, dotted 16th rest, 32nd-note
19 / bottom; 20 / top	US Wc: 2-flag apps. added before last three notes of each bar, as in bars 24–5	47 / top / 8	P 359, B Bc, 3872/2, P 369: tr not + US Wc: ⁓
20 / bottom / 1	P 775 a. corr., US Wc, 43753: no app.	*Third Movement*	
21 / top / 1	P 775 a. corr., US Wc, 43753: no app.	—	P 775 a. corr., US Wc, 43753: 'Presto' P 775 p. corr.: 'o' erased, 'issimo' added
22 / top / 1–3	P 775 a. corr., US Wc, 43753: two 8th-notes (*bb'*, *f''*) not two 16ths and 8th	8 / top / 4	P 775 a. corr. (?),

bar / stave / note-and-rest no.	source: remark
	43753: t not tr
	US Wc: 〜
9 / bottom	all sources: two dotted quarters, tied (no source has dotted half)
19 / top / 4	P 775 a. corr., US Wc, 43753: preceded by *d'* (2-flag app.)
	P 775 p. corr.: app. erased
19 / top / 4	P 775 a. corr. (?), 43753: t not tr
	US Wc: 〜
33–5 / bottom / 4	P 775 a. corr., US Wc, 43753: all notes assigned to one part (no downstems; whole rest in each bar for lower part)
35 / bottom / 3	B Bc: orig. half-note, notehead filled in
38 / bottom	43753: whole rest
	P 775 p. corr.: erasure, *e* and probably rests are autograph; orig. reading illegible
41–3 / bottom / 4	P 775 a. corr., US Wc, 43753: as in bars 33–5
46 / bottom	43753: whole rest
	P 775 p. corr.: orig. whole rest, autograph correction
	P 369: orig. no *F♯*; added lightly, but rests show no signs of alteration
50 / bottom / 3	P 775 a. corr., US Wc: *A*, not rest
53 / top / 5	♯ only in 43753 and as later addition in B Bc (probably by foreign hand, possibly autograph). No source has any accidental on 4 (*e'*).
54 / top / 4–5	P 775 a. corr., US Wc: no slur
59 / top / 3	P 775, P 359, 3872/2, P 369, US Wc: *e'* not *f♯'*
	B Bc: orig. same, corr. by enlarging notehead
	CPEBE = 43753, B Bc p. corr.
62 / top / 2	US Wc: 〜 not 〰

bar / stave / note-and-rest no.	source: remark
62 / 3	US Wc: fermatas here not over barline
	P 369: no fermatas
63 / top / 3	45753: no ♮
70 / top / 4	P 775 a. corr. (?), 43753: t not tr
73 / bottom / 1–2	P 775 p. corr.: orig. *d* (dotted quarter); dot erased, *c* added
74 / top / 4	P 775 a. corr. (?), 43753: t not tr
	US Wc: 〜
77 / top / 1–3, 4–6	43753: slurs
78 / top / 1–3, 4–5	43753: slurs
78 / top / 4	P 775 a. corr. (?), 43753: t not tr
	US Wc: 〜
82–3 / bottom, downstem	tie only in US Wc, 43753
83–4 / bottom, downstem	tie only in US Wc
85–6 / bottom, downstem	no source has tie across barline, although such reading seems musically appropriate
86 / bottom, upstem / 2	P 775 a. corr. (?), 43753: t not tr
	US Wc: 〰
86 / bottom, downstem / 1	except in US Wc and 43753, *D* and *F♯* are written on a single upward stem beamed together with the following two notes. P 775 shows signs of correction here.
87 / top / 1	P 369: *g♯'*, possibly by confusion with key signature in P 775 p. corr. P 359: perhaps the same error; possibly corrected by erasure
91 / top / 4	P 775 a. corr., US Wc, 43753: preceded by *g'* (2-flag app.)
	P 775 p. corr.: erased
	P 775 a. corr. (?), 43753: t not tr

Variants in the Early Version of the First Movement

—	tempo mark from US Wc
	43753: no tempo mark
	P 775: Allegro (no sign of any earlier reading)

87

bar / stave / note-and-rest no.	source: remark	bar / stave / note-and-rest no.	source: remark
0–1 / top, downstem	tie in P 775 a. corr. and 43753, also in parallel passages (for example, bars 34–5)	83–4, 87–8, 91–2 / top	43753: 16th rests on every beat as in bars 93ff.
8, 10 / top / 1	US Wc: tr not +	84 / top	P 775 a. corr., US Wc: f ♮ not a
13 / top / 1	US Wc: ⌇ not +		US Wc: amended by the addition (in a foreign hand) of the letter 'a' beneath the notehead f
26, 33 / top / 6	US Wc: tr not +		
43 / top / 4	US Wc: ♮ inserted by foreign hand		
	P 775 p. corr.: autograph insertion; ♯ probably intended orig.	84 / bottom	P 775 a. corr., US Wc: no f ♮
		87 / top / 4	US Wc: orig. d'' not e'', corr. by enlarging notehead (foreign hand)
45 / top / 1	US Wc: no +		
48, 50 / top / 1	US Wc: ⌇ not +		
51–2 / top	43753: no tie	90 / bottom / 4	♯ only in 43753
66 / top / 6	US Wc: ⌇ not +	94 / top / 7	43753: f ♮'' (=later version), not e''
67–8 / top / downstem	43753: no tie		
75 / top / 1	US Wc: ⌇ not +	100 / top / 1	US Wc: ⌇ not +
79 / bottom / 1	43753: G/g; upper note possibly a later addition (downward stem)	105 / top / 1	43753: d''' not b''
		110–12 / bottom	US Wc: notes entered in foreign hand
80 / top / 1	US Wc: ⌇ not +	112 / top / 6	US Wc: ⌇ not +
		112 / bottom / 1	US Wc: g not G

SOURCES

H. 46 was composed in Berlin in 1746. Although there is no evidence that the notes themselves were ever substantially revised, a large number of ornaments, accidentals, and other signs were added at various times.   The eleven surviving sources preserve at least three stages of the work, probably representing   different states of revision of the autograph (P 1131), which is the principal source for the edition.

The opening Allegro leads without a break to a section whose fragmentary passages (in different tempos) fulfil the roles of coda, second movement, and transition to the finale. The bars of this section have been counted as a continuation of those of the Allegro, even though the Allegro proper is a self-contained sonata movement. The layout of the autograph suggests that Bach regarded the whole sonata as an unbroken sequence, as there is no double bar either at the end of the Allegro or before the concluding Allegretto.   The latter, however, is referred to here as the 'last' or 'final' movement, and its bars are separately numbered.[63]

P 1131. Berlin, Deutsche Staatsbibliothek, Mus. ms. Bach P 1131, autograph.

P 1131 is one of only five sonata holographs that may date from the 1740s, and one of only two for a work then composed (and not merely revised).[64] P 1131 is the only one of these holographs not now gathered into a larger manuscript, and it is exceptional in the large number of staves per page (twenty) and the resulting minuscule handwriting. The latter may have caused some of the errors in some of the copies, particularly in bars 36–44 of the first movement. Otherwise, however, the format and handwriting are similar to those in other holographs of the period.

The manuscript consists of a single bifolio (34 × 21.5 cm.) written on thick yellow paper, lacking a watermark.[65] The cramped writing was not necessary, since the last six systems (twelve staves) of the last page were unused, and a convenient page turn could have been found at an earlier point on page 2. This suggests that P 1131 was a first draft. But P 1131 contains only two or three alterations that might have been made during the initial entry of the text (I. 22, 83; II. 8). Thus it is more likely to be a hastily written fair copy. The presence of two index numbers in the heading—of which at least the upper number is probably autograph—suggests that P 1131 served Bach continuously as his archival copy from the 1740s onwards.

There is no separate title page. Pagination, probably not autograph, is visible on pages 2–3. The autograph title at the top of page 1 reads: 'Sonata per il Cembalo solo di CPE Bach'. To the right of the title are the index numbers: 'No. 45. / (45.)'. The numeral 5 in the upper number may have been altered, but the original reading (if different) cannot be determined. To the right of the index numbers is a later entry ('[Wotquenne 65,15]'), and at the left, beneath the title, faint entries that include the shelf mark 'Mus. ms. autogr. / Bach P 1131' and a reference (now partly illegible) to the Berlin 'Them. Kat.'

It has proved impossible to determine conclusively from P 1131 alone which entries are original and which represent revisions. But the differing variants in the copies P 775 and B Bc show that P 1131 was probably revised more than once, and certain readings in the other copies probably represent an even earlier state of the autograph. Among the ornaments, the sign + and the turn in vertical or slanting form are often written heavily, while other signs, including the horizontal turn, are somewhat smaller and more lightly drawn. The more lightly drawn ornaments, including most of the *prallende Doppelschlägen* and the very few trills indicated by a squiggle (instead of +), seem likely to be later additions, and the copies of the earlier version tend to confirm this. But even signs from the first (heavier) group are sometimes absent from the copies of the earlier version, suggesting that Bach may have added ornaments on many separate occasions.

---

[63] In abbreviated references to movement and bar numbers, the Roman numeral II will refer to the last movement.

[64] The others are of H. 4 (W. 65/2) and H. 16–17 (W. 65/7–8), all in Mus. ms. Bach P 771 in the Biblioteka Jagiellońska, Kraków; and H. 60 (W. 65/24), in Mus. ms. Bach P 776 in the Staatsbibliothek Preußicher Kulturbesitz, Berlin.

[65] I am grateful to Pamela Fox for the description of the paper.

The many accidentals that appear either above or below their proper position are more clearly insertions. Most of the added accidentals are merely cautionary, but a real change of mind on Bach's part is probably reflected in the variant readings for bar 28 of the first movement, where A Wgm lacks both G sharps and the first sharp is displaced in P 367 just as in the autograph. Apparent revisions involving accidentals are noted in the List of Variant Readings only if confirmed by the absence or the apparent insertion of the sign in one or more other sources.

Except in the ornaments mentioned above, only in a few cases do entries that seem to be insertions show differences in form or handwriting. The most likely instance is in bar 42 of the final movement, where the quarter rest in the inner voice is larger than that in the left hand and has a somewhat different shape; other sources confirm that this was probably a later addition.

P 775. Berlin, Staatsbibliothek Preußischer Kulturbesitz, Musikabteilung, Mus. ms. Bach P 775. Manuscript copy by Michel, with autograph additions (33 × 21 cm., no watermark).[66]

The copy of H. 46 occupies the eight pages of P 775 now numbered 141–8. There is no separate title page. Traces of older (original?) pagination are visible on pages 3 and 7. The eighth page is blank.

The original title appears in the upper left corner of the first page: 'Sonata'. In the top center appears: 'Cembalo solo.' In the upper right is the attribution: 'di / C. P. E. Bach'. Added at various locations in the top margin, each in a different hand, are the following separate entries: 'Nr. 20', '(45)', 'Th. Kat. 63,16 = Nach. 7,45', '[Wotquenne 65,16]', and 'Berlin 1746.' The figure '45' in parentheses, though corresponding with the lower index number in P 1131, is probably not autograph and lacks the full stop. At the bottom of the page appears the letter 'C' in the left corner. Following that are the words 'Von Hering geschrieben', an erroneous reference to the S. Hering identified in other manuscripts as *Präfekt Philipp Emanuel Bachs*.[67]

Bach's hand is easily recognizable in bars 37–9 of the first movement, which Michel had apparently

left blank; the passage is nearly illegible in P 1131. Bach's entry at this point in P 775 is in the shaky handwriting, with short, stubby note stems, characteristic of many Hamburg autographs. Other entries, such as the addition or retracing of the dynamic marking in bar 108 (first movement), may also be autograph. Yet Bach allowed to stand a considerable number of other variants, mostly omissions of ornaments, that distinguish the copy in P 775 from P 1131. The great majority of these variants are readily explained as later additions to the autograph. But P 775 contains too many errors, as in bar 121 of the first movement, to have been carefully checked over by Bach, nor could it have replaced P 1131 as his primary reference copy. It also contains one ornament, the turn in bar 12 of the first movement, which, even if autograph, occurs in no other copy. Thus the copy of H. 46, unlike the copy of H. 43 also in P 775, cannot have served as Bach's archival score, and this may be why it bears only one of the usual index numbers.

B Bc. Brussels, Bibliothèque du Conservatoire Royal de Musique, ms. 5883. Manuscript copy by Michel, with at least one autograph entry.

The one certain autograph entry in the copy of H. 46 is the tempo mark of the first movement. A few other entries appear to be in a foreign hand, conceivably autograph.

The music occupies eight unnumbered pages (two sheets, no watermark); there is no separate title page. The original title at the top of the first page reads: 'Sonata per il Cembalo solo da C. P. E. Bach'. Above this in a foreign hand is the number '16' and, in another hand, the underlined call number 'U, no. 5883'. Added in a third foreign hand beneath the title is: '16e. Sonate du no. 15 de Westphal.' At the bottom of the page the number '10' appears in the lower left, and a faint inscription ('Ms. Michel'?) is in the lower right.

The music is written on six or seven systems per page, and line breaks occur at points different from those in Michel's other copy, P 775, although page breaks in the first movement are the same. The text is that of the latest state of P 1131, with only a few insignificant variants.

P 368. Berlin, Staatsbibliothek Preußischer Kulturbesitz, Musikabteilung, Mus. ms. Bach P 368. Manuscript copy possibly by Homilius (33 × 20 cm.; watermark: crowned coat of arms).

---

[66] Facsimile in Berg, ed., *The Collected Works*, III, p. 283.

[67] On Hering, see Dadelsen, *Bemerkungen zur Handschrift Johann Sebastian Bachs*, p. 22. On the erroneous references to Hering as copyist, see the *CPEBE*, I/24, ed. C. Widgery, p. 110.

The copy of H. 46 falls within the first section of P 368, on pages 42–51. There is no title page, in fact no title, and no original pagination is visible. The top of the first page gives merely the tempo ('Allegro'), followed by additions in two different hands: '[Wotquenne 65,16]' and 'Nachl. Verz. 7,45'.

The somewhat carelessly ruled and notated copy contains several errors as well as some later entries in a foreign hand, a few probably by the same person who edited D KIl 52/4 (see below). The copy appears to be in a deteriorating state, with many noteheads showing through from the reverse side of the page, at times reducing legibility and making readings conjectural. Although the copy has been identified as the work of Homilius, it differs in details of handwriting and orthographic style from the copy of H. 51 also assigned to him.[68] Despite the problematical aspects of the copy, together with P 367 it confirms many of the apparent readings of P 1131 *ante correcturam*.

P 367. Berlin, Staatsbibliothek Preußischer Kulturbesitz, Musikabteilung, Mus. ms. Bach P 367. Manuscript copy by Müthel. Oblong format, 22 × 34 cm. (watermark: lily; countermark: lily).

H. 46 is the fifth of the six Bach sonatas in the final section of P 367, on pages 140–3. The format and handwriting are uniform with those in the immediately preceding copy of H. 40. But the copy of H. 46 lacks the distinctive (and unauthentic) ornament sign used in the copy of the earlier sonata (described in the Critical Commentary for H. 40).

The original headings at the top of the first page are the same as for H. 40. Added in the upper left is the faint entry 'autogr Müthel', probably in the same hand as on pages 125 and 135. To the right of the title are added bibliographic entries as in P 368.

The text is close to that in P 368, but not a copy of it. P 367 lacks the obvious errors of P 368, while containing a few others. Müthel's own music may have been influenced by H. 46, as two of his sonatas contain alternating tempi in the second movement.[69]

M23. Washington, DC, Library of Congress, Music Division, M23.B13.W65(16) (case). Manuscript copy by an unknown copyist. Oblong format, with soprano clef in upper system, in wrapper bearing entries in modern hand.

Though enclosed in a similar wrapper, the copy of H. 46 differs completely in format, in handwriting, and in the accuracy and authority of its text from the copies by Anon. 303 in the same library. The six unnumbered, unbound folios (traces of stitching remain), are ruled uniformly in ten staves—including the last page, which bears no music. In the left margin of page 1, just above the first stave, the copyist wrote the title: 'Sonata.'. Probably in the same hand, across the top centre of the page, is: 'Sonata à Cembalo Solo.'. To this another hand has added 'del Sigr. C. P. E. Bach'. Added in pencil in the upper right corner is the entry 'R iii.i', probably a reference to the 1763 Breitkopf catalogue.[70] Just below this is a pencilled signature in another hand, which is illegible. In another foreign hand, in ink in the upper left corner, is 'No 45.' The number '16' appears in blue pencil in the lower right hand corner. A tab attached to the back of the first page, meant to stand up as an index marker but now turned down inside page 2, reads: 'No: 141. / C. P. E. / Bach.' The handwriting does not match that of any of the entries on page 1.

Both the wrapper and the manuscript itself bear later markings similar to those found in the copy of H. 43, except that the number stamped on the final page is one higher (603054). Also on the last page are two lines added in ink, in a modern hand differ-

---

Sonatas et II Ariosi avec XII Variations pour Clavecin (Nürnberg, 1756), modern edition by L. Hoffmann-Erbrecht, Mitteldeutsches Musikarchiv, vol. i/6–7 (Leipzig, 1954). Transposed extracts from the first movement of H. 46 appear among the entries in Müthel's so-called *Technische Übungen* (Berlin, Staatsbibliothek Preußischer Kulturbesitz Mus. ms. 15762/1.2); facsimile in P. Reidemeister, 'Johann Gottfried Müthels "Technische Übungen", oder Von der Mehrdeutigkeit der Quellen', *Basler Jahrbuch für historische Musikpraxis*, 13 (1989), 85, 87. I am grateful to Joshua Rifkin for bringing this article to my attention.

[70] H. 46 is the first of 'VI. Sonate di C. P. E. Bach, per il Cemb. Solo. Racc. III.' listed in *Catalogo de' soli, duetti, trii, terzetti, quartetti e concerti per il cembalo e l'harpa che si trovano in manoscritto nella officina musica di Breitkopf in Lipsia. Parte IVta. 1763*, page 2, in *The Breitkopf Thematic Catalogue: The Six Parts and Sixteen Supplements, 1762–1787*, ed. B. S. Brook (New York, 1966), col. 116.

---

[68] Though both are assigned to Homilius in Kast, p. 26, the copies of H. 46 and H. 51 show inconsistencies in the forms of the G clef and double bar. Only in H. 51 are the clefs repeated at the beginning of every system. See the discussions of P 368 under H. 40 and H. 51.

[69] The works in question appeared in Müthel's *III*

ent from that on the wrapper: 'No 45 des Clavier-Soli [second word unclear]. comp. 1746. zu Berlin. Ungedruckt. / Nachlass-Verz. 17 [?].' The hand may be the one that added 'No 45' on page 1. At the bottom centre of page 2 is the pencilled accession number '344325 / '25', at the lower left the shelf mark 'M23 / .B13 / W65(16) / (case)'.

The copy contains many emendations of dubious authenticity. A number of (authentic) ornaments have been entered, probably in a foreign hand; also present, though probably written by the original copyist, are several of the long slurs in the third movement also found in P 368 and P 367.

D Mbs. Munich, Bayerische Staatsbibliothek, Mus. ms. 1794. Manuscript copy by an unknown copyist; soprano clef.

Manuscript 1794 from the Bayerische Staatsbibliothek closely resembles manuscript 1795 (described in the critical commentary for H. 40). It contains copies of H. 51, H. 46, and H. 39 (W. 62/5), each of which originally constituted a separate manuscript. The first and last were certainly written by the same copyist, and that of H. 46 either by the same copyist or one with a very similar hand. The copies of H. 51 and H. 39 include separate, nearly identical title pages. The leaves have been numbered lightly in a foreign hand, though there is no general title page.

The copy of H. 46 occupies twelve pages, with no original pagination and no title page. The last page is ruled but unused. The title 'Sonata.' appears at the left margin on the first page, with the attribution 'di C. P. E. Bach.' in the upper right corner. The handwriting shows many similarities with that in M23 in the Library of Congress, although the two copies are independent. Despite the difference in format, page turns occur at identical points. The Munich source appears to be the work of a less practiced copyist working from the same model, and contains a greater number of careless errors.

The text of D Mbs is particularly close to that of M23 in the Library of Congress, sharing many orthographic oddities such as irregular beaming and division of parts between the staves. But the third movement contains markings likely to be in a foreign hand. Among the foreign entries are, probably, all of the dynamic indications, as well as several long slurs corresponding to those in P 368, P 367, and M23.

D KIl. Kiel, Schleswig-Holsteinische Landesbibliothek, Mb 52. Contains ten copies of keyboard sonatas by C. P. E. Bach, in oblong format.

Together with its companion in upright format (D KIl Mb 53, described under H. 47), the Kiel manuscript Mb 52 contains a repertory drawn from Bach's unpublished Berlin sonatas. Most copies are in unidentified hands of the late eighteenth or perhaps early nineteenth century. At least some of the copies once belonged to other collections, as the various paginations show.

Mb 52 contains the following works: H. 21 (W. 65/11, twice), H. 42 (W. 65/14, first movement only), H. 46, H. 51 (three times), H. 78 (W. 65/28), H. 176 (W. 65/39), and H. 143 (W. 65/33). Only two of the scores—the first copy of H. 51 and the copy of H. 143—can be assigned to the same writer. The odd-numbered pages bear a running pagination in the lower right corner; this is in addition to any original pagination in each score.

A number of copies in this collection, including the score of H. 46 (Mb 52/4), contain slurs, ornaments, and other entries added by later editors, sometimes but not always with a citation of the source of the addition. In general, such entries are not noted in the List of Variant Readings. Entries in the Kiel copy of H. 46 include references to P 368 and P 367; P 368 contains a corresponding entry at one point, probably by the same editor. Because the source of the addition is not always given, it is sometimes difficult to distinguish additions from the original text.

Some of the added entries (but not those in the copy of H. 46) bear the initials 'E. P.'—for Erich Prieger (1849–1913)—and one of two dates, 1880 or 1886. The remarks in the copy of H. 46 are in the hand of a different nineteenth-century writer (Scheibler?) who made an entry ending with the date 'Okt 99' in one of the copies of H. 51 (Mb 52/6).

The copy of H. 46 occupies pages 25–32. These pages also bear the presumably earlier (but not original) verso pagination 68–75. The copy is preceded by a title page or cover bearing a label that reads: 'Carl Ph. Em. Bachs / Clavier_Sonate / C. dur.' To this have been added notations in various hands: 'Dublette' (underlined), 'N. 45' (underlined), 'comp. 1746', 'Ms . . . [in square brackets, barely legible:] Rieter-Biedermann Weber', [then:] 'W 65,16', and 'Verglichen mit Berlin Ms: P 367, 368.'

The eight pages of music are neatly ruled in ten staves each. The title, in a different hand from the title on the cover, is at the top left of the first page and reads: 'Sonata Allegro.' The attribution, possibly in a third hand, is at the top, to the right of centre: 'dell Sigr. C. P. E. Bach.' The first two words were possibly added later in yet another hand. A few faint letters, perhaps 'Mot', can be made out in the right corner.

The text contains many errors and is written somewhat carelessly, with hand-drawn extensions of several staves into the right margin and one brief hand-drawn system added in the lower margin.

M20. Washington, DC, Library of Congress, Music Division, M20.A2M684. Eighteenth-century manuscript collection of solo keyboard pieces by an unknown copyist.

Little information is available about this collection, which appears to have been assembled from at least two originally separate manuscripts although it is entirely in one hand. What appears to have been the front cover of one manuscript (prior to binding within modern covers) bears an eighteenth-century label reading: 'Miscellanea / per il Cembalo / 1.) Sonata C♮ di C. P. E. Bach. / 2.) Detta C♭ da G. Benda / 3.) Pieces de Caractère di Bach / 4. Variationi di Weimar / 5. Detti Sopra Ich schlief, da / träumte mir / Raccolta IV'. Added in pencil at the top centre is the figure '1'; pencilled numerical entries also appear in the upper right and bottom centre, above the last line of the inscription. The reverse is blank save for a printed label in the upper left-hand corner reading 'LEO LIEPMANNSSOHN / ANTIQUARIAT / BERLIN / S W. BERNBURGERSTR. 14'. A blank leaf follows; the reverse bears the stamp '223206' and the call number 'M20 / A2M648'.

The manuscript is possibly a compilation assembled by a professional copyist employed by a publisher; similar titles appear in the Breitkopf thematic catalogues, which list H. 46 but include it in a 'selection' (raccolta) of pieces different from those given here.

The twenty-five unnumbered pages bearing music are all in the same hand and all use soprano clef. Contents are as follows: H. 46; a sonata in C minor by Jiří (Georg) Benda (1722–95) which had appeared in that composer's fourth *Sammlung vermischter Clavier- und Gesangstücke* (Leipzig, 1781 or later);[71] Bach's character pieces H. 113 (W. 117/33), H. 111 (W. 117/31), H. 123

(W. 117/29), H. 81 (W. 117/26); six 'Variationes di Weimar'—presumably Bach's student the Erfurt composer Georg Peter Weimar (1734–1800); and a 'Variatio' in da capo form followed by seventeen like variations numbered 16–32, followed by a 'Tamburin'. The latter is over a *bourdon* bass but evidently intended as another variation. The 'Variationes di Weimar' are on the same bass as the Arioso H. 54 (W. 118/4); the second set of variations is on the theme used by Bach in H. 69 (W. 118/1). It is conceivable that the variations here were intended as a continuation of a truncated version of H. 69 (hence the numbering starting with 16). But there is no indication that the manuscript is incomplete, or that any of the variations in the manuscript is by Bach.

The copy of H. 46 may once have constituted a separate manuscript. It occupies seven pages of music; an eighth page (reverse of the last page of music) is blank. There is no title page; the title at the top centre of the first page reads 'Sonata per il Cembalo. Solo.'. Added in the upper right corner is the attribution 'del Sig. C. P. E. Bach'. Added beneath the title is the modern entry 'W 65, 16.'

The text appears to be an edited recension of the early version, containing numerous signs for ornaments and articulation not found elsewhere, as well as alterations of the notes and rhythms (see, for example, the variant readings listed for I. 28, 89). Since there is no sign of correction or alteration in the copy at points where text appears to have been edited, presumably the editing was done in an earlier copy that served as a model for the present one. A few cases in which the source gives ornaments belonging to the later version probably represent fortuitous coincidences (for example, II. 67, 69, 87), since elsewhere in the source other ornaments are substituted (for example, turns in I. 20–1). Such apparently arbitrary substitutions have generally not been included in the List of Variant Readings. Several odd variants in the bass (I. 58–9, 107) appear to represent incompetent attempts to fill lacunae.

A Wgm. Vienna, Gesellschaft der Musikfreunde, VII 43745, also known as H 31221. Manuscript copy written by 'Paxmann'.

This set of six sonatas includes a title page signed

---

[71] Ed. V. J. Sýkora as No. 12 of *Jiří Benda: Sonaten I–XVI*, Musica antiqua bohemica, 24 (Prague, 1978).

by the copyist: 'Sechs / SONATEN / von ver-schiedener Art / fürs / Klavier / von / Carl Pplipp [sic] Emanuel Bach / Erste Sammlung / Paxmann [underlined]'. Added later were the stamp of the current owner ('Gesellschaft / der / Musikfreunde / in Wien') and a stamp reading 'Geschenk / HOBO-KEN / 1932', indicating that the manuscript was from the collection of Anthony van Hoboken.

The manuscript also includes a cover or wrapper bearing this title (in another hand): 'Sex / Sonaten / von / verschiedner [sic] / Art fürs Clavier / von / Carl Philip [sic] Emanuel Bach / Poss: W. L. Andrae' to which have been added numerous markings: the stamp 'WOTQUENNE 65/28 U.A.'; the handwritten shelf mark 'VII 43745'; a pencilled (?) '62' and 'S. B. [L. B. ?]'; the stamps 'Geschenk / HOBOKEN / 1932' and 'Gesellschaft / der / Musikfreunde / in Wien'; and in the lower right corner a handwritten '221'.

The original title draws upon that of Bach's 1765 publication *Clavierstücke verschiedener Art* (W. 112), but the contents are evidently the copyist's own selection: H. 78 (W. 65/28), H. 46, H. 116 (W. 62/16), H. 39 (W. 62/5), H. 58 (W. 62/9), and H. 131 (W. 62/21). A copyist of the same name is represented in the Berlin Bach collections by two small manuscripts and appears to have worked in the late eighteenth or early nineteenth century.[72] The pages are ruled in ten to sixteen staves; the handwriting is professional in appearance, but the copy of H. 46 is inaccurate. The music occupies a total of thirty-eight pages; no pagination was observed. Each work is designated 'SONATA I', 'SONATA II', etc.; the only entries in a foreign hand are indications to the right of each title giving the work's number, and date and place of composition, as given in the Wotquenne catalogue.

H. 46 is written on six pages and is designated 'SONATA II.'. Added beside the title is the pencil entry 'Berlin 1746 / (65) No 16'. The garbling of the bass line in the bars 84–6 of the first movement is independent of the other copies. While an error in bar 16 of the same movement suggests that it was copied from an exemplar using soprano clef, another error in bar 17 of the last movement contradicts this.

D GOl. Gotha, Forschungs- und Landesbibliothek, Mus. 2° 21a/3 (90). Copy of H. 46 by Johann Friedrich Gräbner.

Mus. 2° 21a/3 (89–97) is a bound volume (34 × 21 cm., twenty-four sheets, pp. 1 and 96 pasted onto covers, no watermark) containing twelve sonatas: H. 59 (W. 62/10), H. 46 (W. 65/16), H. 17 (W. 65/8), H. 121 (W. 65/31), H. 23 (W. 65/12), H. 3 (W. 65/1), H. 139 (W. 50/5), H. 139 (W. 50/4), and H. 23 (W. 65/13). Gräbner (1714–94), organist at St Wenzel's, Naumberg, copied the manuscript around 1770. It was subsequently in the collection of Christoph Ernst Abraham Albrecht von Boineburg (1752–1840), an avid collector of Bach's music, the main parts of whose Bach collection are now divided between the Gotha Forschungs- und Landesbibliothek and the Gorke collection in Leipzig (on loan to the Bach-Archiv). The cover title reads: '89–97 / von / P. E. Bach'. The copy of H. 46 is on pp. 12–23 and bears the heading 'Sonata. II:'.[73]

Establishing the text
None of the copies is assuredly dependent on another, and only Michel's copies clearly depend directly on the autograph, P 1131. The original text of B Bc includes readings present only as later insertions in both P 1131 and Michel's other copy, P 775. Although it contains at least one autograph entry, B Bc still makes some of the same omissions as P 775; thus P 1131 remains the most authoritative source.

P 775 is clearly earlier than B Bc, but, while a copy of P 1131, its relationship to the autograph is somewhat problematic. Although P 775 contains at least a few autograph emendations, Bach seems not to have finished correcting it, and no further copies stem from it.

P 367 and P 368 form a group of sources distinct from M23, D Mbs, and D Kll. A Wgm and D GOl make significant departures from both groups but are clearly allied with them. The same can be said of M20. Both it and A Wgm seem closer to the group that includes M23, D Mbs and D Kll. But

[72] Listed in Kast, pp. 47, 50, are Mus. mss. Bach P 799 (BWV Anh. 177) and P 829 (the ricercars of the Musical Offering), both in the Staatsbibliothek Preußischer Kulturbesitz, Berlin.

[73] The description of D GOl was supplied by U. Leisinger. Although a copy of the source became available to the editor too late for its readings to be incorporated in the list of variant readings, D GOl provides important evidence about the early version of H. 46 (see below). For more on Boineburg's collection, see U. Leisinger, *Die Bach-Quellen der Forschungs- und Landesbibliothek Gotha: Handschriften und frühe Drucke* (Gotha, 1993).

each of these five sources contains occasional puzzling concordances with the P 368 / P 367 group, making it impossible to determine the precise relationships between the manuscripts under consideration. Some readings common to all these sources, most of them involving the absence of ornaments, slurs, and appoggiaturas in bars 91–126 of the first movement, must represent an authentic version earlier than that of P 775. But it seems unlikely that any of the variants distinguishing these sources from one another are authentic.

That P 367, P 368, M23, D Mbs, D KIl, and M20 might all stem from P 1131 is suggested by the misreadings in bars 36–9 of the first movement, where the autograph is difficult to read. Yet D GOl and the otherwise inaccurate copy A Wgm give this passage correctly; A Wgm also lacks the errors of the other copies in bars 103–4. Hence the variants at these points in the other copies may stem from independent misreadings of the lost composing score. All of the copies in these groups, including A Wgm, share a number of variants of which there is no trace in P 1131 (for example, the inner voice in I. 96, the chord in I. 108, and the lower stave in I. 112). That these readings stem from a lost composing score is evident from the Gotha source, which lacks all octave doublings in the lower stave in II. 24–30 and 87–91 (the lower note is absent in each case, except in bars 87 and 90, where the upper note is omitted). The octaves are present in P 1191, which shows no signs of revision at these points, and partially in the other sources under discussion, suggesting that the latter stem from partially revised states of the composing score. D GOl also confirms the early reading at I. 37 (e♮, not e♭, on the fourth beat). All of the early readings, even the avoidance of low A, in bar 112, are plausible, although the note already occurs in the first of the Württemberg sonatas (H. 30 = W. 49/1), published in 1744.

Variants found only in some of these sources must be regarded as much more doubtful. The P 368/P 367 group contains a few divergent indications of ornaments (mostly the substitution of specific signs for +) that are stylistically plausible. But the long slurs in the last movement (bars 1–2, 13–14, etc.) are not typical of Bach's writing during the 1740s; these probably were original entries only in P 368, P 367, and M20, and were later additions in M23, D Mbs, and D KIl. Even less credible are readings confined to M23, D Mbs, and D KIl, including the banal emendations of the last movement (bars 25–30, 37, etc).

Ornament signs

As with H. 43, the List of Variant Readings does not distinguish between the signs *t* and +. In P 1131 the + appears to be followed by a full stop in I. 79 and 82.

LIST OF VARIANT READINGS
(Music examples can be found on p. 107)

bar / stave / note-and-rest no.	source: remark
First Movement	
—	B Bc: tempo marking: autograph addition
1 / top / 1	D KIl: no arp.
2 / top / 3	P 367: no +
	M23, D KIl, A Wgm: tr
3 / top / 5	P 367, M20, A Wgm: no +
	P 368, M23, D KIl: tr
4 / 1	D Mbs: dotted 16th-note
4 / 1; 4–7	M20: dotted 16th; 32nds

bar / stave / note-and-rest no.	source: remark
4 / 2–7	D KIl: 32nds
4 / 4–7	D Mbs: 32nds
4 / upstem / 6	D KIl: ∞ not +
	M23, A Wgm: tr
5 / top, upstem / 1	P 368, P 367, M23, D Mbs, D KIl, M20, A Wgm: no ↷
	P 1131: orig. possibly + or tr; trace of vertical stroke remains
5 / top, downstem / 1	B Bc, A Wgm: both C' and E' are preceded by 8th rests (one above the other)

bar / stave / note-and-rest no.	source: remark
6 / top, upstem / 1	P 368, P 367: ∿ not *c*∿
	M23, D Mbs, D KIl, M20, A Wgm: no orn.
7 / top, upstem / 1–2	P 368, M23, D Mbs: no slur
	P 368: slur added lightly
7 / top, upstem / 4–5	A Wgm: no slur
7 / top, upstem / 6	M20: no ♮
7 / top, upstem / 8	A Wgm: no *a''*
8 / top, upstem / 1–2	A Wgm: no slur
8 / top, upstem / 6	P 775, B Bc (?): tr not +
	P 368, P 367, M23, D Mbs, D KIl, A Wgm: no orn.
8 / top, downstem / 5	M23, D Mbs, D KIl: *d'/d''*
	A Wgm: 8th rest in middle voice
9 / top, upstem / 1, 9	P 775, B Bc: tr not +
	P 368, P 367, M23, D Mbs, D KIl, A Wgm: no orn.
9 / bottom	M20: first chord (*d/f*♯) directly beneath that in top stave (*d'/f*♯')
11 / top, downstem / 1	M20: *c''* (=bar 12) not *a'*
11 / top, downstem / 2	P 368, P 367, M23, D Mbs, M20, D KIl, A Wgm: no app.
	P 1131: app. a later addition (if present; unclear)
	B Bc: app. probably inserted; top stave line broken at this point (slur erased?)
	P 775: app. inserted?
11 / top, downstem / 9	M23, D Mbs, M20, A Wgm: *a'* not *c''*
11 / bottom / 1	M20: *a* not *g*
11, 12 / top, downstem	P 368, P 367, M23, D Mbs, D KIl, M20, A Wgm: no slur
12 / top, downstem / 2	∾ only in P 775 (autograph addition?)
	A Wgm: no ♭
12 / bottom / 6	M20: no ♭
12 / bottom / 7	♮ only in M23, D Mbs
13 / top, upstem / 1–2	P 368, P 367, M23, D Mbs, D KIl, A Wgm: no slur
14 / top, upstem / 1–2	D Mbs: no slur
15 / top, upstem / 1	D KIl: *d''/a''/c'''*; *a''* possibly a correction in foreign hand
15 / top, upstem / 1–2	D Mbs, D KIl, A Wgm: no slur
15 / top, upstem / 1–3	A Wgm: dotted quarter, two 16ths
15 / top, downstem / 1–2	M23: tied
15 / top, downstem / 2–3	M20: no *d''*, *c'*
16 / top / 1–2, 4–5	D Mbs, M20: no slurs
16 / top / 3	A Wgm: *d*♭''' not *b*♭''
17 / top / 3–4	D KIl: no tie
	A Wgm: end of line following 3, tie om. at beginning of next line
17 / top / 10	P 367: no ♯
	P 368: ♯ is a later insertion (also on 17)
17 / bottom / 1	A Wgm: no ♭
17 / bottom, downstem / 4	M20: no *B*♭
18 / top / 1, 5, 9	P 775, P 368, P 367, M23, D Mbs, D KIl, A Wgm: no strokes
	M20: stroke on 1 only
18 / top / 2–4	M23, D Mbs, D KIl, M20, A Wgm: slur
18 / top / 6–8	P 775, D Mbs, M20, A Wgm: slur
	M23: added lightly, extends to 9 (*d'''*)
18 / bottom, upstem / 1–2	P 368, P 367, M23, D Mbs, D KIl, M20, A Wgm: no slur
18 / bottom, upstem / 1	D KIl: ∿
18 / bottom, upstem / 2–4	P 775, M23, D Mbs, D KIl, M20, A Wgm: slur
19 / top / 3	P 367: ♯ (!)
	P 368, D KIl: ♯ added in foreign hand above note, in D KIl with notation '367'
20 / top, upstem / 3	P 775, A Wgm (?): tr not +
	P 368, P 367: ∿
	M23, D Mbs, D KIl: no orn.
	M23: tr added in foreign hand
	M20: ∾

bar / stave / note-and-rest no.	source: remark	bar / stave / note-and-rest no.	source: remark
21 / top, upstem / 3	P 775, M23, D KIl, A Wgm: tr not + P 368, P 367: ⁓ D Mbs: no orn. M23: ∞	28 / top / 11–15	M23, D Mbs, D KIl:
21–2 / top, downstem	P 368, P 367, M20: no tie		
22 / top, upstem / 4–5	P 1131: orig. *g'* (8th)? A Wgm: two 16ths	28 / top / 13, 20	P 775, P 368, P 367, M23, D Mbs, D KIl, M20, A Wgm: no accidentals (on *g''*). P 1131, B Bc: accidentals inserted above stave
22 / top, downstem / 1	P 775, P 368, P 367, M23, D Mbs, D KIl, M20, A Wgm: no dot (quarter) M23, D Mbs, D KIl: followed by *f♯'* (quarter)	28 / top / 15	P 775, B Bc: 64ths begin here (*b''*) This reading from confusion in P 1131 between fourth beam and top stave line; *CPEBE* follows bar 89
23 / top / 1	M23, D Mbs, D KIl, M20: no app. A Wgm = 2-flag app.		
23 / top / 5	M23, D Mbs, D KIl: no + P 368: unclear, possibly t P 367, A Wgm: tr M20: ∞	28 / top / 16–21	A Wgm:
24-5 / top, upstem	P 368, P 367, M23, D Mbs, D KIl, M20, A Wgm: dotted quarter-note, two 16ths (four times) P 1131: orig. the above?		
		28 / bottom / 2–4	M20: quarter rest, *c* (quarter)
25 / top, upstem / 3	D KIl: no ♮	29 / top / 2	P 368, P 367, D KIl: ⁓ not ≋ M23, M20, D Mbs: no orn.
26 / top, downstem / 1	dot only in P368, M23 M20: no *g'*	29 / top / 10	P 368, P 367: ⁓ not + P 775, M23, D KIl, A Wgm: tr M 20: ≋
27 / top / 9–10	extent of slur unclear in copies; cf. remark for last movement, bar 42 P 368, P 367, M23, D Mbs, D KIl, A Wgm: no slur		
27 / top / 10	D Mbs: no app.	30 / both / 2	M20, A Wgm: followed by half rest
27 / bottom, downstem / 6	M20: no ♯	31 / top / 1	P 368, P 367: no arp.
28 / top / 3–9	D KIl: slur	31 / top / 3–5	M23, D Mbs: slur
28 / top / 4	P 368, P 367: no ♯ P 1131, P 775: ♯ inserted (?) beneath stave	32 / top / 3	D Mbs, D KIl: *g''* not *b''* (corr. in D Mbs)
28 / top / 5	M20, A Wgm: no ♯ P 1131, P 367: ♯ squeezed in between notes	32 / bottom / 1	D Mbs: no rest
		33 / upstem / 8	D Mbs: no ♮
		33 / bottom, upstem / 3	M20: *a* not *b*
28 / top / 10–13; 14–21	M20: 16ths (!), no slur on 10-11; 32nds (!)	33 / bottom, downstem / 1	B Bc: whole rest (here, not in centre of bar) P 368, P 367, M23, D Mbs, D KIl, M20: no rest
		33 / bottom, downstem / 2	P 368, P 367, M23, D Mbs, D KIl: 8th (no dot)

bar / stave / note-and-rest no.	source: remark
33 / bottom, downstem / 3–6	D Mbs (only): 32nds
33	M20: last four notes all beamed together, downstem
35 / bottom	M23, D Mbs, D KIl: no rest
36–44	Sources inconsistent in use of separate stems for each note-head. In P 1131 separate stems are distinct only in bars 36, 37 (fourth beat), 38 (bottom), and 44; the lowest note in the top stave always has a separate stem throughout bars 37 and 40.
36 / bottom	M23, D Mbs: whole rest
37 / top / 2	M23: no ♭ on e'
37 / top / 4	P 1131, P 775, B Bc, A Wgm: ♭ repeated on e'
	P 1131: perhaps orig. ♮
	P 368, P 367 (?): ♮
	M23: no acc.
	D Mbs, D KIl: ♮, but on 1 of bar 38 D Mbs has ♭ (possibly a later addition), D KIl repeats ♮
37 / bottom	D Mbs: only a whole rest
37 / bottom, upstem / 1	M23, D Mbs, D KIl: no quarter rest
37–9 / bottom	P 1131 very unclear here
	P 775: lower stave entirely autograph; no sign of previous erasure
37–9 / bottom, upstem	M20: substitutes b♭ for each d♭'
38 / top / 4	P 368: added above stave lightly (foreign hand): 'x (e)'
38 / bottom	M23, M20: no rests
38 / bottom, upstem / 1	D KIl: no rest
38 / bottom, downstem / 1–2	D Mbs: no rests
38 / bottom, inner voices / 2–4	P 368, P 367, M23, D Mbs, D KIl: no d♭'
	P 1131: d♭' probably a later addition
39	M 23, D Mbs: as Ex. 20a; D KIl: as Ex.

bar / stave / note-and-rest no.	source: remark
	20b; P 368, P 367: as Ex. 20c; all remaining sources as Ex. 20d (=CPEBE)
39 / top / 4	D Mbs: as Ex. 20a, but ♭ orig. on d'' not b'; corr. (possibly in a later hand) to Ex. 20d
39 / bottom / 1	M23, D Mbs, D KIl, M20: no rest
39 / bottom / 2	M23, D KIl: no ♭ (later addition in D KIl)
39 / bottom / 3	D Mbs: as Ex. 20a but g erased (=Ex. 20c)
40 / top / 4	P 368, P 367, M23, D Mbs, D KIl, M20, A Wgm: no ∞
40 / bottom	M20: two untied half-notes (the second tied to the following note)
41 / top / 1 (e♭')	D Mbs: no ♭
44	M23, D KIl: as Ex. 21a; remaining sources as Ex. 21b (=CPEBE) except that D Mbs has a♭' instead of g♯' on the first beat
45 / top / 1	P 368, P 367, M23, D Mbs, D KIl, M20: no arp.
45 / top, downstem / 1	M20: b not d'
46 / top / 1–6	D KIl: 1 (chord) as dotted quarter, 2–6 as 32nds
	D Mbs: 1 (chord) as dotted quarter, 2–4 as 32nds, 5–6 as 64ths
	M23: erasures, orig. probably same as D Mbs
46 / top / 2–6	M20: dotted 8th, 64ths
47 / top / 1	A Wgm: no arp.
47 / top, downstem / 1	A Wgm: f♮'(!)
47 / top / 2	P 368, P 367, M23, D Mbs, D KIl, M20, A Wgm: no f♯'
48 / top / 1	P 368, P 367: ⁓ not +
	M23: ⁓⁓
	D Mbs, D KIl, A Wgm: no orn.

bar / stave / note-and-rest no.	source: remark
	M20: ∞
48 / top / 2–4	M23, D Mbs, M20, A Wgm: slur
48 / top / 5	P 775, P 368, P 367, M23, D Mbs, D KIl, A Wgm: no stroke
48 / bottom	Despite upward stems on notes in latter half of bar, only M23, D Mbs, D KIl have half rest in lower voice
48 / bottom, upstem / 1–2	P 368, P 367, M23, D Mbs, D KIl, M20: quarter not 8th-note, 8th rest
48 / bottom, upstem / 3–5, 7–9	M23, D Mbs, M20, A Wgm: slurs (g♯–d♯, G♯–d♯)
48 / bottom, upstem / 6, 10	P 775, P 368, P 367, M23, D Mbs, D KIl, M20, A Wgm: no strokes
49 / top / 1	P 368, P 367, D KIl, M20: no c∿ ; A Wgm: ∿, drawn through stem of note; M23, D Mbs: ∿; misunderstanding of reading in A Wgm?
49 / top / 3	D KIl: no ♯
50 / top / 1	P 1131: perhaps orig. + or tr as in bar 5, altered to c∿; M23, A Wgm: ∿, drawn through stem; P 368, P 367, D Mbs, D KIl: ∿; misunderstanding of reading M23, A Wgm?; M20: no orn.
50 / top / 4–5	A Wgm: no slur
51 / top / 2	M23, A Wgm: no ♮; M23: ♮ added lightly
51 / top / 5	A Wgm: no ♯ (also on 1 in bar 52); M20: ♯ on 6 not 5
52 / top / 4–5	D Mbs, D KIl, M20: no slur
53 / top / 1	D KIl: arp. probably a later addition
53 / top / 1–2	M20: no tie; ∞ between notes
53 / bottom / 1	P 368: ♭ probably a later insertion; above note: 'B'
54 / bottom, upstem / 4	M20: no ♮
54 / bottom, downstem / 1–2	P 775, B Bc, P 368, P

bar / stave / note-and-rest no.	source: remark
	367, M23, D Mbs, D KIl, M20, A Wgm: no rests
55 / top / 9–10	D KIl, M20, A Wgm: no slur
55 / top / 10	M23, D KIl, A Wgm: tr not +; P 368, P 367: ∿; M20: ≈
56 / top / 1–2	M23, D Mbs, D KIl, M20: no slur
57 / top / 8	D Mbs, M20: a'' not c''
58 / top / 13 (d')	M23, D Mbs, D KIl, M20: no ♮
58 / top / 14 (f')	P 368, P 367, D KIl: no ♮; P 1131: ♮ a later insertion; P 775: ♮ a later insertion (probably autograph)
58 / bottom	M20: last two beats are g♯–g♯ 8ths, f♮ quarter (!)
59 / top / 1	P 368: ♮ in foreign hand
59 / top / 9–10	P 368, P 367: slur
59 / top / 10	P 368, P 367: ∿ not +; B Bc, D KIl, A Wgm, M23: tr; D Mbs: no orn.; M20: ≈
59 / bottom	M20: e–d–c–B (16ths), c–d (8ths), e–E (quarters)
61 / top / 1, 4	D Mbs: no apps.
61–7 / top	P 368, P 367, D Mbs, M23: all apps. as 2-flag apps.; D KIl: same, in bars 62–7 only; A Wgm: same, in bar 61 and in bar 62 (on 1, 5, and 13) only; M20: 2-flag apps., except for 1-flag apps. in bar 61 and on 5 in bar 62
61, 63 / top, upstem / 12–13	P 368, P 367, M23, D Mbs, D KIl, M20, A Wgm: no slur
62, 64 / top, upstem / 17–18	A Wgm: no slur
63 / top, downstem / 1–2	P 368: quarters (no beam)
64 / top, downstem / 1	P 368, P 367: no e'
64 / bottom / last	A Wgm: g not e

bar / stave / note-and-rest no.	source: remark
65 / top / 17–18	P 367: no slur
	M23: slur a later entry?
67 / top / 9–12, 23–6	M23, D Mbs: slurs
68 / top / 1–2	D Mbs, D KIl: no slur
68 / top / 2	P 368, P 367, M23, D Mbs: no ⁓
	P 1131: added above slur
68 / top / 6–7	M23, D Mbs, D KIl, A Wgm: no slur
	M23: tr on 6
69 / top / 8	M20: no ♮
69 / top, upstem / 21–3	D Mbs: a″–b″–c‴
	M23: orig. = D Mbs; corr. (probably by copyist)
	A Wgm: 16th–16th–8th
	M20: 32nd-notes [sic]
69 / bottom / 1	P 775, B Bc, P 368, P 367, M23, D KIl, M20, A Wgm: no rest
70 / top / 2	P 368, P 367, D KIl, A Wgm: ⁓ not +
	B Bc: tr
	M23, D Mbs: no orn.
	M20: tr on 5 not 2
72 / top / 3	B Bc, P 367, D KIl, A Wgm, M20: tr not +
73 / top / 5	B Bc, P 367, D KIl: tr not +
	A Wgm: no orn.
	M20: ⁓
74 / bottom / 5	M23, D Mbs, D KIl: ♮
	M23: corr. to ♭ (probably not by copyist)
79 / top / 9	P 368, P 367, M20: no +
	M23, D Mbs, D KIl: ⁓
	A Wgm: tr
80 / bottom / 1	A Wgm: c not C
81, 82 / top, upstem / 3	P 368, P 367: ⁓ not +
	M23, D Mbs, D KIl: no orn.
	A Wgm: tr
	M20: ∞
82–3 / top, downstem	M20: no tie (bar 83 = new line)
	A Wgm: no tie; no c″ in bar 83 (bar 83 = new line)
83 / top, downstem / 1	quarter (no dot) in all sources except A Wgm (which lacks c″ altogether); cf. bar 22
	M23, D Mbs, D KIl: followed by b′ (quarter)
83 / top / 4–5	P 1131: orig. c″ (eighth)?
	M23, D Mbs: slur
	A Wgm: 32nd–32nd–8th [sic]
84 / top / 1	P 1131, P 775, B Bc, P 368: no ♭, though at start of new line; cf. bar 23
84 / top / 1	B Bc: 2-flag app.
	A Wgm: 3-flag app.
	M23, D Mbs, D KIl, M20: no app.
84 / top / 5	B Bc, A Wgm: tr not +
	P 368, P 367, M23, D Mbs, D KIl: no orn.
	M20: ∞
84–6 / bottom	A Wgm: these bars garbled. Bar 85 in place of bar 84; bar 85: C–C–C–C D–D–D–D; downbeat of bar 86: E (8th) / G (quarter)
85–6 / top	P 1131, P 368, P 367, M23, D Mbs, D KIl, M20, A Wgm: as in bars 24–5
87 / top, downstem / 1	M20: no c′
88 / top / 10–12	M20: 8th-note, two 16th-notes; preceded by two-flag app. e′
88 / top / 10	A Wgm: t not ⁓
	M23, D Mbs: no orn.; instead, t on 12
88 / bottom / 2	M20: f (no ♯) not F[♯]
89 / top / 10–11	M23, D Mbs: no slur
89 / top / 10–13, 14–21	M20: 16th-notes (slurs on 10–11, 12–13); 32nd-notes
89 / top / 11–15	M23, D Mbs, D KIl: rhythm:
89 / top / 15–16	A Wgm: between these two notes: f″

bar / stave / note-and-rest no.	source: remark
89 / top / 20	P 775, M23: no ♮
89 / bottom / 2–4	M20: quarter rest, f (quarter)
90 / top / 1–2	M23, D Mbs, D KIl: no slur
90 / top / 2	P 368, P 367, D KIl, A Wgm: no ∾ M23, D Mbs, M20: ⁓
90 / top / 10	B Bc, P 367: tr not + D KIl: no orn. M20, A Wgm: ∾
90 / bottom / 2–4	M23, D Mbs: no b
91a / both / 1	M20, A Wgm: followed by half rest
91a / bottom / 1	A Wgm: E not c
91a, 91b	M20: no indication of first and second endings
92, 93 / both / 1	A Wgm: 2-flag apps.
92 / top, downstem / 9	M23, D Mbs, M20, A Wgm: no ♮
93 / top / 1	P 1131, B Bc: apps. on single upward stem P 368, P 367, M23, D Mbs, D KIl, M20: no apps. A Wgm: upper app. (d'') only
93 / top, upstem / 2	P 368, P 367: ♮ on c'' A Wgm: ♯ (♮ on following c'' in inner voice)
94 / top, upstem / 1–2	P 775, P 368, P 367, M23, D Mbs, D KIl, M20, A Wgm: no Anschlag P 1131: Anschlag probably inserted; reading unclear
95 / top, both / 1–2	M23, D Mbs, D KIl: no slurs
95 / top, upstem / 8–9	P 368, P 367, M23, D Mbs, D KIl, M20, A Wgm: no Anschlag P 1131: Anschlag possibly inserted
95 / top, upstem / 11	P 368, P 367, M20: 2-flag app. M23, D Mbs, D KIl, A Wgm: no app. M23, D KIl: 1-flag app. added later (foreign hand)
95 / top, downstem / 1–2	P 775: no slur
95 / top, downstem / 9	M20: preceded by

bar / stave / note-and-rest no.	source: remark
	app. c'' (on same stem as app. in upper voice)
96 / top, upstem / 1–2	P 368, P 367, M23, D Mbs, D KIl, M20, A Wgm: no ∾ P 1131: possibly added later. Smaller, less heavily written, than following orn., and in horizontal, not leaning, form
96 / top, upstem / 5	P 775, P 368, P 367, M23, D Mbs, D KIl, M20: no ∾ B Bc: ∾ A Wgm: ⁓
96 / top, upstem / 6	P 368, P 367, M23, D Mbs, D KIl, M20, A Wgm: f' as quarter with separate downward stem
97 / top, upstem / 1–2	M23, D Mbs, M20, A Wgm: no slur
97 / top, upstem / 3	P 1131, B Bc, P 775: 'cautionary' ♭
97 / top, upstem / 6	P 368, P 367, M23, D Mbs, D KIl, M20, A Wgm: no apps. P1131: app. possibly inserted
97 / top, downstem / 1–2	slur only in D KIl
98–9 / top	D Mbs: no tie
98 / top, upstem / 5	P 775, P 368, P 367, M23, D Mbs, D KIl, M20, A Wgm: no ∾
98 / top, upstem / 6–7	P 368, P 367, M23, D Mbs, D KIl, M20, A Wgm: no ∾
98 / top, upstem / 8	M23, D Mbs, D KIl, M20: 8th-note, 8th rest A Wgm: 8th-note only (no rest)
98 / top, downstem / 1–2	M23, D Mbs, D KIl: f' (dotted quarter)
99	M23, D Mbs, D KIl: as Ex. 22a, except as noted below; remaining sources as Ex. 22b (=CPEBE)
99 / top / 10	B Bc, A Wgm: tr not + P 368, P 367, M23 (Ex. 22a) (?): ⁓ M23 (Ex. 22a): later addition? D Mbs (Ex. 22a): no orn.

bar / stave / note-and-rest no.	source: remark
	D KIl (Ex. 22a): ≋ M20: ∞
99 / bottom / 4	D KIl (Ex. 22a): *c* not E
100 / top / 3	D Mbs, D KIl, M20, A Wgm: no app.
100 / top / 5–6	M23, D Mbs: no slur
101 / top / 1	P 368, P 367, M23, D Mbs, D KIl, M20, A Wgm: no ∞
101 / top / 1–2	P 368, P 367, M23, D Mbs, A Wgm: no slur
101 / bottom / 5	M23, D Mbs, D KIl, M20: *d'/d''*
102 / top / 4–5	P 367: no slur
103 / top / 5	P 368, P 367, M23, D Mbs, D KIl, M20, A Wgm: no +
103–4 / top	P 368, P 367, M23, D KIl: *g''* tied over barline
	M23, D Mbs, D KIl: 8th rest (for inner voice) beneath penultimate *g''*; upstem and downstem on last *g''*
104-5 / top, downstem	M20: no tie (page break)
105-6 / top, downstem	M23, D Mbs, D KIl, M20: no tie
105 / top, upstem / 8–10	D Mbs, D KIl: dotted 8th, two 32nd-notes
105 / top, upstem / 9–10	M23: two 16th-notes
105 / top, downstem / 1–2, 4–5	M20: 16th-notes
105 / top, downstem / 6–7	P 368, P 367: no tie (P 368: new line after 6)
105 / top, downstem / 9–10	D Mbs, D KIl, M20: two 16th-notes
106 / top, upstem / 1–2	P 368, P 367, M23, D Mbs, D KIl, M20, A Wgm: no slur
106 / top, upstem / 2	P 775, P 368, P 367, M23, D Mbs, D KIl, A Wgm: no ≋
106 / top, both / 7–10	M23, D Mbs, D KIl, M20: dotted rhythm continues
106 / top, upstem / 8	♮ in P 368, P 367, M23, D Mbs
106 / top, upstem / 11–12	P 368: *f'–e'* (?)
106 / top, upstem / 12	P 368, M23, D Mbs, D KIl, M20, A Wgm: no ∞ P 367: mark over note probably = turn
106 / top, downstem / 11–13	A Wgm: 16th rest, three 16th-notes (= bass)
106 / bottom / 4–5	M23, D Mbs, D KIl: *G–A* M23: corr. by enlarging noteheads
107	P 368: *p* on second beat M23, D Mbs, D KIl, M20: no *p*
107 / top, upstem / 8	P 368, P 367, M23, D Mbs, D KIl, M20, A Wgm: no +
107 / top, both / 7 from end	M23, D Mbs, D KIl: *d'/f'* not *e'/g'* M23: orig. *d'/f'* corr. by enlarging noteheads
107 / bottom / 1–5	M20: *e–f–g–G* (8ths), *c* (quarter)
108	P 368, P 367, A Wgm: as Ex. 23a; M23, D Mbs, D KIl, M20: as Ex. 23b, except as noted below; remaining sources as Ex. 23c (=CPEBE), except as noted below
108 / 1	B Bc, P 775, P 1131: *f* is beneath lower staff; dyn. is in P 775, P 1131 either added or retraced heavily
108 (Ex. 23b)	D Mbs, D KIl: tempo mark begins between 1 and 2
108 / top / 1 (Ex. 23b)	D KIl, M20: no arp.
109 / 9	P 368, P 367: 1-flag apps.
110 / top, downstem / 8	M23, D Mbs, D KIl, M20, A Wgm: no ♮
111 / top / 1	M23, D Mbs, A Wgm: 2-flag apps.
112 / top, both / 1–2	P 368, D KIl: slurs, probably added later
112 / top, upstem / 1	B Bc, A Wgm: tr not + P 368, P 367, M23, D Mbs, D KIl, M20: no orn.
112 / bottom / 1–2	P 368, P 367, M23, D Mbs, D KIl, M20, A Wgm: half-note: *A*
113 / top, both / 1–2	M23, D Mbs: no slurs
113 / top, upstem / 8	P 775, P 368, P 367,

bar / stave / note-and-rest no.	source: remark
	D Mbs, M20, A Wgm: no app.
	P 1131: app. inserted
	D KIl: 1-flag app. (apparently original)
113 / top, upstem / 10–11	P 368, P 367, M23, D Mbs, D KIl, M20: two 16th-notes
113 / top, downstem / 1–2	P 368, P 367, A Wgm: no slur
113 / top, downstem / 5	P 1131, B Bc, P 775: 'cautionary' ♭; possibly an insertion in P 1131
114 / top, upstem / 1–2, 5	P 775, P 368, P 367, M23, D Mbs, D KIl, M20, A Wgm: no ∞, no ≋
114 / top, downstem / 3	P 368, P 367, M23, D Mbs, D KIl, M20, A Wgm: quarter, with separate downward stem
	M20: no ♭
115 / top, both / 1–2	M23, D Mbs, D KIl, A Wgm: no slurs
115 / top, upstem / 3	P 1131, B Bc, P 775: 'cautionary' ♭
115 / top / 4	no ♭ in any source, except possibly as an insertion in B Bc (unclear)
115 / top, upstem / 6	P 368, P 367, M23, D Mbs, D KIl, M20: no +
	A Wgm: tr
116 / bottom / 1	D KIl: B♭ / b♭
117 / 1	A Wgm: no apps.
117 / top / 1	P 775: 3-flag app.
	D Mbs: 2-flag app.
117 / top, downstem / 7	A Wgm: no ♭
117 / bottom / 1	app. from P 368, P 367, M20
119 / top, upstem / 6–7	P 775, P 368, P 367, M23, D Mbs, D KIl, M20, A Wgm: no ∞
120 / both / 13	M23, D Mbs: no ♭
121 / both / 1	M23, D Mbs, D KIl: no app.
121 / bottom / 4–7	P 775: last two beats om. (empty stave)
122, 124	A Wgm: no tempo marks
123 / top / 10	M23: tr (later addition?)
123 / bottom / 5–6	flats in M23, D Mbs, D KIl, A Wgm; flat on 5 also in M20
124 / top / 4	M23, D Mbs, D KIl: ♮
124 / top / 5–6	D Mbs: no slur
124 / top / 6	only B Bc has ↝, probably as later addition (written above slur)
124 / top, downstem / last	M23, D Mbs, D KIl: b not d'
125	A Wgm, M20: no pp
125 / top, upstem / 1	M20: ♭
125 / top, upstem / 2	♮ only as addition (autograph?) in B Bc; possibly also in P 367 (unclear)
125 / top, downstem / 1	P 368, P 367, M23, D Mbs, D KIl, M20: no ♯
126 / top / 1–2	slur only in B Bc (unsteady; autograph addition?), P 368, P 367
Last Movement	
1–2 / top, upstem	P 368, P 367, M20: slur, g' to c''
	D Mbs: slur, g' to d''; added in foreign hand?
6 / top, upstem / 1	P 368, P 367, M23, D Mbs, M20, D KIl: no +
	A Wgm: tr
6, 8 / top / 1–2	P 368, P 367, M23: slur (upper part)
	M23: also in lower part (bar 6 only)
8 / top, downstem / 1	M23, D Mbs, D KIl, A Wgm: e'
	M23, A Wgm: e' and slur to next note
8 / top, downstem / 1–2	P 1131: d' orig. half-note. Altered to quarter; tie and dotted 8th added—hence the notes of the middle part in beat 2 are not beamed together.
	P 368, P 367: no tie
9 / top, upstem / 5	M23, D Mbs: d'' not b'
11 / top / 4	M20: no ♮
11 / top, upstem / 4–7	M23, D Mbs, D KIl: 32nds; top beam erased in M23, D KIl
12 / top / 1–2	D Mbs: slur
13–14 / top, upstem	P 368, P 367, D Mbs, M20: slur as in bars 1–2

bar / stave / note-and-rest no.	source: remark
	M23: slur added lightly
13	M23, D Mbs, D KIl: no *p*
	D Mbs: *p* added in foreign hand
16 / top, downstem / 2	dot in P 775, P 368, M23, D Mbs, D KIl; followed by 16th rest in P 368, M23, D Mbs, D KIl
	M20: 8th-note, 8th rest
16 / bottom / 2	P 368, A Wgm: followed by quarter rest; hence the last *eb'* (which in all sources is written in the top stave) falls in an inner voice
16–17 / top	M23 (?), D Mbs, D KIl (?): no tie
	M23, D KIl: present as later (?) addition
17 / top / 1–2	P 368, M23, D Mbs, D KIl, M20: no tie
	P 368, M23, D KIl: present as later addition
17 / top, upstem / 4	A Wgm: *b''* not *d'''*
19 / top / 1–3	P 368: orig. no tie, added lightly; M20: no tie, no ♭
20 / top / 1	P 1131, P 775: app. lacks flag
20 / bottom / 1	M23, D Mbs, D KIl: no ♮
21–2 / top	M20: no tie
24	D KIl, M20, A Wgm: no *f*
24 / bottom / 2–3	M20: no *G*, no *B♭*
25–30	M23, D Mbs, D KIl: as Ex. 24a, except as noted below; remaining sources as Ex. 24b (=*CPEBE*), except as noted below
25–6 / top, upstem	P 368, P 367: slur, *g'* (bar 25) to *b♭'* (bar 26) (=Ex. 24a). The slur in M23, DKIl (Ex. 24a) is a later addition
26; 28 (Ex. 24a)	D KIl: *p* on 1 of bar 26; *f* between 1 and 2 of bar 28
26 / top / both	M20: no flats
26 / top, upstem / 3	P 368, P 367: ⁓ not ≋
	P 775, M23, D Mbs, D KIl, M20, A Wgm: no orn.
29 / top, upstem / 2	P 368, P 367: 1-flag app.
29 / top, upstem / 3	P 775, P 368, P 367, M23, D Mbs, D KIl, M20, A Wgm: no ≋
31 / top, upstem / 2	P 775, P 368, P 367, M23, D Mbs, D KIl, M20, A Wgm: no ♮
	P 1131: ♮ added? (unclear)
	B Bc: ♮ added (autograph?)
33, 38 / top, upstem / 4	P 775, P 368, P 367, M23, D Mbs, D KIl, M20, A Wgm: no ≋
34 / top, downstem / 1	M23, D Mbs, D KIl: quarter not dotted half
35–6 / top, downstem	M23: tie
37 / top, upstem / 1–2	M23, D Mbs, D KIl: doubled in thirds: *b'–a'*
37 / top, upstem / 2	P 775, P 368, P 367, D Mbs, M20, A Wgm: no ≋
37 / bottom, downstem / 3	M20: *c'* not *b*
38 / top, upstem / 2	D Mbs: *a'* not *c''*
38 / top, downstem / 1–2	M20: no *e'*, no *f♯'*
38 / top, downstem / 2	M23, D Mbs, D KIl, A Wgm: preceded by quarter-note app.: *g'*
38 / bottom / 2	P 367: no *d'*
39	M23, D KIl, M20: no *p*
39 / bottom, upstem / 1	M23, D Mbs: no *g* (*g'* in top stave has two stems)
39 / bottom, downstem / 1	M20: quarter rest not *g'*
42 / top	slur positioned variously in sources. Though covering only 1–2 in P 1131, this type of slur may have been understood as pertaining to all three notes; hence the ambiguity in the copies.
	P 368, P 367, M23, D Mbs, D KIl, A Wgm: no slur

bar / stave / note-and-rest no.	source: remark
42 / top / 2	B Bc, M23: 2-flag app.
	P 1131: unclear, probably 1-flag app.
	D Mbs: no app.
42 / bottom, upstem / 1	P 775, M23, D KIl: no rest
	P 1131: The rest is a later autograph addition, distinct in size and form from that in bass.
43	D Mbs, M20: no *f*
43 / top / 6	D Mbs, A Wgm: no ♯
44 / top / 3	P 368, P 367, M23, D Mbs, D KIl, M20, A Wgm: no stroke
44 / top, downstem / 2	A Wgm: ♯ on 5 not on 2
45 / top / 1–3	M23, D Mbs: '3'
45 / top / 4	P 367, D KIl, A Wgm: tr not +
46a, 46b	M20: no indication of first and second endings
46a, 46b / top / 1–2	M23, D Mbs, D KIl: half–note, no rest
	A Wgm: same, but in bar 46b only
52 / top, upstem / 1	M23, D Mbs, D KIl, M20: no +
	A Wgm: tr
52 / top, both / 1–2	M23, D Mbs, D KIl: slurs
54 / top, downstem / 1	M23, D Mbs, D KIl: *b'* (slurred to next note)
	M20: *b'* (no slur)
54 / top, downstem / 2	M20: no dot
56–7 / top, upstem	P 775: no tie
60 / top, downstem / 2	P 775, P 368, P 367, M23, D Mbs, D KIl, M20: no ♮
	P 1131: ♮ inserted?
	B Bc: ♮ an addition (autograph?)
61–2 / top, upstem	P 367, M23: no tie
62 / top, upstem / 2	B Bc, P 775, P 1131: 'cautionary' ♯
64 / bottom, downstem / 1	M20: no rest
67 / top / 1	P 367: 2–flag app.
67 / downstem / 1	D Mbs: no *e'*
67 / top / 1	D Mbs, M20: no app.
67, 69 / top / 2	P 775, P 368, P 367, M23, D Mbs, D KIl,

bar / stave / note-and-rest no.	source: remark
	A Wgm: no ≈
68 / downstem / 1 (*f♮'*)	M23, D Mbs: orig. no ♮ (added later)?
	D KIl: ♯
	A Wgm: *e'* not *f♮'*
69 / top / 1	D Mbs: no app.
70 / top / 6	A Wgm: no ♮
70 / downstem / 1	B Bc: no dot after *e'*
	P 1131: unclear; dot present in P 775
70 / downstem / 1	P 368, P 367: no *c'*, no ♮
	P 775, A Wgm: no ♮
71 / both / 4–5	M20: 8th rest, 8th–note
71 / downstem / 3	A Wgm: *f♯'* not *g♯'*
72 / downstem / 6	M23, D Mbs, D KIl, A Wgm: no ♯
	M23: ♯ inserted
73 / top / 6	D Mbs: *f'* (no ♯)
74 / top / 3–4	P 775, P 368, P 367, M23, D Mbs, D KIl, M20, A Wgm: no slur
	P 1131: slur is a later addition (unsteady)?
74 / top / 4	B Bc, P 367, D KIl: tr not +
	M23, D Mbs, M20, A Wgm: no orn.
	M23: orn. added lightly in foreign hand
74 / bottom / 1–2	M20: 8ths
74 / bottom / 2–3	M23, D Mbs: *a–b* not *A–B*
75 / top / 1–2	P 368, P 367, M23, D Mbs, D KIl, M20: dotted half, no rest
76–7 / top, upstem	P 368, P 367, M20: slur, *g'* to *c''*
	P 368: slur only to *d''*
81 / top, upstem / 1–2	slur only in P 367, M23, D Mbs
83 / top / 3	P 1131, P 775, B Bc: ♯ on *a''*
	P 367: ♯ on both *a''* and *c'''*
84 / top / 5	P 775, P 368, P 367, M23, D Mbs, D KIl, M20, A Wgm: no ⤳
85–6 / top	A Wgm: no tie
85 / top, downstem / 1–2	M23, D Mbs, D KIl: dotted half, no rest
86 / top	M23: *a'* (dotted half) in inner voice

bar / stave / note-and-rest no.	source: remark
86 / top / 4–7	D Mbs, D KIl: 32nd-notes; probably also in M23 orig., erased
87 / top / 1	P 368, P 367, D KIl, A Wgm: 1-flag app.
87 / top / 2	P 775, P 368, P 367, M23, D Mbs, D KIl, A Wgm: no ≋
87 / top / 2–3	M23, D Mbs: dotted half, no rest
89 / bottom	M23, D Mbs, D KIl: E/e
89, 92 / top, upstem / 3	P 775, P 368, P 367, M23, D Mbs, D KIl, M20, A Wgm: no ≋
91 / top	M23, D Mbs, D KIl: as Ex. 25a; remaining sources as Ex. 25b (=CPEBE)
92 / top, downstem	D Mbs: a' not f♯'
92 / bottom	M23, D Mbs: D/d
93 / top / 2	M23, D Mbs: a'/c'' not b'/d''
93–4 / top, both	M23, D Mbs, D KIl: no ties
95 / bottom / 2–3; 96 / bottom / 1	P 368: orig. G,G,G (quarters), written over by rests
96 / top, downstem / 2	P 775, P 368, P 367, M23, D Mbs, D KIl, M20, A Wgm: no ♮ / P 1131, B Bc: ♮ inserted
96 / top, downstem / 3–4	D Mbs, D KIl: no tie
97–8 / top	D Mbs, D KIl: no ties (both parts) / M23: orig. no tie (upper part only), added lightly
100 / top, both / 3	D Mbs: no apps.
100, 105 / top, upstem / 4	P 775, P 368, P 367, M23, D Mbs, D KIl, M20, A Wgm: no ≋
101 / top, downstem / 1	M23, D Mbs, D KIl: quarter not dotted half
104 / top / 1	P 368, P 367: 1-flag app.
104 / top / 2	P 775, P 368, P 367, M23, D Mbs, D KIl, A Wgm: no ≋
104 / bottom / 2	P 368: e'/g' not f'/g'
	M23, D Mbs, D KIl: d'/f'
104 / bottom, upstem / 2	P 775, A Wgm: no g' / P 1131: unclear, but probably not an addition
104–5 / top	D Mbs: no tie (end of system)
105 / top, downstem / 1	M20: b' preceded by no-flag app. c'', in addition to app. on e''
105 / top, downstem / last 106	D KIl, A Wgm: no b' M20: no p
106 / bottom / 1	D KIl: blank stave; both parts added (foreign hand)
106 / bottom, upstem / 1	M23, D Mbs: no dotted half (c') M20: half-note, no dot
108 / bottom, upstem	A Wgm: no c'
109 / top	Placement of slur as in bar 42
109 / top 1–2	P 368, P 367, M23, D KIl, A Wgm: no slur
109 / top / 2	D Mbs: no app. D KIl, A Wgm: 1-flag app. M20: no app.; ∞ on 3
110	P 368, P 367, M23, D Mbs, D KIl (?), M20: no f D KIl: f present as probable later addition
110 / bottom, upstem / 1	D Mbs: no c'
110 / downstem / 2	D Mbs: d''
111 / 3	P 775, P 368, P 367, M23, D Mbs, D KIl, A Wgm: no strokes
111 / bottom / 5	P 1131: altered, orig. B?
112 / top / 1–3	D Mbs, D KIl: 8th-note, 16th-note, 16th-note not triplet
112 / top / 4	B Bc (?), P 367, M23, D KIl, A Wgm: tr not +

MUSIC EXAMPLES

Ex. 20: H. 46, I. 39

Ex. 21: H. 46, I. 44

Ex. 22: H. 46, I. 99

Ex. 23: H. 46, I. 108

Ex. 24: H. 46, II. 25–30

Ex. 25: H. 46, II. 91

Sonata in G minor, H. 47

SOURCES

H. 47 seems not to have undergone any major revision after its composition in 1746. But the text was subject to many small changes in ornamentation and other performance indications. A few alterations affecting the notes also occurred, including the addition of a considerable number of accidentals (most of them cautionary rather than essential). Certain dynamic markings also were added.

The first movement contains five unmeasured passages, the earliest such passages in Bach's music.[74] The most authoritative sources place no barline before the Adagio, which begins in the middle of a line following an unmeasured passage. But (unlike the middle section of H. 46) the Adagio is sufficiently distinct to be considered an independent second movement, and bars have been numbered accordingly.

P 775. Berlin, Staatsbibliothek Preußischer Kulturbesitz, Musikabteilung, Mus. ms. Bach P 775. Copy of H. 47 by Michel, with autograph entries.[75]

The copy of H. 47 in P 775, which serves as the principal source for the present edition, shows signs of having been carefully reviewed by Bach, who probably added at least some of the inserted accidentals and perhaps altered several ornament signs as well. The most extensive autograph entry is a two-bar passage in the last movement, written over an erasure at a point (following bar 74) where Michel apparently had omitted a bar. The composer's handwriting here is similar to that in the autograph entry in the first movement of H. 46 (bars 37–9), also in P 775. At the end of the second movement (page 5), the last word in the expression 'Volti allegro assai' is clearly in Michel's handwriting, but is somewhat smaller and possibly a later addition. (In B Bc it is an autograph addition; see below.) Many other entries, such as the numerous inserted accidentals and the corrected or retraced

ornament signs, are also likely to be autograph, but no note of this possibility is made in the List of Variant Readings except where the handwriting of the entry is clearly distinct from Michel's.

The copy of H. 47 consists of eight pages (two sheets, 33.5 × 21 cm., no watermark) now numbered 149–56. There is no title page, but traces of earlier (original?) pagination remain on pages 3, 5, and 7. Seven or eight systems appear on each page except the last, which is blank save for the library stamp reading 'Ex Bibl Regia Berlin.'

The headings at the top of page 1 include the same information as in other copies in P 775. The original title is: 'Sonata per il Cembalo solo. di. C. P. E. Bach.' Beneath the composer's name is the same ornamental underline found in Michel's copies of H. 43 and 47 in A Wgm. Beneath this is the date '1746'; above the title are the index entries 'No. 46 / (46.)'. Other entries, in foreign hands, are: 'Nr. 21', 'Th. Kat. 63,17 = Nachl. 7,46', 'No. 46', and '[Wotquenne 65,17]'. At the bottom of the page is the letter 'C' and the incorrect inscription 'Von Hering geschrieben', each in a foreign hand.[76]

The text, as revised by Bach, agrees in all essentials with B Bc and A Wgm, both also by Michel. Hence the copy appears to have served as Bach's own reference score.

B Bc. Brussels, Bibliothèque du Conservatoire Royal de Musique, ms. 5883. Copy of H. 47 by Michel, with additions probably by the composer.

The copy of H. 47 consists of eight unnumbered pages (two sheets, page 8 blank, no watermark). There is no title page; the original title at the top of the first page reads: 'Sonata per il Cembalo solo. da C. P. E. Bach.' To this have been added annotations similar to those in other copies in B Bc: '17', '17e. Sonate du No. 15 de Westphal', 'U, no. 5883'. At the bottom left is the numeral '11', at the right a faint entry 'Ms Michel'.

The music contains a few entries that are probably in the composer's hand. The most important (and most probably autograph) is the addition of the word 'assai' in the rubric 'Volti allegro assai.' at

---

[74] A possible exception is a work preserved in Bach's autograph from the 1740s; see D. A. Lee, 'C. P. E. Bach and the Free Fantasia for Keyboard: Deutsche Staatsbibliothek Mus. ms. 103 (Nichelmann 1 N)', in *C. P. E. Bach Studies* (Oxford, 1988), pp. 177–84.

[75] Facsimile in Berg, ed., *The Collected Works*, III, 291.

[76] For explanations of some of these entries, see the discussions of P 775 under H. 43 and H. 46.

the end of the second movement (page 5). Together with the reading of ENK and D Kll (see below), this provides evidence that the original tempo mark in the last movement was simply 'Allegro'. Other possibly autograph entries are confined to insertions of accidentals and dynamics. The text contains a few errors, but it also gives at least two readings that are superior to those of P 775 (see below under 'Establishing the text').

A Wgm. Vienna, Gesellschaft der Musikfreunde, VII 3872/1. Copy of H. 47 by Michel.

The manuscript 3872/1 closely resembles Michel's copy of H. 43 in the Gesellschaft der Musikfreunde (3872/2). It consists of twelve unnumbered pages, including the title page and the blank twelfth page. The entries on the title page and the headings at the top of the first page of music are similar in most respects to those in the copy of H. 43. The sole difference lies in the use on the title page of manuscript 3872/1 of the preposition *di* instead of *da* before the composer's name.

The manuscript 3872/1 contains only one entry in a foreign hand (an accidental in I. 74, first triplet group), probably not autograph. There are very few errors, but the one in bar 18 of the first movement is sufficient to demonstrate that this manuscript was the basis for a romanticized edition of the first movement—designated 'Fantasie' and ending incongruously on a dominant harmony—by Adolf Prosniz (*Historische Klavierliteratur aus dem XVI., XVII. und XVIII. Jahrhundert*, Heft 9 [Vienna and Leipzig, 1908]).[77]

P 359. Berlin, Staatsbibliothek Preußischer Kulturbesitz, Musikabteilung, Mus. ms. Bach P 359. Copy of H. 47 by Michel, with probably autograph additions.

Including the original title page, the copy of H. 47 occupies twelve pages (three sheets, 32.5 × 21 cm., no watermark) now numbered 17–27. No original pagination was observed. The title page bears the following original markings: 'Sonata / per il / Cembalo solo. / di / C. P. E. Bach.' followed by an incipit on two staves. Added in a foreign hand beneath the composer's name is the date 'Berlin 1746'. A faint entry at the very top centre appears to read '46 Nachlass'. The music is found on pages 2–11. The top of the first page of music reads 'Cembalo solo.' The last page is blank.

P 359 gives an earlier version of the piece than Michel's other copies (P 775, B Bc, and A Wgm) either before or after correction. A number of corrections are likely to be autograph. As in Michel's copies of H. 43 and H. 46 in P 775, there are several indications, apart from the early version of the text, that P 359 is one of his earlier products. The layout, which does not match that of any of his other copies of H. 47, is poorly planned; a clumsy page turn follows bar 11 of the Adagio. There are also several careless errors.

Some faint markings have been added, probably by a later annotator. These include several of the dynamics missing in this version of the sonata, as well as numerals at the end of each page indicating the number of bars on the page.

P 212. Berlin, Staatsbibliothek Preußischer Kulturbesitz, Musikabteilung, Mus. ms. Bach P 212. Collection of keyboard works by J. S., W. F., and C. P. E. Bach, partly in the hand of Johann Nicolaus Forkel (1749–1818). In oblong format. Copy of H. 47 by an unknown copyist.

The works by J. S. Bach in P 212 include the Chromatic Fantasia and Fugue (BWV 903), the Goldberg Variations (BWV 988; incomplete), and movements from the Well-Tempered Clavier and the French and English Suites. Near the end of the manuscript are two sonatas of W. F. Bach (F. 5 and 3)[78] and seven of C. P. E. Bach: H. 47, H. 260 (W. 56/1), H. 261 (W. 56/3), H. 278 (W. 58/7), H. 276 (W. 58/1), H. 267 (W. 58/5), and H. 283 (W. 59/4).[79] Although some pages earlier in P 212 appear to have been bound or rebound at some point in incorrect order, it is clear that the section containing works by the Bach sons formed an integral unit, since each work in this section begins on the back of the final page of the preceding copy.

The manuscript appears to have served Forkel as a selection for pedagogic purposes of pieces copied

---

[77] An exemplar of this edition in the Gesellschaft der Musikfreunde bearing the shelf-mark VII 38402 has been described in H. as a manuscript source. I am grateful to Dr Otto Biba, Archivdirektor, for furnishing information about VII 38402 as well as a copy of the edition.

[78] As numbered by M. Falck (see the List of Abbreviations).

[79] Complete inventory in *J. S. Bach: Neue Ausgabe sämtlicher Werke*, V/6.1, *Kritischer Bericht* by A. Dürr (Kassel, 1989), pp. 89–91. Dürr does not identify the copyist of BWV 988 (and H. 47), named as C. F. G. Schwenke in G. Stauffer, ed., *The Forkel–Hoffmeister & Kühnel Correspondence: A Document of the Early 19th-Century Bach Revival* (New York, 1990), p. 113 n. 134.

from various sources, including other copies in Forkel's possession. Although it is not an important source for the music of J. S. Bach, all of whose works survive in earlier and more dependable copies, P 212 is of great interest as having belonged to the first biographer of J. S. Bach and a correspondent and admirer of C. P. E. Bach.

The title on the cover, in Forkel's hand, reads: 'Auswahl einiger vorzüglichen / Clavier-Compositionen / von / Joh. Sebastian—Wilhelm Friedemann und / Carl Phil Emanuel / Bach.' Above this is an entry in a foreign hand, 'acc 2162', twice underlined. Facing the inside of the cover is a general title page (unnumbered), also in Forkel's hand, reading: 'Sammlung / einiger auserlesenen [sic] Claviercompositionen / aus den grösseren Werken / von / Johann Sebastian, Wilhelm Friedemann und Carl / Phil. Emanuel Bach gezogen.'

The copy of H. 47 occupies pages 144–51 and, together with the other sonatas by C. P. E. and W. F. Bach, was the work of an unidentified writer. The title across the top of the first page of H. 47 appears to be in Forkel's hand: 'Sonata von C. Ph. Em. Bach. (Ungedruckt.)'. H. 47 is the only one of the works by C. P. E. Bach in the collection that was unpublished during Forkel's life. The remaining six sonatas appeared in the second, fourth, and fifth collections *für Kenner und Liebhaber*. Forkel's name appears in the printed lists of subscribers to the fourth and fifth collections (Leipzig, 1783 and 1785, respectively). The two sonatas by W. F. Bach also were published, in the 1740s.

Forkel served as Bach's agent in Göttingen for the sale of printed music, and their correspondence, which began no later than 1773, includes references to various keyboard sonatas, including some that Forkel had obtained on his own and some that Bach sent to Forkel in manuscript. A letter of 10 February 1775 from Bach to Forkel mentions six sonatas that have been identified as being from the 'Württemberg' set (W. 49),[80] but this is open to question. At the time of Bach's writing, the first two sonatas mentioned were already in Forkel's possession, and Bach, evidently answering an inquiry from Forkel, describes them as having 'something in common with a free fantasy' (*etwas gleiches von einer freyen Fantasie*), adding that

these are the only such sonatas he has written. Bach's description fits H. 46–7 more closely than any of the Württemberg set. In his biography of Sebastian Bach, Forkel later mentioned having searched in vain for pieces resembling BWV 903/1 (the Chromatic Fantasia).[81] Evidently he had carried out a similar search for works by Emanuel Bach.

Bach's letter states that the two sonatas 'belong with' (*gehören zu*) four others, of which only two are specifically named as 'from the Haffner-Württemberg collection' (*aus der Hafner-Würtemburgischen Samlung [sic]*). 'All six' were, according to this letter, composed at Töplitz in 1743 on a clavichord with a short (bass) octave. But the *Nachlassverzeichnis* lists only three sonatas as having been written in 1743 at Töplitz: H. 32.5 (W. 65/13), H. 33 (W. 49/3), and H. 34 (W. 49/5). None is playable on a keyboard with a short octave. Either Bach later changed his records or failed to consult them before writing this letter. In any case, it seems possible that Forkel already possessed his copy of H. 47 at the time of the letter. The copy in P 212 gives an inaccurate text for a version of the piece earlier than that found in any of Michel's copies; thus it cannot have been obtained from the composer. Nevertheless, this copy is of some importance, as the two other copies giving early readings (ENK and D KIl) preserve an even earlier state of the text.

ENK. Greenwich, Connecticut. Manuscript copy by an unknown copyist, in private possession (Elias N. Kulukundis).

This copy is the work of a professional eighteenth-century copyist, as the ornate title page and the calligraphic verbal and numerical entries elsewhere suggest. The same hand appears in D KIl, and the writing is in most respects identical with that of the copyist known as 'J. S. Bach I' of the Amalienbibliothek, who was responsible for a copy of H. 51 (Amalienbibliothek 54). The only clear distinction in handwriting between ENK and D KIl, on the one hand, and that in H. 51 on the other, is in the form of the treble clef. Foreign entries in pencil, including fingerings and other markings, suggest that the copy was put to practical use.

The copy was acquired by its present owner from the firm of Otto Haas in about 1973; its previous

---

[80] E. Suchalla, ed., *Briefe von Carl Philipp Emanuel Bach an Johann Gottlob Immanuel Breitkopf und Johann Nikolaus Forkel* (Tutzing, 1985), pp. 549–50.

[81] J. N. Forkel, *Über Johann Sebastian Bachs Leben, Kunst, und Kunstwerke* (Leipzig, 1802), p. 55.

whereabouts are unknown. The original reading of the title page is: 'Sonata / per il / Cembalo Solo. / Dal Sig^re. / C: P: E: Bach.' Added in the upper left is the following, which the present owner believes to be in the hand of Albi Rosenthal: 'Wotquenne 65 17 (Ungedruckte Werke) / (Berlin 1746)'. In the upper right is an owner's signature in another hand that appears to read 'S: vander Does' (underlined). The paper beneath the signature is discoloured and may have been chemically treated to remove an earlier entry. The back cover bears a diagram representing the name Bach in musical notation.[82]

There are twelve pages (three bifolios) in all, including the title page; the music appears on pages 2–11, which bear original pagination and are ruled in six or seven systems each. Most pages bear pencil entries, mainly fingerings and emendations of accidentals; most are probably the work of a subsequent owner and most are not noted in the List of Variant Readings.[83]

Despite the handsome appearance of the manuscript, the text contains frequent errors as well as apparently arbitrary alterations, most of them also found in D Kll. Several pencil markings further emend the text (not always correctly); one of these (II. 7) is of a type found in copies of other works from the Amalienbibliothek.[84] Nevertheless, the two copies together establish the earliest known version of H. 47.

D Kll. Kiel, Schleswig-Holsteinische Landesbibliothek, Mb 53. Manuscript copy by an unknown copyist.

Mb 53 from the Schleswig-Holsteinische Landesbibliothek bears many resemblances to Mb 52, described above under H. 46. It contains the following works (in this order): H. 32.5 (W. 65/13), H. 42 (W. 65/14), H. 47 (W. 65/17), H. 48 (W. 65/18), H. 52 (W. 65/21), H. 56 (W. 65/22), H. 61 (W. 65/25) (twice), H. 64 (W. 65/26), and H. 143 (W. 65/33). Each originally formed a separate manuscript; running pagination has been added in the upper right corners of the odd-numbered pages. The title pages of H. 32.5 and H. 42 are signed by Ernst Ludwig Gerber (1746–1813) and are dated Leipzig, 1768 and 1767, respectively; the handwriting in these signatures matches that of the verbal rubrics in the musical texts of these two copies.

The remaining copies are all in different unidentified hands, except for the copies of H. 52, H. 64, and H. 143, and the second copy of H. 61, which are all in the same hand. Numbers in the titles of these last four copies suggest that they originally formed part of a single set. The title page of H. 61 bears an owner's signature, probably 'Zippora Itzig nee Wulff'. The latter is most likely Zippora Wulff (d. 1830) of Berlin, who married into the Itzig family in 1780. Her husband Benjamin Daniel Itzig (1756–1833), also of Berlin, is listed among the subscribers to the last two volumes of the *Kenner und Liebhaber* series. This Zippora Wulff is therefore distinct from the 'Mad. Zippora Wolf' listed as a Berlin subscriber to all six volumes—evidently Cäcilie (Zippora) Itzig (1759–1818), sister of Sara Itzig (later Levy).[85] The only other possessor's mark in any of the copies is the signature 'Leining' at the end of the copy of H. 22. The name occurs (without title or first name) among the Berlin subscribers to the first set (only) *für Kenner und Liebhaber*.[86]

Mb 53/3, the copy of H. 47, consists of eight pages (now numbered 17–24), including the title page and the blank last page. Pages 3–7 bear original pagination. The copyist is the same as in ENK, and the text and the style of the calligraphy of the original entries on the title page are virtually identical, although the layout of the musical text is not, each page of Mb 53/3 being ruled in eight systems. The title page bears numerous additions in many

[82] Diagrams of this type occur elsewhere; one is reproduced as Example 2 in M. Boyd, s. v. 'B-A-C-H', in *The New Grove Dictionary of Music and Musicians* (London, 1980), vol. 1, p. 877.

[83] I am grateful to the present owner for furnishing a detailed description of the manuscript, including the reading of the signature on the title page, of the diagram on the back cover, and of many of the pencil additions.

[84] For example, AmB 94 in the Staatsbibliothek Preußischer Kulturbesitz, Berlin, a copy of the concerto H. 428 (W. 24). On Kirnberger and the Amalienbibliothek, see below under H. 51. The entries in ENK and AmB 94 are too brief for a positive identification of the hand.

[85] Zippora Wulff married Benjamin Daniel Itzig on 11 January 1780; her sister Sara married Itzig's brother Jakob Daniel (1764–1838) in 1785 and is probably the 'Sara Wolf' listed as a subscriber to four of the *Kenner und Liebhaber* volumes. On both, see Max Freudenthal, *Aus der Heimat Mendelssohns* (Berlin, 1900), p. 282. Cäcilie (Zippora) Itzig married Simcha Bonem (Benjamin) Wulff in 1777, divorcing him and at the age of forty marrying Bernhard von Eskeles; see Hilde Spiel, *Fanny von Arnstein, oder Die Emanzipation* (Frankfurt, 1962), p. 263. On Zippora Wulff, see the forthcoming article by P. Wollny in *Jüdische Aufklärung* (Wolfenbütteler Studien zur Aufklärung, 22).

[86] There is also a 'Gräfinn von Leining' or 'Leiningen' among the Hamburg subscribers to the first five sets.

different hands, including an entry noting that the text has been compared with that of P 359 and P 212. Further entries in the same hand appear throughout the copy, giving readings from P 359 and P 212. In many instances, these entries can be distinguished as later additions only after comparison with ENK.

Establishing the text
Bach's autograph is lost, but, like that of H. 46, it must have received small revisions on several occasions. P 359 and P 775 are probably independent copies of the autograph made at different times (see variants listed for I. 6, 17, 22, and 46). While the layout of P 359 differs from those of Michel's other copies (P 775, B Bc, and A Wgm), the last page turn in P 359 occurs at the point in the final movement where Michel omitted a bar in P 775 (following bar 74). Possibly there was also a page turn at that point in the common model for both copies.

Bach himself appears to have altered P 359, P 775, and B Bc. Only a few of the alterations represent substantive revisions—additions or changes of dynamics or ornaments. The rest are mostly insertions of accidentals or corrections. A different set of alterations occurs in each of the three sources, and it cannot be assumed that all of the alterations in each source were made at the same time. For example, P 775 has at least two corrections in common with P 359, and seven with B Bc. Only one correction occurs in all three copies. This, together with some independent readings in B Bc, suggests that the copies in P 359 and P 775 were made from and checked against a fourth (lost) source—presumably the autograph—which Bach continued to revise even after Michel wrote the copy in P 775. But P 775 was almost certainly the immediate model for A Wgm, and probably also for B Bc, in which line and page breaks coincide with those of P 775 for about half the piece.

Two readings in P 775 traceable to the autograph do not occur in B Bc. The first is the easily overlooked mistake in the first movement, bar 61, first note in the treble clef. The second is in the fourth unmeasured passage of the first movement (bar 74), where a long flourish of a sort usually given in

thirty-seconds appears in P 775 as sixteenths.

Although the provenance of P 212 and of the closely related ENK and D KIl is cloudy, the three sources clearly stem from earlier states of the autograph. Despite errors and signs of arbitrary emendation, many variant readings in P 212 are authenticated by concordances with ENK, D KIl, P 359, or P 775 *ante correcturam*. The most important concordance of P 212 with ENK and D KIl is the reading of the inner part at bar 82 of the first movement. The second note, a', is replaced in P 775, B Bc, A Wgm, and P 359 by $f\sharp'$. While P 775 shows no sign of alteration at this point, the sharp is repeated in P 775, B Bc, and A Wgm on the following note (also $f\sharp'$), showing that the previous note originally was something else, presumably a'. Since that note leaves an open fifth on the second eighth of the bar, it was probably an error, even if Bach's own. Likewise, some of the dynamics and ornaments missing in ENK and D KIl, while possibly the result of omissions by the copyist, could have been absent in the earliest version of H. 47.

Certain dynamic markings are omitted or are imprecisely placed in the sources, suggesting that these were additions squeezed into the autograph at different times. While in some instances Bach merely added a *forte* following an existing *piano*,[87] in several cases he appears to have added *piano* markings as well. Even some of the original dynamic markings do not appear in precisely the same place in every copy. The most glaring inconsistency is between bars 9 and 46 of the slow movement. The reading adopted here for both bars is found in only two copies—and only in bar 9. In this reading, the change in dynamic level occurs after a leap in the melodic line, and thus is somewhat more plausible that the other readings. The ambiguous placement of the dynamic signs may, however, be an indication that at such points Bach no longer confined himself to the 'terraced' dynamics of the harpsichord. Even in the sources giving the earliest known readings, some of the dynamic markings can be performed effectively only on clavichord or fortepiano.

---

[87] Bach overlooked the necessity for doing so in I. 84.

LIST OF VARIANT READINGS

bar / stave / note-and-rest no.	source: remark
First Movement	
1	P 212, ENK, D KII: time signature: ¢
1 / top / 20	♮ on *f''* only as pencil insertion in foreign hand in ENK
1 / top / 28–9	P 212, ENK, D KII: no tie from *c''*
1 / top / 29	ENK, D KII (?): no 'arpeggio' in top stave
	ENK: *a'* altered in pencil to *g'*
	P 212: preceded by barline
1 / top / 55	P 212, ENK, D KII: no ♭ before *b''*
1 / top / 71	P 212: no *eb''*
1 / top / 90	P 212: no *eb'*
6 / both / 1	P 212, ENK, D KII: tr not c⟿
	P 359: ∞
	P 775, B Bc: orig. ⟿ (?), retraced or corr. (by Bach?)
17 / both / 1	P 212: tr not ⟿
17 / bottom / 1	ENK, D KII: ⟿
17 / 7	P 359, P 212, ENK, D KII: *c/c'* (no ♯)
	P 775: ♯ inserted (both staves)
18 / 7	accidentals only in P 212
18 / bottom, downstem / 7	A Wgm: 8th-note
22 / bottom, downstem / 3–4	P 212: no tie
22 / adagio	P 359, ENK: no *pp*
	D KII: *pp* above B♭ instead of a 16th earlier
	P 359, P 212, ENK, D KII: no slur (either stave)
22 / bottom / adagio	ENK, D KII: *g* not *a*
	ENK, D KII: no ⟿
22 / allegro	P 212: no tempo, no time signature
28 / top / 1–2	P 212: dotted 16th and 32nd-note, instead of two 16ths
31 / bottom, downstem / 1	P 775, A Wgm: no tr
38 / top / 2	ENK, D KII: ♯ (!)
46 / both / 1	P 359, P 212, ENK, D KII: tr not c⟿

bar / stave / note-and-rest no.	source: remark
	(P 359: ⟿ in top stave?)
	P 775: orig. ⟿ (?), retraced or corr. (by Bach?)
47 / both / 4	naturals in P 212, ENK, D KII
47, 48 / top, downstem / 2	P 359: no tr
51 / bottom, downstem	ENK, D KII: as Ex. 26a; remaining sources as Ex. 26b (=CPEBE)

Ex. 26: H. 47, I. 51

bar / stave / note-and-rest no.	source: remark
52 / top / 12	ENK, D KII: *c♮''* not *b'*
55, 57–8	P 359: dyns. possibly autograph
58	B Bc, P 212, ENK, D KII: no *f*
58 / bottom / 1	♮ only in ENK, D KII
61 / top / 1	P 775, A Wgm, P 359, ENK, D KII: *f'* not *d'*. *CPEBE* = B Bc, P 212
61 / bottom, upstem / 9	P 359, P 212, ENK, D KII: no ♯ on g
61 / top / 84	ENK, D KII: no ↝ on *f''*
61 / top / 84–5	P 212: 84 (*f''*) as quarter-note; orn. on 85 (*e''*)
61 / top / 90	P 212: no ♮ on *d'''*
	P 775, P 359: ♮ inserted (autograph?)
61 / 91–100	ENK, D KII: all 32nds, as small notes
	P 359, P 212: normal 32nds
73 / both / 5	P 212, D KII: no ♮
	P 775, P 359: ♮ inserted

113

bar / stave / note-and-rest no.	source: remark
74 / top / 23	ENK, D KIl: no ≋
74 / top / 30–5, 38–43	ENK, D KIl: half these values (including apps.)
74 / top / 77, 80	P 359, P 212, ENK, D KIl: no ♭ on first *a'*, no ♮ on second *a'*
	P 775, B Bc: both accidentals inserted
74 / top / 94–115	P 775, A Wgm, P 359, P 212, ENK, D KIl: 16th-note group, not 32nds. *CPEBE* = B Bc
74 / top / 112	♯ (on *f'*) in all sources; no source has any accidental on the following note
79 / both / 1	P 212, ENK, D KIl: tr not *c⁀*
	D KIl: tr in top stave only
	P 775: orig. ⁀ (?), retraced or corr. (by Bach?)
81	ENK, D KIl: no *p*
81 / top / 7–8	P 775, A Wgm: slur (possibly just a stray line in P 775)
82 / bottom / 2 (inner voice)	P 212, ENK, D KIl: *a'* not *f♯'*
83 / top / 3	P 212: no ♮
	P 775: ♮ inserted
85 / bottom, downstem / 4	P 775: ♮ inserted; autograph?
90–1	ENK, D KIl: no dyns.
93 / bottom, upstem / 1–2	P 359, P 212, ENK, D KIl: no slur
94 / top / 6	P 212: 8th-note app.
	ENK, D KIl: no app.
94 / top / 7	ENK: no ≋
	D KIl: orn. present but probably added by editor
94 / top / 18–22, 33–7 (*eb'* to *b♮*, *c♯''* to *f♯''*)	ENK, DKIl: half these values
94 / top / 36	P 212: *ab''* not *bb''*
94 / top / 38–9	ENK: first *g''* as 16th, second *g''* as 32nd, both notes beamed with the following 32nds
	D KIl: both notes as 32nds, beamed as in ENK (tie *g''* to *g''* remains in both sources)
94 / bottom, upper part / 12–15	ENK, D KIl: 32nd-

bar / stave / note-and-rest no.	source: remark
(*g* to *d*)	notes
94 / bottom, upper part / 19–20 (*bb* to *a*)	P 212: *bb* tied to previous note; no slur between *bb* and *a*
	ENK, D KIl: orn. between 19 and 20, not on 20
94 / bottom, upper part / 20–22	P 212, ENK, D KIl: *a* (*a–bb–g*) as dotted 8th followed by *g–bb–g* (16ths)
94 / bottom, upper voice / 24	ENK, D KIl: no *pp* (*f♯*)
94 / bottom, inner voice / 1	P 212: no *c♯*
94 / bottom, inner voice / 2	P 212, ENK, D KIl: no *d*
94 / bottom, lowest voice / 3	ENK, D KIl: *Eb* (breve) placed beneath 17–18 of top stave (app. *f'*, *eb'*)
	ENK: *Eb* (breve) tied to previous *Eb* (pencil addition)
94 / bottom, lowest voice / 4	D KIl: no *D*
Second Movement	
1	D KIl: no tempo mark
1 / top, downstem / 3–4	A Wgm: no slur
2 / top, upstem / 4–5	P 359, P 212, ENK, D KIl: no slur
3 / top, upstem / 7–8	ENK, D KIl: no ∾
5 / top, upstem / 1	ENK, D KIl: ∾ on 1 not between 1 and 2
5, 6 / top / last	ENK, D KIl: no ≋
7 / top / 9	ENK: ♯ cancelled (in pencil)
8 / top, upstem / 1–2	P 359, P 212, ENK, D KIl: no slur
8 / top, upstem / 2	P 212, ENK: ⁀ not ≋
	D KIl: ⁀ (?)
9–10	position of *p* as in *CPEBE* only in P 359, P 212
	ENK, D KIl: dyn. on third beat
	P 775, B Bc, A Wgm: *p* on downbeat of bar 10; in P 775 and B Bc it is inserted (autograph?)
10 / top / 1–2	P 359, P 212: no slur (upper voice)
	P 359, P 212, ENK, D KIl: no slur (inner voice)
13 / top / 1	P 359, ENK, D KIl: no arp.

114

bar / stave / note-and-rest no.	source: remark
13 / top / 4	P 212: *p* repeated here
15–16 / bottom, upstem	ENK, D KIl: no *d–d*
17 / bottom, upstem / 1–2	P 359, P 212, ENK, D KIl: no slur
18	ENK, D KIl: no *f*
19 / top, upstem / 4–5	P 359, P 212, ENK, D KIl: no slur P 775: slur ambiguous, perhaps on 4–6 B Bc: slur on 4–6 A Wgm: slur on 5–6 (or perhaps 4–6)
20 / top, upstem / 5	P 359, P 212, ENK, D KIl: 2-flag app. P 775: quarter-note app. (lacks flag)
20 / top, upstem / 4–5	P 359, P 212, ENK, D KIl: no slur A Wgm, B Bc: slur on 4–6
20 / top, upstem / 7–8	P 212: ∞ on 7 not between 7 and 8 ENK, D KIl: no orn.
23 / top, upstem / 1–2	P 212: ∞ on 1 not between 1 and 2 ENK, KIl: no orn.
24	P 212, ENK, D KIl: no *p*
25	ENK, D KIl: no *f*
26 / top / 2–7	B Bc: double these values
27	ENK, D KIl: no *f*
27 / bottom, upstem / 2	P 359, P 212, ENK, D KIl: no ⌣
28 / top, upstem / 1–4	P 212: as Ex. 27a; remaining sources as Ex. 27b (=*CPEBE*), except as noted below **Ex. 27: H. 47, II. 28**
28 / top, upstem / 1–2	slur only in ENK, D KIl
28 / top, upstem / 2–4	ENK, D KIl: dotted 8th, 16th
28 / top, upstem / 5, 7	ENK, D KIl: no apps.
28 / top, upstem / 6	P 212: ⌣ not ≋
	P 359, ENK, D KIl: no orn.
28 / top / 8	P 359: no ♮
29 / top / 2	ENK, D KIl: no orn.
29 / top / 4	ENK, D KIl: no apps. (either part)
31 / top / 3	♮ only in P 212 and as addition in foreign hand in ENK and (by editor?) in D KIl
32 / bottom	*CPEBE* = ENK, D KIl; all other sources: quarter tied to half
33 / top / 5	ENK, D KIl: tr not ⌣ᴡ P 775, A Wgm, P 212: ⌣ᴡᴡᴡ P 359: ᴡᴡ? (indistinct)
33 / bottom / 4	ENK, D KIl: *e'* not *d'*; pencil correction in ENK
34	P 212: *p* on third beat ENK, D KIl: no dyn.
34 / top / 3–6	ENK, D KIl: 64ths
36 / top / 1	P 212, ENK, D KIl: ∞ on 1 not between 1 and 2
37 / top / 1	P 359, P 212, ENK, D KIl: no ♮ P 775: ♮ inserted (autograph?)
37, 39 / top / 2	P 359, P 212, ENK, D KIl: no ≋
39 / top / 8–9	ENK: no slur D KIl: slur drawn lightly, probably by editor
39 / top / 9; 40 / 2	P 359, P 212, ENK, D KIl: no ⌣, no stroke
42 / top / 1	ENK, D KIl: ♯ (!)
42 / top / 5	P 359, P 212, ENK, D KIl: no ⌣
44	P 775, P 359: *f* inserted? (autograph?)
46	*p* on third beat in all sources; *CPEBE* = P 359, P 212 in bar 9
47	B Bc: *f* added (autograph?)
48 / top / 9	P 359, P 212, ENK, D KIl: no ⌣
52	P 359: *f* on third beat
53 / bottom, downstem / 2	B Bc: double-stemmed (upward

bar / stave / note-and-rest no.	source: remark
	stem in P 775, P 212)
55 / top, upstem / 4–5	P 359, P 212, ENK, D KIl: no *Anschlag* P 775: *Anschlag* inserted
Third Movement	
1	ENK, D KIl: tempo mark: Allegro (no 'assai') P 775, B Bc: page turn rubric at end of second movement orig. 'Volti Allegro', 'assai' added (autograph)
9 / top / 1	P 359, P 212, ENK, D KIl: *g'/e*♭*''* (no *a'*). cf. bar 70
10, 22	P 359, P 212, ENK, D KIl: no dyns. P 359: dyns. added faintly in foreign hand
12 / top / 5	♮ only in ENK, D KIl
19–20 / top, upstem	slurs in P 212, ENK, D KIl
20 / top, upstem / 9	P 212, ENK, D KIl: no ♭ P 775, B Bc, P 359: ♭ inserted
21 / top, downstem / 2	P 359, P 212, ENK, D KIl: no ♭
25 / top / 2	P 212, ENK, D KIl: tr not *c*⤳
29 / downstem / 3	♮ (on *g'*) only in P 212
30	P 212, ENK, D KIl: *f* on second beat A Wgm: no dyn.
37 / bottom, downstem / 2	rest only in ENK
50 / bottom, upstem / 7	P 775, B Bc, A Wgm, 3872/1, P 212: 32nd (no dot)
51 / top / 3	P 359, P 212: no ♮ P 775: ♮ inserted
54 / top / 2	P 359, P 212, ENK, D KIl: no ♮ P 775, B Bc: ♮ inserted
54, 58 / bottom, upstem / 7	P 775, B Bc, A Wgm: 32nd (no dot)
58–9 / top	tie on *bb'* and downward stem on *c*♯*''* only in ENK, D KIl P 359: tie on *c*♯*''* only
59 / top / 1	P 359: bottom note: *a'* (!)
60 / bottom	P 359, P 212: no rest
70 / top / 1	P 359, P 212, ENK, D KIl: *d'/bb'* (no *e'*)
70 / top / 5	♮ only in ENK, D KIl
71, 75	P 359, P 212, ENK, D KIl: no dyns. P 359: dyns. added lightly in foreign hand
72 / top, downstem / 1	P 359: ♭ inserted (neither Michel nor Bach?)
75–6	P 775: these bars autograph
79 / top / 4	P 359, P 212: no ♮ P 775: ♮ inserted, possibly autograph
85 / top / 1	P 212, ENK, D KIl: 2-flag app.
85 / top / 2	P 212: no ⤳ P 359: orn. small, light, probably inserted
85 / top / 2–3	P 775: correction? Notes retraced, orig. reading unclear
94–6 / bottom	Rests only ENK, D KIl
95 / bottom, upstem / 1	P 359, P 212: no ♮ P 775: ♮ inserted
97, 101	P 359, P 212, ENK, D KIl: no dyns. P 359: dyns. added lightly in foreign hand
101 / top, upstem / 1–2	P 359, P 212, ENK, D KIl: no slur
101 / top / 4	ENK, D KIl: *d''* not *c''* ENK: preceded by ♮
104 / top, upstem / 2	P 212, ENK, D KIl: tr not *c*⤳
104 / top, downstem / 1	ENK, D KIl: *d'* not *c'* D KIl: *d'* preceded by ♮ (*sic*)
105 / bottom / 2	Fermata only in ENK, D KIl P 212: no rest
108 / top, upstem / 1–2	B Bc, P 359 (and P 212): no slur
109 / top / 1	ENK, D KIl: no orn.
109 / top / 1–2	ENK, D KIl: slur
109	ENK, D KIl: *f* on second beat
113 / bottom	B Bc, P 359, P 212: no rest
114 / bottom	B Bc, P 359, P 212, ENK, D KIl: no rest
116 / bottom, downstem / 2	Rest only ENK, D KIl

Sonata in F major, H. 48

SOURCES

H. 48 was composed in 1746 and, to judge from the extant sources, thereafter underwent small but significant revisions affecting mainly the slow movement. The sonata was published, probably in 1761, by the Parisian firm of Antoine Huberti, but the print was not authorized by Bach and contains numerous arbitrary alterations of the text. The only reliable sources of the work are three manuscript copies by Anon. 303, one of which (in P 775) serves as the principal source for the present edition for both the early version and, with Bach's revisions, for the later version. Despite the somewhat puzzling variants in the other copies, there is no good evidence that the work was revised more than once.[88]

P 775. Berlin, Staatsbibliothek Preußischer Kulturbesitz, Musikabteilung, Mus. ms. Bach P 775. Manuscript copy by Anon. 303, with autograph revisions. Soprano clef in upper stave.[89]

The copy of H. 48 is the very last of the once independent manuscripts now incorporated into P 775. The twelve pages (three sheets, 35 × 21.5 cm., watermark: octagonal star; countermark: W [?]), now numbered 157–68, show traces of earlier pagination on pages 3 and 5. The last page is blank, and so originally was the first page, evidently, although it bears in the top centre the usual double index entries of this source, possibly in Bach's hand: 'No. 47. / (47.)'. Entered later, in different foreign hands, are several additional entries. In the upper right corner there is a large digit '1' followed by at least one smaller digit (3?). Below that is 'C P E Bach' in hasty cursive script. This is very light, and no sign is visible to suggest that it once belonged to a title; it is not in the hand of Bach or Anon. 303. In the lower centre is 'Th. Kat 63,18 = Nachl. 7,47' and directly below that is '[Wotquenne 65,18]'. Near the bottom is the erroneous remark 'Von Hering geschrieben' and, in the lower left corner, the letter 'C'.[90]

The ten pages of music are each ruled in six systems; the bottom system is blank at the ends of the first two movements. There is no title at the top of the first page of music.

The versions of the copy *ante* and *post correcturam* are treated as distinct sources in the List of Variant Readings. Since at least one of the two other copies by Anon. 303 (US Wc; see below) is in all likelihood a copy of P 775 *ante correcturam*, a comparison of the two sources aids in identifying the alterations that Bach subsequently made in P 775. The handwriting and the manner in which the revisions were entered are similar to those described in the copy in P 775 of H. 43.

Only those revisions that are clearly autograph are noted as such in the List of Variant Readings. These always occur at points where US Wc and D Kll (see below) give simpler readings than P 775 *post correcturam*. Conversely, US Wc and D Kll always agree with P 775 *ante correcturam* where the readings of the latter remain legible. Thus it is safe to assume that, as with many other works of C. P. E. Bach, the absence of slurs and similar variants of omission occurring in both US Wc and D Kll correspond with readings in P 775 *ante correcturam*.

Although the first movement contains several traces of correction, only one of these (bar 13) is likely to have been made by the composer. The earlier reading of $b\natural'$, which was later changed to $b\flat'$, was probably an error. The ascending form of what is now referred to as the melodic minor scale often occurs even in descending passages in works from the Bach circle. The change probably represents the composer's greater tolerance for the melodic interval of the augmented second later in his career, after the composition of H. 48.

The second movement was more thoroughly revised than the first, the composer having added

---

[88] Not seen here was the copy by Johann Mederitsch (1752-1835; also known as Gallus) in Salzburg, Dom-Musikarchiv, Mn 96, reported as item 3O in T. Aigner, *Thematisches Verzeichnis der Werke von Johann Mederitsch detto Gallus*, Musikwissenschaftliches Schriften, Band 3 (=Publikationen des Instituts für Musikwissenschaft der Universität Salzburg, Band 8) (Munich, 1974), 212. I am grateful to Ulrich Leisinger for referring me to this publication. Many of the works attributed to C. P. E. Bach in Aigner's item 3 are of doubtful authenticity; most of the remainder (including H. 48) appeared in eighteenth-century prints.

[89] Facsimile in Berg, ed., *The Collected Works*, III, p. 299.

[90] On the significance of these entries, see the discussions of P 775 under H. 43 and H. 46.

appoggiaturas, ornament signs, and other markings, and embellishing or altering the actual notes at several points. The autograph character of the alterations is clearest in bars 19 and 35, in which the melodic line was varied.

No revisions at all appear to have taken place in the last movement.

A Wgm. Vienna, Gesellschaft der Musikfreunde, VII 3872/14. A copy by Michel, using soprano clef.

Manuscript 3872/14 closely resembles Michel's other copies in this collection. It is a nearly exact copy of P 775 *post correcturam*, following the model precisely even in the layout of each page and the ornamental designs at the ends of movements. In fact the similarities are great enough to suggest that Anon. 303 might have been the same person as Michel. However, the quarter rests and *custodes* in manuscript 3872/14 are very distinct from those in the copies by Anon. 303, and only Michel repeats the clefs at the beginning of every system. Among the few differences in format are the presence in manuscript 3872/14 of the title 'Sonata' at the top left of the first page of music, and 'Cembalo solo.' at the top centre, as in other copies in manuscript 3872. There are no signs of correction or any other entries in a foreign hand.

US Wc. Washington, DC, Library of Congress, Music Division, M23.B13. W65(18)(case). Copy of H. 48 by Anon. 303, using soprano clef, in wrapper bearing modern entries.

This copy of H. 48 closely resembles the copy by Anon. 303 of H. 43 in the same collection. The wrapper and the manuscript itself bear later markings similar to those described for the copy of H. 43, although the wrapper of H. 48 includes an additional line, subsequently crossed out: 'Dieselbe Sonate in Abschrift von andrer alter [corrected in lighter ink to 'alten'!] Hand'. The number stamped on the final page of the manuscript is two higher (603055) than in the copy of H. 43, and page 2 bears librarian's entries in pencil similar to those in the other copies in the Library of Congress.

The manuscript consists of twelve pages stitched together and is nearly identical in all respects to P 775 *ante correcturam*, except that the first page serves as a title page, reading at the upper centre: 'Sonata / per il Cembalo / Solo'. Immediately below this, offset to the right, is the attribution: 'dell Sigl: C. P. E. / Bach'. At the top in two foreign hands are the entries 'N. 1.' and 'F. dur.' The former ('N. 1') corresponds with the numbering of the incipit for H. 48 in the Kiel manuscript Mb 61/2 (previously described; see entry for US Wc in the critical commentary for H. 43). Like the copies of H. 48 in the Library of Congress and the Kiel manuscript Mb 53/4 (see below), the incipit in Mb 61/2 lacks the ornament on bar 1. Unlike those copies the incipit also lacks the mordent on bar 2, note 1, instead giving a mark of uncertain meaning (trill?) on note 3. Nevertheless it seems likely that the copy in US Wc once belonged to the collection indexed in Mb 61/2, and that it is the 'doublette' mentioned on the title page of Mb 53/4.

At several points in the second movement the text has been emended by a foreign hand, in a brown ink that is darker than the ink used for corrections in the copy of H. 43 now in the Library of Congress; this ink has also not eaten into the paper as deeply. Bar 35 shows extensive erasures; the corrector may have begun to enter the later version, although the present reading gives essentially the earlier version. Other corrections (bars 16, 20) do not coincide with either version. Apart from these presumably later entries, US Wc appears to be a faithful copy of P 775 *ante correcturam*.

D Kll. Kiel, Schleswig-Holsteinische Landesbibliothek, ms. Mb 53/4. Copy of H. 48 by Anon. 303, using soprano clef.

The Kiel copy of H. 48 occupies pages 25–35 of Mb 53 and is the only copy by Anon. 303 in either Mb 53 or Mb 52. The ruling and layout of the pages are close to those of P 775 *ante correcturam* and US Wc, but there are a few small divergences in the placement of line breaks. There are also variations in the wording of *volti* indications and in the ornamentation of double bars. The title page reads as in US Wc, but the attribution is centred.

An entry in the upper left corner reads: 'No. 1. ist doppelt geschrieben'. This is presumably in a foreign hand, although the source contains no other entries in German cursive script with which to compare it.[91] Beneath the title is the Wotquenne number: 'W. 65, 18'.

Although it gives every indication of being a copy of US Wc, D Kll contains a few careless errors not found there, such as the omission of the bass for a whole bar (27) of the slow movement. D Kll also

---

[91] The hand appears much older than that on the wrapper of US Wc, which bears a somewhat similar entry.

gives specific graphic ornament signs at many points where P 775 *ante correcturam* and US Wc have only *t* or *tr*. Since the copy of H. 43 in the Library of Congress shows the same practice, it appears that Anon. 303 supplied his own interpretations of some ornament signs in copies not prepared for Bach. However, the ornaments in this copy are subject to further considerations (see below).

B Bc. Brussels, Bibliothèque du Conservatoire Royal de Musique, ms. 5883. Copy by J. J. H. Westphal. Soprano clef in the upper stave.

The copy of H. 48 has been reported to be by Michel,[92] but it is in fact in the hand of J. J. H. Westphal, the original owner of all or most of 5883. The most obvious differences between this copy and those of Michel lie in the lettering, including the metrical indication 'C' and the capital 'A' in *Allegro*; the more compressed, sometime coiled form of the bass clef; and such matters of style as the different ornamentation of double bars and the absence in the copy of H. 48 of clefs at the beginnings of all but the first system on each page.[93] Westphal's apparent tendency to confuse ornament signs (see below) supports the assignment of the copy to him.

The copy of H. 48 consists of eight unnumbered pages, including the title page, which reads: 'Sonata / F dur / per il Cembalo / Dal Sigr. C. F. E. Bach'. Added in later hands are the usual indications of 5883. Beneath the title appears: '12e. Sonate du no. 15 de Westphal'. The incorrect number 12 has been changed to 18. In the upper left corner a stamped 12 has also been crossed out and replaced by a written 18. The title at the top left of the first page of music is simply 'Sonata'. The last page is blank.

B Bc gives a distinctive and markedly inferior text characterized by copying errors such as misplaced ornaments (II. 4, 30) and several faulty notes. There are also signs of emendation by the copyist, as in the presence of extra rests (and stems) to produce a clearer indication of voice-leading in inner voices; substitutions of ornament signs; and the redistribution of a passage in the last movement

(bars 26–8) between the two hands. Since these readings occur only in B Bc, they are unlikely to represent late revisions by the composer.

P 1134. Berlin, Staatsbibliothek Preußischer Kulturbesitz, Musikabteilung, Mus. ms. Bach P 1134. Copy possibly by Borsch, using soprano clef.

The hand in P 1134 has been described as 'Su, 18. Jh., ähn[lich] Borsch'.[94] Johann Stephan Borsch (*c*.1744–1804) was organist at the Heilig-Geist-Kirche in Hamburg from 1777,[95] and the handwriting in P 1134 indeed resembles that in P 289, in the Staatsbibliothek Preußischer Kulturbesitz, Berlin.[96] But in fact the copies in P 289 of canons from BWV 1079 show widely varying forms of clefs, rests, and other signs, few of them matching P 1134 precisely.

P 1134 consists of eight pages, the first of which is a title page reading: 'Sonata / per il / Cembalo Solo / di Sig: C. P. E. Bach'. The last line is offset to the right. Another hand has added beneath: 'Berlin, 1746'. Added in a third hand beneath the title is: '[Wotquenne 65,18]'. An illegible cursive entry appears above the title, and another, perhaps a price, in the upper left corner.

Pages 2–7 are each ruled in eight systems. At several points the copyist entered notes a tone too high; these have been corrected (not necessarily by the copyist himself) by enlarging the noteheads and occasionally adding letters above. The most significant corrections, however, were made in the slow movement, where certain passages originally given in the early version have been altered to the later version. Yet some of the earlier readings remain, in particular the bass in bars 17 and 23–4, and one passage that underwent revision (bar 10, and the parallel bar 32) occurs in an otherwise unattested form. Although the latter appears to be an original entry, alterations clearly occurred in bars 19–20 and 35, where erasures and cramping are evident. A few added accidentals elsewhere in P 1134 appear to be in a foreign hand.

A peculiarity of this copy, possibly one that it shared with the lost autograph (see below), is that many of the indications for ornaments are very

---

[92] Berg, *The Collected Works*, III, p. xxv.

[93] The sonata does not contain a single half-note with downward stem, the character that presents the most obvious difference generally between Westphal's and Michel's musical hands.

[94] In Kast, p. 64.

[95] H.-J. Schulze, *Studien zur Bach-Überlieferung*, p. 26.

[96] One of two 'weitere Hss.' listed in Dadelsen, p. 22, as confirmed copies by Borsch. The other was not seen here.

small. This makes it occasionally difficult to distinguish between the various ornament signs.

HB. *Six Sonatas pour le clavecin.* Engraved print of six sonatas by C. P. E. Bach, published by Antoine Huberti (Paris, *c.*1761).[97]

The title page of this unauthorized print reads:

SIX / SONATES / POUR LE CLAVECIN / COMPOSÉES / PAR M[r.] C. P. E. / BACH / Premier M[tre.] de clavecin de la chambre de S. M. le Roy de Prusse. / Mises au jour par M[r.] Huberti de l'academie Royale de Musique. / OEUVRE [Ier.] / Gravées par Ceron. / Prix 9[th.] / A PARIS, / Chés l'Editeur rüe du Chantre á [*sic*] l'hotel du S[t.] Esprit chés le M[tre.] / D'armes. Et Aux Adresses Ordinaires. / A LYON chés M[rs.] les Freres le Goux Place des Cordeliers. / A ROUEN chés les Marchands de Musique. / Avec Privilege du Roy

This print was first listed in a catalogue probably dating from 1761; it was advertised 9 November 1761, and reprinted around 1765.[98] According to later catalogues, Huberti (=Anton Huberty, *c.*1722–91) also issued as 'Op. 2' a 'Concerto de Clavecin' attributed to Bach, and as 'No. 2' the concerto H. 404 (W. 2) in what has been identified as an early version.[99] The first five works in Huberti's print are H. 18 (W. 65/9), H. 19 (W. 65/10), H. 56 (W. 65/22), H. 55 (W. 62/8), and H. 67 (W. 62/13), the latest of which was composed in 1752.

H. 48 appears on pages 25–31, entitled 'Sonata VI' at the head of the first system. Like several other sonatas in the print, it appears in an arrangement that shows no sign of stemming from the composer. Only the first movement of H. 48 is included, with numerous substitutions and additions of ornaments as well as harmonic filling out of certain passages. In place of the last two movements is the Arioso with variations H. 54 (W. 118/4), in the same key as H. 48 and composed a year later, in 1747. Although H. 54 is given without additional harmonic filling out, the text otherwise shows alterations similar to those in the first movement of

H. 48. Several errors show that it was derived from a text that employed soprano clef for the upper stave, as do Michel's copy and the incipit in the *Nachlassverzeichnis*.[100]

Inconsistencies between parallel passages in the harmonic filling out and in added ornaments reveal the unauthentic nature of those readings, which are not found in any source independent of the print. Although the Arioso was composed within a year of H. 48, there is no reason to think that it ever constituted an alternate ending to the sonata. The opening of the Arioso bears a similarity to the opening theme of the sonata H. 43, but this probably reflects Bach's adoption in both works of a simple *galant* style and provides no evidence for Bach's having originally conceived H. 54 as a sonata movement.

The print by Huberti is thus of no value to the text, but is of great interest for the evidence it sheds on the state in which Bach's music was received in Paris at a relatively early date. For this reason, readings unique to the print are given in a separate list following the main List of Variant Readings. Of special interest are the dynamic markings in bars 7–8, which indicate that Huberti's arrangement was carried out with the fortepiano in mind.

P 673. Berlin, Staatsbibliothek Preußischer Kulturbesitz, Musikabteilung, Mus. ms. Bach P 673. Copy of the Huberti print by an unknown copyist, in oblong format.

The same Viennese hand found in P 673, from the group designated Su (*Schreiber unbekannt*) VI, has also been discerned in P 674 in the Staatsbibliothek Preußischer Kulturbesitz, Berlin, a manuscript containing the six sonatas of the *Fortsetzung* of Bach's *Reprisen-Sonaten*, W. 51 (Berlin, 1761). Both P 673 and P 674 belonged to the Viennese pianist and collector Josef Fischhof (1804–57).

The copy of H. 48 is the second work in P 673, on pages 13–28. The title page (page 13) reads: 'Sonata. / per / Cembalo. / Del Sige: Carlo Fil: Em: Bach.' and is followed by an incipit on two staves. The music is written on pages 14–27. Page 28 is blank.

Despite the change in format and title, the text is very close to that of the Huberti print, differing

---

[97] The print was examined in an exemplar belonging to the Österreichische Nationalbibliothek, Vienna.

[98] C. Johansson, *French Music Publishers' Catalogues of the Second Half of the Eighteenth Century* (Uppsala, 1955), pp. 43–4.

[99] See Wade, *The Keyboard Concertos*, p. 90. There is no indication in Huberty's catalogue that the works designated 'Op. 2' and 'No. 2' are the same.

[100] Michel's copy, ms. 19035 in the Österreichische Nationalbibliothek, Vienna, is reproduced in Berg, ed., *The Collected Works*.

(apart from a very few trivial variants) only in details of orthography.

Establishing the text

Two of the copies by Anon. 303, P 775 *ante correcturam* and US Wc, are so similar as to pose difficulties in determining which was copied from the other, or whether both stem from a third manuscript. Although US Wc contains some errors of omission, it is impossible to say for certain that these were not also present in P 775 *ante correcturam*. Nevertheless, in the absence of sure evidence to the contrary it seems reasonable to assume that US Wc was copied from P 775 *ante correcturam*. Despite its substitutions of ornament signs, D KIl is clearly a copy of US Wc, perhaps made at a somewhat later date. The copy by Michel, A Wgm, just as clearly stems from P 775 *post correcturam*, despite two minor discrepancies.

Although Westphal appears to have been unaware of the Huberti print,[101] his copy (B Bc), together with P 1134 and the print by Huberti, belongs to a less dependable tradition than the copies by Anon. 303. Even when the arbitrary emendations in B Bc are disregarded, this copy, together with P 1134, poses great puzzles. Both are faulty,[102] and P 1134 contains an odd mixture of old, new, and revised readings in the slow movement.[103] A number of readings in both sources cannot have been derived from P 775 either before or after correction.[104]

The most likely explanation for the eclectic or transitional readings in P 1134 is that it is a copy of a now lost autograph, one containing roughly sketched revisions that the copyist of P 1143 did not fully understand. That copyist's tempo for the first movement, Allegro non molto, might have been another misreading of Bach's script, and at least some of the errors and omissions in P 1134 might be explained in similar fashion. Other variants, especially the many omissions of slurs and ornaments, could have resulted from Bach's own

failure to enter such signs into the autograph even though he entered them into the copy by Anon. 303. While there is no evidence that Borsch, possibly the copyist of P 1134, studied with Bach, both he and Westphal might have been given access to the autograph either before or after Bach's death.

Although B Bc gives the slow movement without the eclectic mixture of readings seen in P 1134, the two copies do form a significant number of concordances in all three movements. While most of these are substitutions of ornament signs, which could have been carried out independently by the two copyists, several more substantial variants, notably those in bars 4 and 28 of the last movement, seem unlikely to have arisen in both copies through chance. Hence B Bc might also have been copied, perhaps at a later date and by a more expert writer more experienced in reading Bach's hand, from the same revised autograph.

The Huberti print, which (with P 673) contains only the first movement of H. 48, leaves little to go on. But its time signature, tempo, and inclusion of the ornament in the first bar (see below) suggest that it, too, stems (indirectly) from the autograph rather than P 775.

Ornament signs

The varying indications for ornaments pose more questions in this sonata than in any other edited in this volume. Particularly problematical is the very first note in the upper stave. There is no sign in US Wc or D KIl, and the sign in P 775, though possibly a mordent, is minuscule and could be interpreted as +. The indication in P 1134 is even more likely to be +, which is certainly the reading of the print.[105] Yet, as is clear from the *Nachlassverzeichnis* (page 7), and also from parallel passages, Bach intended a mordent.

While the sign + does occur in Bach's autographs from the 1740s, it is rare or unknown in contexts that call for a mordent; thus it is surprising to find the sign used in contexts implying both trills and mordents in the sources of H. 48. In P 775, the sign occurs only in the first bar, and, as it differs in form from the other ornament signs in the manuscript, may be a late addition in a foreign hand. Many occurrences of the sign + in the Huberti print (and P 673) are clearly the work of the arranger. But its use

---

[101] There is no reference to the print in the entry for H. 48 in the latest version of Westphal's catalogue (B Br II 4104, fo. 33ᵛ).

[102] See variants listed for I. tempo mark and time signature, and bars 24, 60; III. 4, 16, 17, 19, 29, 30, 31, and 34.

[103] See variants listed for II. 8, 10, 11, 12, 18, and 32.

[104] See variants listed for I. 27, 71, 72; II. 33, 34; III. 4 and 28.

[105] The plus sign is definitely present in P 1134 at bar 31 of the first movement, where it forms a clear contrast with the mordent in bar 32.

in P 1134 and B Bc requires further explanation; most likely the copyists were unaware of Bach's use of + to indicate a trill, and confused it with the mordent in the opening bars of the first movement while copying from the (lost) autograph. J. J. H. Westphal, the likely copyist of B Bc, in fact used the sign normally employed for the mordent as an indication for trills in copying at least one other work.[106]

Since the copies of Anon. 303 lack the cross or plus sign, this copyist, while working from the same autograph, may have substituted *t* or *tr* in making the copy now present in P 775. Since this copy was revised by Bach, the substitutions (if such they were) must have had his authorization. This is less likely to be true of the further substitutions of ornament signs (for *t* or *tr*) in D KIl, P 1134, and B Bc. Since many of these substitutions occur in only one of the three sources, they may have been the work of the copyists. Even so, they are usually validated by the prescriptions in Bach's *Versuch* concerning the usage of orna-

ments.[107] But none of these substitutions can be regarded as authentic. Even less credible are the ornaments added in P 1134 and D KIl at several points (for example, I. 33, 62–3).

A slighter problem is that of the written-out *Nachschläge* at two (possibly three) points in the slow movement (bars 30 and 35, and in P 1134, bar 12). That these may have been inserted into the original text is suggested by the misplacement of one of them in B Bc, although they already occur in P 775 *ante correcturam*. While Bach rarely wrote out such *Nachschläge*, he might have included them here for the benefit of beginners lacking even a 'mediocre ear',[108] a group Bach might have had in mind in composing this relatively easy sonata. The same holds for the slurs, normally left to the player's understanding, that are present on several appoggiaturas (e.g., in II. 2).

---

[106] Westphal apparently followed a practice described in an unpublished *Abhandlung von der Musik* by Hertel. See the facsimile and discussion in R. Hertel's edition of Johann Wilhelm Hertel, *Keyboard Concertos in E-flat and F minor* (Ann Arbor, 1988), p. xii.

[107] Westphal seems to have understood a longer trill with *Nachschlag* by the sign used in bar 10 of the first movement, where the context indeed calls for such an ornament. See *Versuch*, I, pp. 74–6 (Theil I, Das zweyte Hauptstück, dritte Abteilung, 13–16); Mitchell, pp. 103–5.

[108] 'Ein mittelmässig Ohr', *Versuch*, I, p. 76 (Theil I, Das zweyte Hauptstück, dritte Abteilung, 17); Mitchell, p. 105.

LIST OF VARIANT READINGS
(Music examples can be found on p. 126)

bar / stave / note-and-rest no.	source: remark	bar / stave / note-and-rest no.	source: remark
First Movement		2, 3 / top / 1	P 1134: + not ⌇
—	B Bc, HB, P 673: tempo: 'Allegro'	10 / top / 1	B Bc: ⌇ not tr
	P 1134: 'Allegro non molto'	13 / top / 1	B Bc: 3-flag app.
—	P 1134, HB, P 673: time signature: ¢	13 / top / 4	P 775 a. corr., US Wc, D KIl: *b♮*
	P 1134: possibly an orthographic variation of C		P 775 p. corr.: erased, remnant of ♮ altered to ♭
1 / top / 1	P 775 p. corr. (?), P 1134 (?), HB, P 673: + not ⌇	24 / top / 11	P 1134: ♮ added in foreign hand
	P 775 p. corr.: later addition? CPEBE = Nachlassverzeichnis, B Bc	26 / top / 2	P 1134: unclear, possibly ⌇
		27 / top / 1–2	B Bc: slur
	P 775 a. corr., US Wc, D KIl: no orn.	27 / top / 2	B Bc, P 1134: ⌇ not tr
		30 / bottom, lower part / 3	rest in A Wgm, B Bc, P 113
		31 / top / 1	P 1134, HB, P 673: + not ⌇

122

bar / stave / note-and-rest no.	source: remark
33 / top / 1	P 1134: ⁓
33 / top / 8	P 775 a. corr.: orig. b'(?), erased and over-written (by copyist)
52 / top	P 775 p. corr.: stave line broken between 4 and 5; accidental orig. on f''?
53 / top / 9	B Bc: no rest
57 / top / 5–6	B Bc: slur
57 / top / 6	B Bc: ⁓ not tr
59 / top / 9–10	P 1134, HB, P 673: no slur
59 / top / 10	P 1134: no tr
60 / bottom / 2	P 1134: no quarter rest
62 / top / 1	D KIl: ⁓
63 / top / 1	P 1134: ⁓
65 / top / 1	P 1134, HB, P 673: no ⁓
70 / top / 9–12	P 775 a. corr., US Wc, D KIl, A Wgm: slur imprecisely placed, could be read on 10–12
71 / top / 1	B Bc, P 1134: ⁓ not tr
72 / top / 3	B Bc: ⁓ not tr / P 1134 (?): ⁓
83 / top / 1	D KIl, HB: 1-flag app.
83 / top / 6–8	P 1134: orig. bb''–a''–g'' 'a g f' written above notes

Second Movement

bar / stave / note-and-rest no.	source: remark
1 / top / 3	P 775 a. corr., US Wc, D KIl: no app. / P 775 p. corr.: app. added (probably autograph)
1 / top / 3–4	B Bc: slur
2 / top, upstem / 1–2	P 1134, US Wc: no slur
2 / top, upstem / 2	P 775 a. corr., US Wc, D KIl: no ⁓
4 / top / 1–3	P 1134: no slur
4 / top / 6	B Bc: ∞ on 6 not afterward / P 775 a. corr., US Wc, D KIl: no orn.
5 / top, upstem / 2–3	P 1134: no tie
6 / top, upstem / 1–2	B Bc, P 1134: no slur
6 / top, upstem / 2	B Bc: ∞ not tr / D KIl: no orn.
7 / top, upstem / 3	B Bc: ⁓ not tr / P 1134: orn. on 2 not 3

bar / stave / note-and-rest no.	source: remark
7 / downstem / 1	P 775, US Wc, D KIl, B Bc, A Wgm: lower note: f' not d'. The latter only in P 1134 and as correction (probably in foreign hand) in US Wc
8, 11	P 1134, P 775 a. corr., US Wc, D KIl: no dyns. / P 775 p. corr.: added (autograph)
9 / top, upstem / 1	D KIl: ⁓ not ⁓
9 / top, upstem / 5	P 775 a. corr., US Wc, D KIl, P 1134: no ⁓
10–11 / top	P 775 a. corr., US Wc, D KIl, P1134 a. corr. (?): as Ex. 28a; remaining sources as Ex. 28b (= CPEBE), except as noted below / In bar 10, P 1134 p. corr. remains as Ex. 28a but note 1 is preceded by four *petites notes* (same pitches as notes 1–4 of Ex. 28b); in bar 11, P 1134 p. corr. lacks f
11 / top / 7	D KIl, B Bc, P 1134: ⁓ not tr
12 / top / 3	D KIl, B Bc: ⁓ not tr
12 / top / 5–6	P 1134: no slur
12 / top / 6	P 775 a. corr., US Wc, D KIl: no ≋ / P 1134: a *Nachschlag* is added in *petites notes* (e', f', 16ths)
14, 16	P 775 a. corr., US Wc, D KIl, P 1134: no dyns. / P 775 p. corr.: dyns. added (autograph)
15 / top / 3	P 775 a. corr., US Wc, D KIl, B Bc: no app. / P 775 p. corr.: app. added
16 / top / 2	B Bc: + not tr
16, 20 / bottom / 1	B Bc: 8th rest (for inner part) above note / US Wc: inner part: c' (bar 16), d' (bar 20), added in lighter ink
17–20	P 775 a. corr., US Wc, D KIl, P 1134: as Ex. 29a except as

bar / stave / note-and-rest no.	source: remark
	noted below; remaining sources as Ex. 29b (= *CPEBE*) except as noted below
18, 20	P 775 p. corr.: dyns. added (autograph)
18 / top / 1	P 1134: as Ex. 29a, but has ⁓ instead of tr, preceded by *Anschlag*: a'–c'' (small 16ths)
19–20	P 775, P 1134: revised to read as *CPEBE* (autograph revision in P 775)
20 / top / 3	B Bc: +
20 / top / 7	US Wc: 8th rest (no dot)
21 / top / 2–3	P 775 a. corr., US Wc, D KIl: no tie
23–4	P 775 a. corr., US Wc, D KIl, P 1134: as Ex. 30a, except as noted below; remaining sources as Ex. 30b (= *CPEBE*) except as noted below
	All sources include two additional 8th rests for the inner voice in bar 24.
23–4 / bottom	P 775 p. corr.: d' (bar 23), g' (bar 24) added; erasure above 4 in bar 24
24 / top / 10	D KIl, B Bc: ⁓ not tr
25 / top / 7	US Wc: no tr
	D KIl, B Bc, P 1134: ⁓
25 / top / 10	D KIl, B Bc, P 1134: ⁓ not tr
26	P 775 a. corr., US Wc, D KIl: no *p*
	P 775 p. corr.: *p* added (autograph)
26 / top / 1	D KIl, B Bc: ⁓ not tr
27 / bottom	D KIl: bass entirely om.
28 / top, upstem / 1–2	A Wgm, P 1134: no slur
28 / top, upstem / 2	P 775 a. corr., US Wc, D KIl: no ♮
	P 775 p. corr.: ♮ inserted (autograph?)
	P 1134: ♮ added (foreign hand?)
29 / top, upstem / 7, 10	D KIl, B Bc, P 1134: ⁓ not tr
30 / top / 4	D KIl, B Bc, P 1134: ⁓ not tr
30 / top / 8	B Bc, P 1134: ⁓ not tr
30 / top / 9–10	B Bc: *Nachschlag* follows barline
31	P 775 a. corr., US Wc, D KIl: no *f*
	P 775 p. corr.: *f* beneath stave, large, in Bach's hand, written over an earlier entry. Orig. reading unclear, perhaps a smaller *f*
31 / top / 5	P 775 a. corr., US Wc, D KIl: no ⁓
31–2	US Wc: barline om.
32–5	P 775 a. corr., US Wc, D KIl, P 1134 a. corr. (?): as Ex. 31a except as noted below
	P 1134: as Ex. 31a in bar 32, but preceded by *petites notes* as in bar 10; orig. as Ex. 31a in bars 33 and 35, corr. to read as Ex. 31b. Remaining sources as Ex. 31b (= *CPEBE*) except as noted below.
	P 775 p. corr. = autograph revision
33 / top / 5	B Bc, P 1134, D KIl: ⁓ not tr
33 / top / 7	B Bc, D KIl: ⁓ not tr
34 / top / 7	D KIl, B Bc, P 1134: ⁓ not tr
35 / top	US Wc: water damage at this point; erasures, emended in foreign hand. Reading after corr. = Ex. 31a but with extra beam on notes 4–6.
35 / top / 10	B Bc: + not tr
Third Movement	
2 / top / 1–2	B Bc: slur
2 / top / 5–6	D KIl: no slur
4 / top / 1	B Bc: + not tr
4 / bottom / 2–4	B Bc, P 1134: F (dotted 8th), c' (16th), beamed together

bar / stave / note-and-rest no.	source: remark
5 / 12	B Bc: *d''* (!)
10 / bottom / 1	P 1134: no rest
14 / top / 1–2	P 775 a. corr., US Wc, D KIl: no slur
16 / top / 1	B Bc: + not tr
16 / bottom	P 1134: erasures; orig. reading unclear
17, 19 / downstem / 1, 2	P 1134: orig. one step lower (?), corr. by enlarging note-heads
22 / upstem / 9	D KIl, B Bc: ⁓ not tr / P 1134: no orn. / B Bc: slur (?) crossed out above note; similar sign in B Bc copy of H. 51
24 / bottom / last 2	B Bc: slur
25 / top / 8	P 1134: ⁓ (?)
26, 28 / top / 4	B Bc: downward stem
26, 28 / top / 8 (*f'*)	B Bc: downward stem, beamed with 5–7
26 / top / 10 (*f'*)	B Bc: downward stem
26 / bottom / 1	B Bc: followed by 8th rest
27 / top / 8	B Bc, P 1134 (?): ⁓ not tr
28 / top / 10–12	B Bc: beamed together, downward stems
28 / bottom / 1	B Bc, P 1134: followed by 8th rest
29, 30, 31	P 1134: first note of top stave directly above bass note
30 / top / 7 (*b'*)	P 1134: preceded by ♮ (in foreign hand?)
34 / bottom / 1	P 1134: quarter-note, quarter rest
34 / bottom / 2	B Bc: no rest

Readings from the unauthorized print

The following variants in the first movement are found in both HB and P 673.

bar / stave / note-and-rest no.	source: remark
1–6 / bottom	as Ex. 32
2 / top / 1	no ⁓
2, 4 / top / 3	+
3 / top / 1	no ⁓
3, 5 / top / 3–5, 6–8, 9–11	slurs, '3'
6 / top / 1	preceded by 2-flag app.: *b♭'*
6 / top / 1–3	slurs, '3'
7, 8	*p* on first beat, *f* on second

bar / stave / note-and-rest no.	source: remark
10–13 / top	as Ex. 33
18 / top / 1	+ not tr; followed by *Nachschlag*: *b[♭]'*, *c''* (16ths)
22 / top / 16	♮
23–5 / bottom	doubled an octave higher
26 / top	as Ex. 34
27 / top / 1	1-flag app.
27 / top / 2	no tr
28 / top / 1	+
29 / top / 10	+ not tr, followed by *Nachschlag*: *c'–d'* (16ths)
31–3 / bottom	as Ex. 35
32 / top / 1	no ⁓
32, 34 / top / 3	+
33 / top / 3–5, 6–8, 9–11	slurs, '3'
37	as Ex. 36
41	as Ex. 37
42 / top / 2	no ♮
48 / top / 3	no ♮
49 / top / 2–3	no accidentals
50 / top / 9	no stroke
51–2 / top	no slurs
52 / top / 1	preceded by 1-flag app.: *b'*
57 / top / 6	no tr
59 / top / 10	+ not tr
61 / 1	'F[orte]'
61 / top / 1	+ not ⁓
61–6 / bottom	as in Ex. 32, except as noted below
61 (see Ex. 32, bar 1) / 1	F, not *f/a/c'*
62, 64 / top / 3	+
63, 65 / top / 3–5, 6–8, 9–11	'3' (not slurred)
65 (see Ex. 32, bar 5) / 1–2	neither *d* is present
66 / 1 (Ex. 32)	no *f* upstem
66 / top / 1	preceded by 2-flag app.: *b♭'*
71 / top / 1	no tr
71, 72 / top / 5	⁓
72 / top / 1–4	slur
72 / top / 3	no tr
74 / top / 1	preceded by 2-flag app.: *f'*
75, 77 / top / 5	+
79–82 / bottom	as Ex. 38
82 / top	as Ex. 39
84 / top / 1	+
84 / top / 1–3	slur (not in P 673)
85 / top / 9–10	no slur
85 / top / 10	+ not tr (not in P 673)

MUSIC EXAMPLES
Authentic Early Readings

Ex. 28: H. 48, II. 10–11

Ex. 29: H. 48, II. 17–20

Ex. 30: H. 48, II. 23–4

Ex. 31: H. 48, II. 32–5

Other Variant Readings

Ex. 32: H. 48, I. 1–6

Ex. 33: H. 48, I. 10–13

Ex. 34: H. 48, I. 26

Ex. 35: H. 48, I. 31

Ex. 36: H. 48, I. 37   **Ex. 37: H. 48, I. 41**

Ex. 38: H. 48, I. 79

Ex. 39: H. 48, I. 82

SOURCES

H. 49 survives in only three sources, of which the late autograph P 771 probably served as the direct model for the two copies; P 771 is the principal source for the present edition. Although P 771 shows a few corrections, they do not appear to have involved substantial changes to the text. Nevertheless it is unlikely that the surviving version is the original one of 1746, to judge from the catalogue numbers associated with the work and the handwriting of the autograph (see below).

P 771. Kraków, Biblioteka Jagiellońska, Mus. ms. Bach P 771. Autograph.

P 771 contains eleven sonatas of C. P. E. Bach, mostly autographs.[109] Each appears to have originally constituted a separate manuscript, and many if not all served as Bach's reference scores. The volume was removed from the Berlin Staatsbibliothek in 1941 and is thought to have reached its present location in 1946, although its whereabouts were not generally known until the 1980s.[110]

The copy of H. 49 is a holograph written on a single folded sheet (bifolio). Traces of pagination, including a probable '1' on the first page and perhaps '25' on page 3, are faintly visible. The title at the top of page 1 is: 'Sonata per il Cembalo solo. di CPEBach.' To the left are the index numbers 'No. 211. / (48.)' of which the first appears to be autograph, the second possibly not. Above the title in a foreign hand is the usual bibliographic entry, 'Th. Kat. 63,19 = Nachl. 7,48.' At the bottom left, in other hands, are the word 'autogr.' and the letter 'C'.

The wide gap between the first and second index numbers is striking in a work that the *Nachlassverzeichnis* lists as having been composed in 1746. For most keyboard works, the two index numbers diverge by no more than two or three except in the very earliest sonatas.[111] The last entry in the *Nachlassverzeichnis* for a solo keyboard work bears the number 210; it is the fantasia H. 300 (W. 67), composed in 1787. Thus it would appear that Bach at first regarded this sonata to be one of the last, perhaps the very last, of his keyboard works. It was later assigned, either by him or someone else, to the 1740s. Such a drastic change is most likely to have occurred if the autograph of H. 49 is the product of a very late and unusually thorough revision of a much earlier piece, such as Bach apparently carried out on at least one other work whose autograph is also in P 771.[112]

The score of H. 49 is a rapidly written fair copy in Bach's handwriting in its latest known form.[113] Although the characteristic shakiness is not as extreme as in some late autographs, the stems are very short, the noteheads small and point-like, the clefs minuscule. Throughout Bach uses the ornament signs described in the *Versuch*, never *t*, *tr*, or **+**. A number of slurs and dynamic markings were entered rather imprecisely, creating problems for the writers of the two copies as well as for the modern interpreter.

The autograph of H. 49 contains evidence of several corrections of detail. Among these are two corrections of entries that originally may have been a third too high (I. 36b; III. 33). These, coupled with the uncorrected error of *d'''* for *f'''* in bar 13 of the last movement, show that Bach may have been copying from a score or sketch that employed treble

---

[109] For a list of the sonatas and their movements in the order in which they now appear in the manuscript, see *CPEBE*, I/24, ed. Claudia Widgery (Oxford, 1989), p. 97. The contents and handwriting were first noted in the entries for the individual sonatas in Berg, *The Collected Works*. One sonata, H. 212 (W. 65/45), includes an alternate final movement in Bach's autograph (overlooked in the list of contents in H. J. Marx, 'Wiederaufgefundene Autographe von Carl Philipp Emanuel Bach und Johann Sebastian Bach', *Die Musikforschung*, 41 (1988), 155). Another sonata, H. 298 (W. 65/49), is present together with remnants of an early version (this one work appears under items 10, 11, and 12 in the list in *CPEBE*, I/24).

[110] See Marx, 'Wiederaufgefundene Autographe', p. 150.

[111] See Berg, 'Towards a Catalogue', pp. 282–5.

[112] On Bach's revisions in H. 298, see P. Fox, 'C. P. E. Bach's Compositional Proofreading', *The Musical Times*, 129 (1988), 653. H. 298 was assigned a high number (205) in the *Nachlassverzeichnis*, possibly because Bach himself dated it to 1786 on the first page of the autograph. No such indication appears for H. 49.

[113] The handwriting is similar in all respects to that in the autograph of the Saint Matthew Passion H. 802 (W. 235; Mus. ms. Bach P 339 in the Deutsche Staatsbibliothek, Berlin). This work is listed in the *Nachlassverzeichnis* (p. 61) as 'Die letzte Arbeit des Verfassers.'

clef in the upper stave. (In the latter instance, the note *f'''* is clearly demanded by the context and the error is easily overlooked.)

It is impossible to say whether the corrections were made during or after the initial entry of the text. Nor do any of the corrections, or the text itself, offer much evidence concerning the nature of the revisions that Bach may have carried out while making this copy. But the sonata in its present state bears a closer resemblance to some of the pieces of the Hamburg collections *für Kenner und Liebhaber* than to works dated to the 1740s. The first movement is a gigue, a type reserved for the finale in earlier works (such as H. 43), and the coda resembles the closing passages of several late symphonies, such as H. 657 (W. 182/1). Both the short Andantino and the closing polonaise with varied reprises recall movements in some of the more concise late sonatas, such as H. 291 (W. 61/6), written in 1786, although none of these closes with a dance labelled as such.

To be sure, H. 46, of which the autograph can be safely dated to 1750 or earlier, also contains a quasi-symphonic coda at the end of the first movement. Dances or dance-like final movements with variations or varied reprises do occur among the early sonatas, notably the revised versions (1744) of the sonatinas H. 8, H. 11, and H. 12 (W. 64/2, 5, and 6). Yet polonaises do not otherwise occur among Bach's dated keyboard works until the 1750s, beginning with *La Borchward* H. 79 (W. 117/17) of 1754. The rapidly changing figuration in the varied reprises here accords more with Bach's later works than with the homogeneous style of variation movements from the 1740s, such as in the Sonatina H. 11 or the Arioso with variations H. 54 (W. 118/4). The note *f'''* occurs five times in H. 49: twice in a passage in the first movement that might originally have lain an octave lower (bar 13), and three times in the varied reprises of the last movement (bars 13, 33, 34). Although the note also occurs once in H. 54 (in variation 6), it does not occur in any other sonata from the 1740s. As late as 1753, Bach appears not to have regarded *f'''* as an essential note on the keyboard, and its presence in a relatively simple, easy sonata would seem unlikely before that date.[114] Thus there is a strong possibility that H. 49 consists partly or even largely

of late material. It is likely that at least the varied reprises of the last movement are late additions.

B Bc. Brussels, Bibliothèque du Conservatoire Royal de Musique, ms. 5883. Manuscript copy by an unknown copyist, using soprano clef.

This copy, written like the autograph on a single bifolio, is similar in format and orthographic style to Michel's copies of sonatas in B Bc 5883. The title is: 'Sonata. per il Cembalo Solo. di C. Ph. E. Bach'. Beneath this appears in a foreign hand: '19e. Sonate du No. 15 de Westphal.' The number '13' is stamped at the left foot of the page.

P 369. Berlin, Deutsche Staatsbibliothek, Mus. ms. Bach P 369. Manuscript copy by an unidentified copyist, in oblong format, using soprano clef.

The copy of H. 49 begins on the fourth system of page 76, immediately following the conclusion of the symphony arrangement H. 45 (W. 122/1). The title is given as 'Sonata 20.' This is followed by a light entry ('Nachl. Verz. 48'?) and a darker one ('[Wotquenne 65,19]') in two different hands. The copy contains a convenient page turn at the end of the first movement, and concludes on the second system of page 79, followed immediately by H. 60 (W. 65/24). The copy is less accurate than the one in B Bc and contains at least one correction possibly in a foreign hand.

Establishing the text
Both copies (B Bc and P 369) are fairly accurate, the chief variants involving misplaced slurs and accidentals. The copyists misunderstood Bach's notation in bars 28 and 30 of the slow movement, where his tie is easily misread. Several further common errors make it clear that B Bc and P 369 stem from P 771.

The orthographic variants in B Bc and P 369 in bar 9 of the slow movement suggest that the copies—at least P 369—could have been made before Bach had entered all of the corrections in P 771. One or two slurs missing in P 369 might also have been late additions to the autograph.

---

[114] In the first volume of the *Versuch*, Bach recommends a clavichord whose compass extends *wenigstens von dem grossen C bis ins e''''*. See *Versuch*, I, p. 9 (Einleitung, 12); Mitchell, p. 36.

LIST OF VARIANT READINGS

bar / stave / note-and-rest no.	source: remark
First Movement	
1 / top / 2–3	B Bc: slur on 2–3 not 2–4; a possible reading of P 771. Also in Westphal's catalogue (B Br II 4104), but the *Nachlassverzeichnis* gives slur on 2–4
10 / top	B Bc, P 369: *p* beneath 5
13 / top / 1–4	all sources orig. a third too low, correct letter-names added lightly above notes (foreign hand?) in P 369
24 / top	all sources: extent of slur unclear; possibly on 1 to 3
34 / top / 3	P 771: ♮ inserted
36b / top / 5–6	P 771: orig. *g'–e'*, erased and overwritten
Second Movement	
9 / top / 2–3	B Bc, P 369: slur on 2–3 not 2–4
9 / bottom, downstem / 1–2	B Bc, P 369: upward stems / P 369: double stem on 2
	P 771: erasures above these notes; orig. upward stems?
9–10 / bottom, upstem	P 369: no tie
18 / bottom / 2–4	all sources: slur thus
23 / top / 1–4	P 369: slur on 1–4 not 2–4; possible reading of P 771
28, 30 / top, downstem / 2–3	B Bc, P 369: ties misunderstood as slurs
38 / bottom / 2–3	P 771: erasures above these notes, orig. reading unclear (*d♭–e♮*?)
Third Movement	
8 / top / 6	B Bc: ∿ not ∿∿
12 / 3	P 771: '1' (fingering) very small. Probably misunderstood as stroke in B Bc; om. (?) in P 369
13 / top / 9	all sources: *d'''*
16 / top / 6	B Bc, P 369: ∿ not ∿∿
29 / top / 3	all sources: preceded by ♭
33 / top / last 4	P 771: erasures. Orig. a third higher? Orn. sign unclear; might be ∿∿ as in B Bc. *CPEBE* = P 369

Sonata in Bb major, H. 51

SOURCES

H. 51 was composed in 1747 and was revised at least twice. While the revisions involved no variation on the scale seen in H. 43, they involved the entry of a greater number of performance indications than in any other work edited in this volume. Although H. 51 appeared in two printed editions within fifteen years after Bach's death, these were based on a corrupt transmission of the earliest known version, as was the later nineteenth-century edition in *Le Trésor des pianistes*.

The sources fall into three distinct groups: 1. manuscripts by Bach's copyists, all bearing probably autograph entries (P 775, B Bc, and P 359); 2. several copies of an early version (P 368, D Mbs, and D KIl ms. Mb 52/5); and 3. the two prints (RL, KN) and several related but independent manuscript copies (D KIl mss. Mb 52/6 and 52/7, GOl, and AmB 54). Most of the revised readings occur only in the first group, the text of which will be referred to in the following as the 'late' or 'later' version, as opposed to the 'earlier' versions presented by the other groups of sources.

Because of the great number of variants, especially those involving ornaments and other signs absent from groups 2 and 3, the List of Variant Readings is divided into two sections. Section A lists, in condensed form, readings common to all eight sources of groups 2 and 3. These readings are likely to belong to an authentic early version of the work. Section B lists other readings as well as autograph entries in the sources of group 1.

Group 1: Sources of the later version

P 775. Berlin, Staatsbibliothek Preußischer Kulturbesitz, Musikabteilung, Mus. ms. Bach P 775. Manuscript copied by Michel, with autograph entries.[115]

The copy of H. 51 occupies pages 73–80 of P 775. There is no title page; traces of earlier pagination are visible on pages 3 and 7. All eight pages (two sheets, 33 × 21 cm., no watermark) are ruled in seven systems and, because of the length of the piece, are written unusually densely. The original title at the top of page 1 is: 'Sonata per il Cembalo.

solo da. C. P. E. Bach.' To the left are these index entries, the upper one possibly autograph: 'No. 49. / (49.)'. Added later in other hands are several bibliographic entries: 'Nr. 10', 'Th. Kat. 61,30=63,20 (Allegro assai) (Nachl. 7,49)', '[Wotquenne 65,20]'. The second catalogue entry is in two different hands; the portion beginning at the equal sign was added by someone who noticed that the first catalogue entry incorrectly referred to the early, printed version, not the late, manuscript version of the sonata. The two versions have different tempo marks in the opening movement and are listed separately in Westphal's catalogue.[116] At the bottom of the page are the usual 'C' and the faulty entry 'Von Hering geschrieben', in unidentified hands.

Although the copy in P 775 appears to have been the second surviving copy of the work prepared under Bach's oversight after P 359, it nevertheless contains a large number of added entries of accidentals and dynamic indications. Also autograph is the tempo marking (Allegro assai) for the first movement; there is no trace of the earlier tempo (Moderato) found in the sources of groups 2 and 3. The List of Variant Readings notes only those entries whose autograph character is clear.

B Bc. Brussels, Bibliothèque du Conservatoire Royal de Musique, ms. 5883. Manuscript copied by Michel, with at least one autograph entry.

The copy of H. 51 consists of ten unnumbered pages; music appears on the first nine, which are ruled in seven systems each. The title is the same as in P 775. Though following almost exactly the same layout as P 775 through the first movement and a half, Michel adopted a more spacious layout for the remainder of the piece, at the expense of an extra leaf.

Added beneath the title is the indication: '20e. Sonate de no. 15 de Westphal'. The shelf mark 'U, no 5883' (underlined) falls at the left beneath the first system. As in P 775, the tempo mark of the first movement is autograph; just above and to the left of it is a shape that might have been Bach's scrawled 'NB'. At the bottom left of the page is the

---

[115] Facsimile in Berg, ed., *The Collected Works*, III, p. 31.

[116] On the catalogues, see note 6.

large number '18' and at the right a faint inscription 'Ms Michel'.

For the most part, B Bc includes as original entries those readings that were inserted into P 775. Although a few dynamic signs and accidentals appear to have been insertions here as well, it is impossible to determine with certainty whether any of them are autograph. They are perhaps more likely not to be, since the text contains a small number of minor discrepancies as against P 775.

P 359. Berlin, Staatsbibliothek Preußischer Kulturbesitz, Musikabteilung, Mus. ms. Bach P 359. Manuscript by an unknown copyist with probably autograph corrections.

This copy appears to have served as the model for the copy in P 775. It is by an unidentified copyist from the group designated Su III.[117] It occupies pages 29–36; there is no title page.

The title is the same as in P 775. Beneath the attribution, in a foreign hand, is the date 'Berlin, 1747'. Lightly written to the left of the title is the number '49', which corresponds with both of the index entries in P 775. But in P 359 the number is certainly not autograph; it might have been entered during the inventory of P 359 (see under H. 43).

Still, the copy does appear to have been corrected by Bach. Many signs entered here as corrections or interpolations appear in the original text of P 775. The dynamic marking *f* (possibly *p* as well) takes two different forms, one of them recognizable as Bach's. It is also likely that two bars entered in the margins (I. 66, III. 27) after being omitted by the copyist are partly or entirely autograph. Turns also appear in two forms, of which the horizontal ones may be autograph additions.

Group 2: Manuscripts of an earlier version

P 368. Berlin, Staatsbibliothek Preußischer Kulturbesitz, Musikabteilung, Mus. ms. Bach P 368. Manuscript copy of the first movement, by a copyist said to be Homilius.

H. 51 occupies pages 146–52 (33 × 21 cm., watermark: crowned coat of arms) in a section of P 368 showing a hand identified as that of Homilius. The first page, which bears no original title, is the reverse of the last page of a copy of a fugue by

W. F. Bach (F. 33). Page 153 is blank, and is followed by the Arioso with variations H. 54 (W. 118/4). There is no indication as to why the copyist omitted the last two movements.

At the top right of the first page the title 'Sonate von C. P. E. Bach' appears in a foreign hand, probably the same one that added just below this 'Nachl. Verz. 7,49'. Added in another hand at the centre is '[Wotquenne 65,20]'.

The copy is careless and contains a number of implausible variants. Nevertheless, together with the other sources of group 2 it preserves many indubitably authentic early readings.

D Mbs. Munich, Bayerische Staatsbibliothek, Mus. ms. 1794. Manuscript by an unknown copyist.

H. 51 is the first of the three separate works making up D Mbs 1794. It is in the same hand as the third manuscript (a copy of H. 39), and occupies pages 1–16, the first of which is the title page. Each leaf is numbered (in a foreign hand?) in the upper right corner of the recto.

The title page reads: 'Sonata / per il / Cembalo solo. / del / Sigl. C. F. E. Bach.' Above is a library stamp reading 'BIBLIOTHECA / REGIA / MONACENSIS', and beneath this the more modern stamp 'Bayerische Staatsbibliothek / Musiksammlung'. At the bottom centre is a handwritten entry '80 = A'.

The text is a generally accurate copy of the same version found in P 368. The copyist occasionally breaks a dotted eighth rest into an eighth and a sixteenth rest, and tends to add slurs between an appoggiatura and the following note. A few slurs are added lightly, probably in a later hand; none correspond with readings in other sources.

52/5. Kiel, Schleswig-Holsteinische Landesbibliothek, Mb 52/5. Manuscript by an unknown copyist, in oblong format.

This is the first of the three copies of H. 51 found in manuscript 52, occupying pages 33–46. Page 35 is the original title page; the previous leaf, pages 33–4, appears to have served as a cover and bears a title in (probably) the same hand seen on the title page and in the text. The latter resembles the copies by E. L. Gerber that are now in Kiel (Mb 53/1–2; see under H. 47), but differs in the shape of the quarter rest and in the inclusion of *custodes* at the end of most lines. The same hand appears in the

---

[117] Kast, p. 25. The writer of H. 51, there designated 'Su III (1)', is distinct from the writers 'Su III' and 'Su III (2)' also represented in P 359, and also from the copyist of H. 40 in P 365 and P 414.

Kiel copy Mb 52/10 of H. 143, composed in 1759.

The original entries on the cover are: 'No: 12. / SONATA / per il / Cembalo Solo / dal Sigl. C. F. E. Bach. / C B. lvii.' Several further entries in later hands are added at different locations on the page: 'gedruckt', '(49)', 'Dubl.', 'W. 65,20', 'Gedruckt von Rellstab.'

The original title on page 35 reads: 'Sonata / per il / Cembalo Solo / dell Sigl. C. F. E. Bach.' Added beneath are remarks probably by Erich Prieger: 'Comp. 1747 zu Berlin (Nachlass-Verz. S. 7, Nr 49 der Clavier-Solis). / Ungedruckt [? crossed out]. 1886: E. P.'

The text is very close to that of D Mbs, but lacks the occasional slurs added there. Despite the entry on the cover, the text is independent of that in the print by Rellstab (see under RL below).

Group 3: Manuscripts and prints of an early version

52/6. Kiel, Schleswig-Holsteinische Landesbibliothek, Mb 52/6. Manuscript by an unknown copyist, in oblong format, in soprano clef.

The second copy of H. 51 in manuscript 52 occupies pages 51–62. Preceding it is a page, evidently part of a cover, bearing a label from the eighteenth or perhaps early nineteenth century with the following generic title: 'Eine / Clavier-Sonate / von / Carl Phil. Em. Bach'. Similar covers precede the copies of H. 21 (D KIl 52/1) and H. 46 (D KIl 52/4), but, unlike the cover for H. 46, this one bears no indication that it originally belonged with the following copy. It does, however, bear added identifying remarks in different hands: 'Dublette', 'B', 'N. 49', 'Comp. 1747', 'gedr. Rellstab . . . [illegible] 1791 / Rieter-Biederman [*sic*]. . . [illegible].'

The original title page is numbered 50 but evidently should read 51. Original entries read: 'Sonata / per il / Clavicembalo / del Sigr. / C. P. E. Bach.' Added beneath this are two sets of remarks, both in the same hand that added annotations in H. 46, but distinct from the 'E. P.' of D KIl 52/5. In ink are the following comments:[118] 'verglichen Okt 99 mit Berliner Ms: P 359 (meist korrekt; wohl späteste Form). / P 368 (hat nur Satz 1); frühe Form, den vor- / liegenden Ms meist entsprechend, mit wenig Verzierungen u[nd] Vortragszeichen / Druck von Hoffmeister, Co . . .'. The last entry continues with some remarks that are much lighter and mostly illegible.

In the upper corners of the pages are older numbers giving the verso pagination 36–47, possibly part of the same series as that found in the copy of H. 46. The text itself bears numerous indications of variants in the hand of Erich Prieger, who also added many ornaments and slurs in ink from P 359; pencil annotations note the source of some of the entries as well as variants in P 368 and the print by Hoffmeister. In many cases it is difficult to distinguish the original from the added entries, although the added ornament signs are given in distinctive forms. In the List of Variant Readings only original readings are noted.

The original text is very faulty but clearly belongs to a tradition distinct from that of 52/5. A number of errors (for example, I. 73 and 117) arose as a result of transferring the upper stave from treble to soprano clef, which is found only in this copy among the manuscript sources.

52/7. Kiel, Schleswig-Holsteinische Landesbibliothek, ms. Mb 52/7. Manuscript by an unknown copyist, in oblong format.

The third copy of H. 51 in ms. Mb 52 in the Schleswig-Holsteinische Landesbibliothek occupies pages 63–9 and is by a third unidentified copyist. There is no title page; the heading at the top centre of page 1 is simply 'Sonata' followed by the attribution 'Del Sigr. C. P. E. Bach.' to the right.

The text, which is independent of that in the two other Kiel copies, appears to be a conscientious copy of a defective exemplar, possibly the same one used by the scribe of the copy in the Amalienbibliothek (see AmB 54 below). There are a few light entries in one or more later hands, including several fingerings.

AmB 54. Berlin, Staatsbibliothek Preußischer Kulturbesitz, Amalienbibliothek Ms. 54. Collection of keyboard works by J. S. and C. P. E. Bach, in the hand designated J. S. Bach I of the Amalienbibliothek (= Anon. 401).[119]

This *Sammelband* contains seven organ works of J. S. Bach in addition to H. 51. These originally

---

[118] Entries of this type, provisionally identified as having been made by Heinrich Schenker (Horn, *Carl Philipp Emanuel Bach: Frühe Klaviersonaten*, p. 151), are more likely by Scheibler (see note above on source D KIl of H. 40 and source D KIl of H. 46).

comprised three separate manuscripts, each entered in the fine calligraphic hand known as J. S. Bach I, which occurs in many other copies in the Amalienbibliothek. The paper has been dated to the period 1775–1808.[120] The copy of H. 51 was originally the second of three separate component manuscripts; the first contains BWV 572, while the third contains BWV 545–8, 583, and 544. Each of these has its own title page; there is no running pagination for the whole volume. Since AmB 54 was not included in the portion of Johann Philipp Kirnberger's estate willed to the Amalienbibliothek,[121] it presumably was prepared expressly for the Princess Anna Amalia (1723–87). She willed her library to the Joachimsthal Gymnasium, from which it passed to the Prussian Royal Library and its successors.

The source contains twelve pages; the first (unnumbered) is a title page and page 12 (unnumbered) is blank. The title page reads: 'SONATA / per il / Cembalo / dal Sig.re. / Carl: Philipp: Eman: Bach.' Added beneath is the entry 'Wotquenne 65 Nr 20'. The title 'Sonata' and the attribution are repeated at the head of page 2.

Although Bach was titular Capellmeister to Princess Amalia from 1768, the text is unlikely to have been obtained from him. AmB 54 contains no entries in a foreign hand, but it appears to be a copy of a text that has been edited, perhaps by Kirnberger, curator of the Princess's collection. Despite the presence of some slurs and dynamics missing in 52/7 and perhaps supplied here by the editor, the underlying text of the two manuscripts is very similar. Among other probable emendations in AmB 54 are added rests (I. 6 and 8), and readings at two points where the common model for the sources of group 3 was either corrupt or illegible (see below). But the copy is not without its own errors of omission, notably of the chord in bar 70 of the first movement.

D GOl. Gotha, Forschungs- und Landesbibliothek, Mus. 2° 21a/3 (67). Copy of H. 51 by Christoph Ernst Abraham Albrecht von Boineburg.

Boineburg's copy consists of twelve pages (three sheets, 34.5 × 20 cm.; paper from the Weilar mill of Johann Joachim Illig; watermark: unicorn; countermark: crowned monogram). The title page (p. 1) reads: '67 / Sonata / di C F. E. Bach.'; the music (p. 2) is headed 'Sonate I di C. F. E. Bach.' The copy is careless, omitting III. 23–4 and portions of III. 71–2; the text is closely related to but independent of that of the Rellstab print.[122]

RL. *OEUVRES POSTHUMES de C. P. E. Bach.* Print from moveable type of three sonatas by C. P. E. Bach, published by Rellstab (Berlin, c.1792). Issued both with soprano and with treble clef in the upper stave.

This print containing H. 51 by the Berlin publisher Johann Carl Friedrich Rellstab (1759–1813) was listed in the Wotquenne catalogue as W. 266. The print was consulted in the exemplar in Brussels, Bibliothèque Royale Albert I (Fétis R. P. 2.970c), which employs treble clef. The title page reads: 'OEUVRES POSTHUMES / de / C. P. E. Bach. / Trois Sonates / pour le / Clavecin ou Pianoforte. / On peut avoir ces Sonates dans la clef de sol & celle d'Ut. / Prix 20 Gr. Op. CXXV. 8 Feuilles. / A BERLIN, / de l'Imprimerie & dans le Magazin de Musique de RELLSTAB.' Added at the bottom of the Brussels exemplar in Westphal's hand is the date '(1792)', which agrees with the entry for the print in his catalogue (B Br II 4104, fo. 32.v). The latter notes the absence of 'Veränderungen' and 'Manieren' in the print and refers to a review in the 'Hamburger Corr[espondent] 1792 No. 90'.[123]

The Rellstab print contains the sonatas H. 121 (W. 65/31), H. 51, and H. 21 (W. 65/11). In a short untitled preface signed 'J. C. F. Rellstab', the pub-

---

[119] On the identity of J. S. Bach I and Anon. 401, see E. R. Wutta, *Quellen der Bach-Tradition in der Berliner Amalien-Bibliothek* (Tutzing, 1989), p. 14, note 16. Wutta, p. 13, tentatively identifies the copyist with one 'Kühn' mentioned by Princess Anna Amalie in an undated note to Kirnberger.

[120] *J. S. Bach: Neue Ausgabe sämtlicher Werke*, IV/5–6, *Kritischer Bericht* by D. Kilian, Teilband 1 (Kassel, 1978), p. 107.

[121] Items from Kirnberger's estate are listed in Wutta, *Quellen der Bach-Tradition*, pp. 21–35.

[122] The description of D GOl was supplied by Ulrich Leisinger; its readings could not be incorporated in the list of variant readings. An additional manuscript source containing H. 51, possibly from mid-eighteenth-century Dresden, was illustrated in a Sotheby's auction catalogue of 23 May 1993 (information from U. Leisinger).

[123] Rellstab's print is dated 'wohl 1791, jedenfalls aber vor dem 2.7.1792' in *Bach-Dokumente, III: Dokumente zum Nachwirken Johann Sebastian Bachs*, ed. H.-J. Schulze (Kassel, 1972), p. 488. For the text of the review, see Ernst Suchalla, ed., *Carl Philipp Emanuel Bach im Spiegel seiner Zeit: Die Dokumentensammlung Johann Jacob Heinrich Westphals* (Hildesheim, 1993), p. 192.

lisher complains of having suffered a substantial loss through his previous issues of the 'Reprisen-Sonaten' (W. 50, 51, and 52) and of the organ works (W. 70). He also mentions possessing 'nearly everything left behind by the great man that is not yet printed.'[124] But the text of H. 51 cannot have stemmed from Bach's estate in the literal sense, since it belongs to the same corrupt line as the other sources of group 3. The text has been edited with some care, but the reading for bar 7 of the first movement is clearly arbitrary, and there are several obvious mistakes. More plausible but still arbitrary are a number of ornament signs (I. 35 and parallel passages; II. 13–14) and the unique dynamic marking *mf* at bar 64 of the opening movement. The authority of the Rellstab edition is further reduced by the slighting reference to the 'liberties taken by publishers, especially Rellstab' ('die Freyheiten, die sich Buchhändler, insonderheit Rellstab, nehmen') in a letter of Bach's widow Joanna Maria to J. J. H. Westphal.[125]

KN. *GRANDE SONATE / pour le Clavecin.* Engraved print of H. 51, published by 'Hoffmeister' (Leipzig: Chez A. Kühnel, Bureau de Musique, *c.*1802).

The 'Hoffmeister' print mentioned by Westphal (see above) was seen here in an exemplar in Munich, Bayerische Staatsbibliothek, bearing the imprint of Ambrosius Kühnel (1770–1813) and the Leipzig 'Bureau de Musique'. It is listed as item 268 in the Wotquenne catalogue. Between 1801 and 1805 Kühnel issued a number of items jointly with the Viennese publisher and composer Franz Anton Hoffmeister (1754–1812); 'Bureau de Musique' was the name adopted for the joint venture. Westphal appears to have added his entry for this print after the completion of the final version of his catalogue; he assigns it the date 1802.[126]

The title page reads: 'GRANDE SONATE / pour le Clavecin, ou Fortepiano / composée par / C. P. E. BACH. / Oeuvres posthumes / No. I / à Leipzig chez A. Kühnel. / (Bureau de Musique) / Prix 16. gg.'

The title page and each page of music bear the plate number 126.

The letter copy-books of the publishing house indicate that the text of the edition was obtained from the organist Christian Friedrich Gottlieb Schwenke (1767–1822), who had succeeded Bach in his Hamburg church position. Schwenke's text belongs to the same tradition as RL and may well have been derived from the latter. Like his edition of *Das wohltemperirte Clavier*, it appears to have been carried out without the benefit of the superior text that presumably could have been obtained from Bach's heirs, implying a lack of communication between the publisher and the composer's family.[127] A letter from Hoffmeister & Kühnel to Schwenke reports the engraving of the sonata but complains of mistakes in it: 'The sonata of Emanuel Bach received from you is engraved and will soon follow.... There were many errors in the sonata.'[128] The implication is that Schwenke had supplied a poor text, and indeed the edition is inaccurate.

Wedge-shaped dynamic indications are only the most obvious of the arbitrary emendations of the text, which are independent of those in Rellstab's print. Although Forkel's editions of keyboard works by J. S. Bach were published by Kühnel and Hoffmeister during the same period, there is nothing in the print of H. 51 to suggest that Forkel had anything to do with it. Indeed, Forkel complained to the publishing house of having been charged for an exemplar of the print, stating that he had owned the work for over twenty-five years ('ich sie schon seit länger als 25 Jahren besitze').[129] Forkel must

---

[124] '*fast alle noch ungedruckte Sachen aus dem Nachlass des grossen Mannes*'.

[125] The letter was actually written by Bach's daughter Anna Carolina Philippina. See letter No. 3 (8 Feb. 1791) in M. H. Schmid, 'Das Geschäft mit dem Nachlass von C. Ph. E. Bach', *Carl Philipp Emanuel Bach und die europäische Musikkultur des mittleren 18. Jahrhunderts*, Veröffentlichungen der Joachim Jungius-Gesellschaft der Wissenschaften, 62 (Göttingen, 1990), p. 490.

[126] Until 1806 the names of both publishers appear in title pages; afterwards Kühnel pasted over his former partner's name on existing exemplars or altered the plate for reprintings, generally without changing the musical text. See R. S. Hill, 'The Plate Numbers of C. F. Peters' Predecessors', *Papers Read by Members of the American Musicological Society at the Annual Meeting, Washington, D.C., December 29th and 30th, 1938* (N. p., 1940), pp. 117, 123. No signs of alteration were visible on the exemplar seen here, which was presumably printed between 1806 and 1814, when C. F. Peters acquired the firm.

[127] On Schwenke's edition of the Well-Tempered Clavier (Berlin, 1801 or 1802), see *J. S. Bach: Neue Ausgabe sämtliche Werke*, V/6.1, *Kritischer Bericht* by A. Dürr (Kassel, 1989), pp. 181–2.

[128] 'Em [*sic*] Bachs Sonate von Ihnen ist graviert und folgt nächstens.... In der Sonate waren viel Fehler.' Letter of 4 August 1802, quoted in Stauffer, ed., *The Forkel–Hoffmeister & Kühnel Correspondence*, p. 112, note 121.

have known the work in a lost manuscript copy; nothing is known about the latter.

The Kühnel print appears to have been an important source for the edition in *Le Trésor des pianistes*, which took from it the distinctive readings for I. 7 and the wedge-shaped dynamic marks at I. 55 and 57–8. This is so despite the fact that the title page of the 1863 installment of *Le Trésor des pianistes* containing H. 51 mentions only the Rellstab edition as a source. While some readings were indeed taken from the Rellstab print, no reference at all seems to have been made to the much better text in B Bc, even though the Brussels sources presumably furnished the text for many other sonatas edited in *Le Trésor des pianistes*.

Establishing the text
The music of H. 51 is in several respects extraordinary even within Bach's varied and imaginative output. This, together with what was probably a hastily written and not entirely legible autograph of the original version, helps explain many of the variants in the copies as well as the later addition of a large number of performance markings. Several passages in the first two movements involve many small note-values that are easily misread and which do not always fill the beat in a numerically correct manner. Especially in the slow movement, the long bars required the addition of many cautionary accidentals in order to make Bach's intentions clear. Even so, several accidentals that today would be regarded as essential do not appear, and the correct reading remains somewhat doubtful at one point (II. 27, upper part, note 13). In addition, small inconsistencies between parallel passages are evident in both other movements. These have been left to stand as they appear in the sources of group 1, except for the dynamic markings in bars 42–3 of the first movement.

The three sources of group 1 contain evidence of at least two distinct layers of revisions. These

involved additions not only of an unusually large number of ornament signs, but also of most of the dynamic indications present in the later versions. The tempo markings in the outer movements also were altered. The two stages of revision are represented by the readings of P 359 *post correcturam* and P 775 *post correcturam*, respectively. Many of the alterations might have been entered only during Bach's proofreading of the later copy P 775 against the earlier copy P 359, since some readings appear as additions to both copies. But whether P 775 was originally copied from P 359 or from the (lost) autograph cannot be determined with certainty. Similarities in layout suggest that Michel at least consulted P 359 in making the copy in P 775.

B Bc bears a relationship to P 775 similar to that of P 775 to P 359. A number of readings in B Bc cannot be traced to P 775 and could stem from either P 359 or the autograph.

Many variants in orthography indicate that neither group 2 nor group 3 stems directly from the same model as group 1. Moreover, groups 2 and 3 probably preserve a version predating P 359 *ante correcturam*, although the ornaments and other signs lacking in groups 2 and 3 could all conceivably have been originally absent from P 359 as well, and subsequently inserted there without leaving visible traces. Yet there are indications that all sources ultimately stem from the same lost autograph, one that contained a page-turn before bar 66 of the first movement (see List of Variant Readings). A page-turn at that point would not be inconsistent with the layout of the surviving autograph of H. 46 (P 1131), whose first page ends after bar 64.

The sources of group 3 are characterized above all by confused, absent, or arbitrary readings at two points: I. 7 and II. 3. Such readings could reflect illegibility or lack of clarity in Bach's autograph. Whether group 2 and group 3 represent two distinct early versions or merely different lines of transmission cannot be completely settled, but the latter seems more likely. Most of the characteristic readings of both groups seem to be the products of carelessness or misunderstanding.

[129] Letter of 12 November 1802; No. 22 in Stauffer, ed., *The Forkel–Hoffmeister & Kühnel Correspondence*, p. 60. The price quoted (16 silver groschen) agrees with that on the title page of KN.

LIST OF VARIANT READINGS

A. Variant readings common to all sources of groups 2 and 3

Note: these readings occur in D Mbs, 52/5, 52/6, 52/7, AmB 54, RL, KN, and P 368 (first movement only). Bar numbers in bold indicate that the reading recurs or is corrected in other sources (see section B below).

movement / bar	source: remark
I. 99; II. 14, 21	no tr
I. 6, 8, 20, 40, 41, 44, 74; III. **64**, 84, 87	no ⌇
I. 2, 3, 24, 26, 28, 31, 46, 47, 72, 76, 86, 89, 90, 91, 100, 102, 106, 109, **113**, 118, 119; II. 20, 25; III. 4, 8, 36, 52, 58, 91, 95	no ⌇
I. 21	no ⌇
II. 7, **25**	no app.
III. 17, 19, 55	1-flag app.
I. 4, **48**, 92,; II. 1, **11, 20**, 24 (both); III. **34, 93, 97**	no *Anschlag*
I. 36, 56, 58, 59 (all), 84, 114; II. 8; III. **2**, 34, 44 (both), 48 (both), 57, 65, **83, 93**	no slur
I. 44; II. 28 (both); III. 20, 22, 24–8, 42–4, 46–51, 59, 61, 71–2, **74**, 79–80, 82, 99, 101, 103–7, 111a	no stroke
II. 4 (both), 15	no fingering
I. 2, 6, 10, 13, 21, **24, 26**, 58 (bottom, both), 65–6 (all), 69–70 (all), 72 (bottom); II. **11, 28, 29**; III. 54, 97, 99	no dyn.
I. 22 (on *b'*), 53 (on *c''*), 104 (on *f*); II. 4 (on *b*, top), 27 (both flats)	no cautionary accidental
I. **1**	tempo mark: Moderato
I. 50 (inner voice), 57 (8th-rest, inner voice)	no rest
II. 20	no '3'
III. **1**	tempo mark: Allegretto
III. **4** / bottom, upstem / 1	no *c'*
III. **36** / bottom, upstem / 1	no *g'*
III. **38** / inner voice / 1–2	*d''–d''* (no accidentals)
III. 80, 81	♮ in these sources only

B. Additional readings

bar / stave / note-and-rest no.	source: remark

First Movement

1	P 359: no tempo mark
	P 775, B Bc: 'Allegro assai' is autograph
—	52/6, 52/7: time signature: ¢
1 / top, upstem / 1	52/7, AmB 54, KN: tr not ⌇
6 / bottom, upstem / 2	P 359: ⌇
6, 8 / bottom, downstem	AmB 54: half rest in second half of bar
7	RL: as Ex. 40a; KN: as Ex. 40b; remaining sources as Ex. 40c (=*CPEBE*) except as noted below

Ex. 40

7 / top, upstem / 1	P 368, 52/5: dotted half (!)
7 / bottom	52/6, 52/7: lower stave blank
7 / bottom / 1	AmB 54: bass: *G* not *B♭*
7, 9 / top, upstem / 2	B Bc, 52/7, AmB 54, RL, KN: no ⌇
8 / bottom, upstem / 1	52/6, 52/7, AmB 54, RL, KN: 64th
8 / bottom, upstem / 2–5	P 775, B Bc, P 359: 32nds (beamed with note 1); *CPEBE* = P 368, D Mbs, 52/5; cf. bar 6
8 / bottom, upstem / 6–8	P 368, D Mbs, 52/5: *d'–c–b♭*
8 / bottom / 7	52/6, 52/7, AmB 54, RL, KN: 64th
13	B Bc: *f* on downbeat
	P 359: *f* is an autograph addition (or retraced)

bar / stave / note-and-rest no.	source: remark	bar / stave / note-and-rest no.	source: remark
13 / top / 11	♮ only in KN	42 / top	P 775, B Bc, P 359, P 368, D Mbs, 52/5, KN: *p* beneath 5, but cf. bar 120
13 / bottom / 8	P 359, 52/6 (?): ♮ inserted; foreign hand?		
18 / top	P 368, D Mbs, 52/5: no tr	42 / bottom, upstem / 1(–2)	P 368: ♮ (!)
19	52/6 (?), 52/7, AmB 54, RL, KN: no *p*	43 / top	P 775, B Bc, KN: *f* beneath 2, but cf. bar 121
19 / top / 7	RL: ♭ not ♮ / P 775: ♭ altered to ♮	47 / top / last	52/6, 52/7, AmB 54, RL, KN: *c*'' not *b*♭'
21 / top / 1	52/6, 52/7, AmB 54, RL, KN: *d*', with ♮	48 / top / 1–2	P 359: *Anschlag* inserted
21 / bottom, downstem / last	P 368, D Mbs, 52/5, 52/6, 52/7, RL, KN: no rest	50	P 368, 52/5: *p* on downbeat
24	P 775: *p* an autograph addition	50, 51 / bottom / 3	P 775, B Bc, P 359: accidental repeated
24 / top / 2 (and 3)	P 368, D Mbs, 52/5: *d*♭''' not *d*'''	52 / top, downstem / 1	P 359, D Mbs, 52/5, KN: ♯ repeated (not a new line) / P 775, B Bc: erasure; orig. illegible / 52/6, 52/7, AmB 54, RL: ♮
25 / top / 8	P 368: *e*'' not *c*''		
25 / top / 11	P 775, B Bc: ♮ on 11 not 12; cf. following variant	53 / top, downstem / 6	P 359: no ♮ / P 775, B Bc: ♮ inserted, possibly autograph
25 / top / 12	P 359: ♮ inserted before stem of previous note	55	KN: crescendo wedge through bar
26	P 359: *f* an autograph addition	56 / 2	*f* beneath lower stave in all sources (probably for lack of space between staves)
28 / top / 1	D Mbs, 52/5, 52/6, 52/7, AmB 54: no ♮ / P 359: ♮ inserted		
30 / top / 1	52/6, 52/7, AmB 54, RL, KN: tr not ≈ / P 368, 52/5: ⁓ / D Mbs: ⁓	57 / top / 3	P 368, D Mbs, 52/6, 52/7, AmB 54, RL, KN: one rest only
35 / top / 8	P 368, Mbs, 52/5, 52/6, 52/7, AmB 54, KN: no ≈ / RL: ⁓	58 / top, upstem / 4	P 368, D Mbs, 52/5, 52/6, 52/7, AmB 54, RL: no ♮
36 / top / 1–2	P 368, D Mbs, 52/5: ∞ on 1 not between 1 and 2 / 52/6, 52/7, AmB 54, RL, KN: no orn.	64	52/6, 52/7, AmB 54: no *p*
		64 / top / 2	RL: 8th rest, 16th rest; *mf* under latter
36 / top / 5	P 368: + not tr	65–6, 69–76, 72	P 775, P 359: dyns. all or mostly autograph
37 / top / 6–7	P 359: crossed-out slur (?) above notes; similar sign in the copy of H. 48 in the Brussels Conservatoire	66	P 359: this bar orig. om., entered in top margin (probably autograph)
38 / top / 7	P 775, B Bc, P 359: ♯ inserted above and to right of notehead, as though referring to 8	66 / top / 1	P 775, B Bc, P 368, D Mbs, 52/5, 52/6 (?): ♭ repeated, not new line
39 / bottom	P 368: bass om.	66 / bottom / 2–8	P 775: erasures, autograph entry; orig. reading illegible
40 / top / 2	B Bc: ∞ or ≈; upper sign unclear	67, 71	KN: crescendo wedge through bar

bar / stave / note-and-rest no.	source: remark
68 / top / 2	P 368, D Mbs, 52/5, 52/6: no tr
68 / bottom / 2	P 368, D Mbs, 52/5, 52/6, 52/7, AmB 54, RL: no dyns.
	KN: *fp* beneath 2
70 / top / 1	AmB 54: no chord
73 / top / 5	52/6: *g''* not *bb''*
76 / top / 1	P 775, B Bc, P 359, D Mbs, 52/6: ♭ repeated; new line
77, 78 / top / 1	52/6, 52/7, AmB 54, AmB 54, KN: tr not ⚬
79 / top / 2	P 368, D Mbs, 52/5, 52/6, 52/7, AmB 54, KN: no ≋
	RL: ⚬
83 / top / 8	P 368, D Mbs, 52/5, 52/6, 52/7, AmB 54, KN: no ≋
	RL: ⚬
84 / top / 1–2	P 368, D Mbs, 52/5, 52/7, AmB 54, RL, KN: ∞ on 1 not between 2 and 3
	52/6: no orn.
88 / top / 16	♭ only in D Mbs
89 / top / 1	B Bc, P 359 (?): 2-flag app.
94, 95 / bottom, downstem / 2–4	P 359: erasure; orig. a third higher
100 / top / 5	♭ only in KN
100 / bottom / 1	52/6, RL, KN: *f/a/c'* 52/7, AmB 54: *a/c'*, no *f*
103 / top / 2	P 775, B Bc, P 359: ♮ on 2 not 3
103 / top / 8	P 368: *a'* not *f'*
103 / bottom, upstem / 1 (*f♯*)	P 359: orig. *g(♯)*? notehead enlarged
106 / top / 1	P 359, D Mbs, 52/5, 52/6, 52/7, AmB 54, RL: no ♭
	P 775, B Bc: ♭ inserted, possibly autograph
106 / bottom / 5	♮ only in KN
108 / top / 1	P 368, D Mbs, 52/5: ⚬ not tr 52/6, 52/7, AmB 54, RL, KN: no orn.
110–13 / bottom	P 359, D Mbs, 52/5, RL: all notes separately stemmed
112 / top / 1	P 368, 52/7, AmB 54, RL: preceded by

bar / stave / note-and-rest no.	source: remark
	quarter-note app.: *d''* KN: preceded by 1-flag app.: *d''*
113 / top / 9	52/7: ⚬ (added lightly)
114 / top / 1–2	P 368, 52/6, 52/7, AmB 54, RL, KN: ∞ on 1 not between 1 and 2
	D Mbs, 52/5: no orn. RL: ⚬ (?)
115 / top / 10	P 368: ♭
115 / bottom, upstem / last	*g'* only in P 368, D Mbs, 52/5; cf. bar 37
116 / bottom / 2	D Mbs, 52/5: *bb* not *c'*
117 / top / 10	52/6: orig. *bb'*, corr. by copyist
118 / bottom / 4	D Mbs, 52/5: quarter rest

Second Movement

In the second movement the terms 'upper part' and 'lower part' refer to separate voices, not to upper and lower staves.

1	52/6: time signature orig. ¢, beam erased
1 / lower part / 8–9	P 359: no *Anschlag*
2 / upper part / 4	D Mbs, 52/5: ⚬⚬ not tr 52/6, 52/7, AmB 54, RL, KN: no orn.
2 / upper part / 11	52/6: no ∞ 52/7, AmB 54: tr on 12, no orn. on 11 RL: ≋ on 12, no orn. on 11 KN: tr on 11
2 / lower part / 13–14	D Mbs, 52/5: ∞ on 13 not between 13 and 14 52/6, 52/7, AmB 54, RL, KN: no orn. P 359: orn. in foreign hand (autograph?) Erasure above 13; orn. orig. misplaced?
3 / first beat	52/6, 52/7, KN: as Ex. 41a (52/7: no tie); AmB 54: as Ex. 41b; the remaining sources as Ex. 41c (=*CPEBE*)

Ex. 41

138

bar / stave / note-and-rest no.	source: remark
3 / upper part / 6	D Mbs, 52/5, RL: ⁓ not tr / 52/6: no orn. / 52/7, AmB 54, KN: ⁓
3 / upper part / 8–10	D Mbs, 52/5, 52/6, RL, KN: no '3' / KN: slur
3 / bottom / 11	52/6, 52/7, AmB 54, RL, KN: no tr
4 / upper part / 1–2	52/6, 52/7, AmB 54, RL, KN: no slur
4 / upper part / 3–4	D Mbs, 52/5: no tie
4 / upper part / 7	P 359: no ♭ / P 775, B Bc: ♭ inserted, possibly autograph
4 / lower part / 7	P 359: no '3' (fingering) / P 775, B Bc: '3' on 8
4 / lower part / 9	B Bc, P 359: no '1' (fingering)
4 / lower part / 25 (c')	D Mbs, 52/5, 52/6, 52/7, AmB 54: no ♮ / P 775, P 359 (?): ♮ an autograph addition
4 / lower part / 25–6	D Mbs, 52/5: slur
5 / upper part / 1–2	P 775, P 359: slur poorly drawn, possibly an autograph addition
5 / lower part / 25	52/6, 52/7, AmB 54, RL: no ♭ / P 775, P 359 (?): ♭ an autograph addition
5 / lower part / 25–6	D Mbs, 52/5: slur
7 / upper part, upstem / 8	D Mbs, 52/5: tr not ≈ / 52/6, 52/7, AmB 54, RL, KN: no orn.
7 / upper part, upstem / 10	P 359: no rest
9 / upper part / 16; 25–6	D Mbs, 52/5: 32nd (f''); 64ths (c'''–d''')
9 / upper part / 24, 26	52/7, AmB 54, RL, KN: 64th (bb''), 32nd (d''')
9 / lower part / last	D Mbs, 52/5: ⁓ not tr / 52/6, RL: no orn.
10 / upper part / 4	P 359: orig. e''? note-head enlarged
10 / upper part / 25	P 775, P 359: ♮ possibly autograph
11	P 775, P 359: f an autograph addition
11 / lower part / 1	B Bc: ⁓
11 / lower part / 8–9	B Bc, P 359: *Anschlag* in 16ths / P 775: third beam unclear, can be read as 16ths
11 / lower part / 12–14	D Mbs, 52/5, 52/6, 52/7, AmB 54, RL: no '3'
12 / upper part / 4	D Mbs: ⁓ not tr / 52/5: ⁓ / 52/6, 52/7, AmB 54, RL, KN: no orn.
13 / upper part / 7	D Mbs, 52/5: ⁓ / 52/7, AmB 54, KN: ⁓ / RL: ⁓
13 / lower part / 1–2	52/6, 52/7, AmB 54, RL, KN: no slur
13 / lower part / 20	D Mbs, 52/5: no ♮ / P 359: ♮ inserted
14 / lower part / 20	D Mbs, 52/5, 52/6, 52/7, AmB 54: 1-flag app.
15 / upper part / 25	P 359, D Mbs, 52/5, 52/6, 52/7, AmB 54, RL: no ♮ / P 775, B Bc: ♮ inserted, possibly autograph
15 / lower part / 1–2	D Mbs, 52/5: slur
16 / upper part / 25	P 775, P 359, D Mbs, 52/5: ♮ / B Bc: ♮ inserted, possibly autograph
17 / both / last	D Mbs, 52/5: ♭
17 / lower part / 2	D Mbs, 52/5: e' not d'
18 / upper part / 1	52/6, 52/7, AmB 54, RL: a' not c''
18 / lower part / 1	RL: c' not a
19 / lower part / 16	P 775: ♯ autograph (?)
20 / lower part / 9–10	P 775, P 359: *Anschlag* (and ♯) inserted
21 / upper part / 4	D Mbs, 52/5: tr not c⁓ / 52/6, 52/7, AmB 54, RL, KN: no orn.
23 / lower part / 6	P 775, P 359: ♭ inserted?
24 / lower part / 1–2, 9–10	P 775, P 359: *Anschläge* inserted (with accidentals)
24 / lower part / 16	P 775: ♭ possibly autograph
25 / upper part / 14	P 775, P 359: app. possibly inserted

bar / stave / note-and-rest no.	source: remark
26 / lower part / 1–2	52/7, AmB 54, RL, KN: no slur
	P 775: autograph? Slur somewhat wobbly
27 / upper part / 3	♮ only in KN
27 / upper part / 6	P 359: no ♭
	P 775: ♭ inserted, possibly autograph
27 / upper part / 13	All sources: no accidental here (c''); ♯ intended? ♯ on 19 in all sources
27 / lower part / 11–12	D Mbs, 52/5: no tie
27 / lower part / 28	P 359: no ♭
	P 775, B Bc: ♭ inserted, possibly autograph
28, 29	P 775, P 359: dyns. autograph additions
28 / lower part / 5	P 359: ♭ inserted
29	D Mbs, 52/5, 52/6, 52/7, AmB 54: no '6'
30 / upper part / 8 (e'/g')	P 359: orig. entered above bass note 6; initially corr. by guideline, then erased and re-entered (autograph?)
30 / upper part, upstem / 14	D Mbs, 52/5: ⁓ not tr
30 / upper part, downstem / 2–5	52/6, 52/7, AmB 54, RL, KN: notes om. (d'–d'–d'–e')
	D Mbs: beam (but not noteheads) crossed out lightly (in later hand?)
30 / lower part / 2	P 775: ♯ autograph
31 / 2	D Mbs, 52/5, KN: followed by half rest
31 / upper part / 1	52/6(?), 52/7, AmB 54, RL: ⁓
	KN: ⁓

Third Movement

bar / stave / note-and-rest no.	source: remark
2 / top / 1–2	D Mbs, 52/5: no *Anschlag*
	P 775, P 359: *Anschlag* inserted
2 / top / 3	52/6: e♭'/c''
2 / top / 3–4	B Bc: no slur
2 / top, downstem / 2	D Mbs, 52/5: followed by quarter rest
7 / bottom / 3	RL: ♮
10 / top, upstem / 1–2	D Mbs, 52/5, 52/6 (?), KN: no slur

bar / stave / note-and-rest no.	source: remark
11 / top, upstem / 5	♮ only in 52/6, 52/7, AmB 54, RL, KN
12 / top / 2	♮ only in RL
14 / top, upstem / 1–2	P 359, 52/6, 52/7, AmB 54, RL, KN: no slur
	P 775: slur possibly an autograph addition
14 / top, upstem / 3	P 775: ♭ is possibly autograph
17 / top / 3–7	KN: decrescendo wedge beneath these notes
18 / top / 1	P 775: *p* autograph
18 / top / 1–2	D Mbs, 52/5, 52/6, 52/7, AmB 54, KN: no slur
18 / bottom / 1–2	D Mbs, 52/5, 52/6: dotted half-note, no rest
18, 19 / top / 2	P 775: erasures beneath these notes: misplaced dyns.?
18, 20 / top	RL: *p* beneath 2
19 / 1	P 359, 52/6: *f* repeated
19 / top / 1	P 775: ♯ repeated (new line)
19 / top / 2	P 359: 1-flag app.
19 / top / 3–7	KN: decrescendo wedge beneath these notes
19 / top / 5	P 359: ♮ inserted
20	P 775, P 359, and B Bc clearly place *f* on 4.
	D Mbs, 52/5, 52/6: *f* between 2 and 3
	AmB 54, 52/7, RL: *p* on 2, no *f*
	KN: *p* on 1, no *f*
26 / top / 4	D Mbs, 52/5: no ♮
	P 359: ♮ possibly inserted
27 / top / 2	P 775: ♮ is possibly autograph
27–8	P 359: bar 27 orig. om. Bar 28 in main text altered to = bar 27, and bar 28 entered in upper margin. Alterations at least partly autograph
34 / top / 1–2	P 775, P 359: *Anschlag* inserted
34 / top / 3–4	B Bc: no slur

140

bar / stave / note-and-rest no.	source: remark
34 / bottom / 3	D Mbs, 52/5, 52/6, 52/7, AmB 54, RL: rest doubled in inner voice
36 / bottom, upstem / 1	P 359: no *g*
	P 775: *g* is an addition (autograph?)
38 / inner voice	P 359: orig. *d''–d♭''–d♮''*? First accidental possibly inserted, second accidental altered to ♮, third note erased and re-entered (autograph?)
39	P 775: *f* possibly autograph
39 / 1	D Mbs, 52/5: no arp.
	P 359: only a small gap separates the arpeggio signs for the two hands
	52/6, 52/7, AmB 54, RL, KN: arp. unbroken between hands
44	D Mbs, 52/5, 52/7, AmB 54, RL, KN: *p* on downbeat
45 / bottom, downstem / 1	52/6, 52/7, AmB 54, RL, KN: *c* not B♭
	P 359: orig. *c*, corr. possibly autograph
48	D Mbs, 52/5, AmB 54, RL, KN: *p* on downbeat
	52/7: *p* on second beat
49	D Mbs, 52/5: no *f*
50 / top, downstem / 1	P 359: erasure; no rest
51 / top, middle voice, *f♯''*	D Mbs, 52/5: no ♯
51 / top, middle voice, *e♮''*	D Mbs, 52/5: no ♮
	P 359: ♮ inserted
52 / top / 1–2	D Mbs: two quarter-notes, no slur
	52/5: quarter-note, half-note [*sic*]; no slur
55 / top / 2	D Mbs, 52/5, 52/7, AmB 54, RL, KN: 1-flag app.
55 / top / 2–3	D Mbs, 52/5, 52/7, AmB 54, KN: slur
57 / top, upstem / 1–2	P 359: no slur
58 / top, inner voice / 1	52/6, 52/7, AmB 54, RL, KN: preceded by 1-flag app. *a'*
59	D Mbs, 52/5, 52/6,

bar / stave / note-and-rest no.	source: remark
	52/7, AmB 54, RL: no *f*
63–4 / bottom	D Mbs, 52/5: no tie
64 / top / 1	P 359: no ⁓
65 / top	P 359: erasures, orig. reading illegible
66 / top / 2–3	P 359: notation in two parts in this source only; rests are autograph
72 / top / 4	D Mbs, 52/5, 52/7, AmB 54, RL, KN: *g'/b'/d''/g''*
74 / top / 1	B Bc: no stroke
75 / top / 3	52/6, 52/7, AmB 54: no ♮
	P 775: ♮ possibly an autograph insertion
75 / bottom, downstem / 3	P 775, B Bc, P 359: *g* not *a*. CPEBE follows DMbs, 52/5, 52/6, 52/7, AmB 54, RL, KN, P 368.
79 / bottom / 3	♮ only in D Mbs, 52/5, 52/6, RL, KN
80 / top / 4	D Mbs, 52/5: *a'/c♯''/e♮''/a''*
82	D Mbs, 52/5: *p* on downbeat
83 / top, upstem / 1–2	P 775: slur possibly an autograph addition
86 / top / 2, 8	P 775: these flats possibly autograph
86 / bottom / 3	P 359: orig. *b♭*; notehead enlarged, but ♭ remains on space above stave
87 / bottom / 1	♮ only in KN
90 / top / 3–4	52/6 (?), 52/7, AmB 54, RL, KN: no slur
93, 97 / top, upstem / 1–2	P 775, P 359: *Anschlag* inserted
93 / top / 3–4	P 775, P 359: slur small and light, possibly added
95 / bottom	No source has *c'* on 1, but cf. bar 4
97, 99	P 775, P 359: dyns. possibly autograph
98 / top / 2	D Mbs, 52/5, 52/7, AmB 54, RL, KN: 1-flag app.
98 / top / 2–7	KN: decrescendo wedge beneath these notes
98 / top / 4	P 775: ♭ possibly autograph

bar / stave / note-and-rest no.	source: remark
107 / top / 1 (lower voice)	P 775, B Bc, P 359, D Mbs, 52/6, 52/7, AmB 54, RL, KN: ♮ repeated (P359, D Mbs: new line)